GAZETTEER OF SCOTTISH AND IRISH GHOSTS

Peter Underwood

Underwood Publishing

For
PAMELA and CRISPIN
with love

CONTENTS

Title Page	1
Dedication	3
ILLUSTRATIONS	11
INTRODUCTION	13
SCOTLAND	19
Aberdeen	20
Abergeldie, BRAEMAR	21
Alves, NEAR ELGIN, MORAYSHIRE	22
Annan, DUMFRIESSHIRE	23
Ardrossan, AYRSHIRE	27
Assynt, SUTHERLANDSHIRE	28
Athelstaneford, EAST LOTHIAN	33
Balgie, GLEN LYON, PERTHSHIRE	35
Ballachulish, ARGYLLSHIRE	40
Ballater, ABERDEENSHIRE	42
Banff, BANFFSHIRE	43
Beauly, INVERNESS-SHIRE	47
Ben Ime, GLENCROE, ARGYLLSHIRE	48
Ben Macdhui, THE CAIRNGORMS	51
Benderloch, NEAR OBAN, ARGYLLSHIRE	56

The Black Isle, ROSS AND CROMARTY (See also Cromarty)	58
Blackness, WEST LOTHIAN	63
Bladnoch, NEAR WIGTOWN, WIGTOWNSHIRE	65
Blairgowrie, PERTHSHIRE	68
Boat of Garten, MORAYSHIRE	70
Bowland, VALE OF GALE, MIDLOTHIAN	73
Braemar, ABERDEENSHIRE	75
Brechin, ANGUS-SHIRE	78
Callander, PERTHSHIRE	80
Castle Douglas, KIRKCUDBRIGHTSHIRE	82
Corrieyairack Pass, INVERNESS-SHIRE	83
Craigmaddie Moor, STIRLINGSHIRE	84
Cramond, EDINBURGH, MIDLOTHIAN	87
Cromarty, ROSS-SHIRE	89
Culloden Moor, INVERNESS-SHIRE	95
Dingwall, ROSS-SHIRE	97
Dornoch, SUTHERLANDSHIRE	98
Drumelzier, NEAR PEEBLES, PEEBLES-SHIRE	99
Drymen, STIRLINGSHIRE	100
Drynachan, NEAR FORT AUGUSTUS, INVERNESS-SHIRE	101
Dumfries, DUMFRIESSHIRE	102
Dunblane, PERTHSHIRE	104
Dunure, AYRSHIRE	105
Dunvegan, ISLE OF SKYE	107
Duror, NEAR BALLACHULISH, ARGYLLSHIRE	109
Earlston, BERWICKSHIRE	112
Edinburgh	116

Edrom, near Duns, BERWICKSHIRE	130
Elgin, MORAYSHIRE	132
Ethie Castle, ANGUS	133
Fearn, ROSS AND CROMARTY	135
Fettercairn, KINCARDINESHIRE	139
Forfar, ANGUS-SHIRE	142
Fyvie, ABERDEENSHIRE	144
Galashiels, SELKIRKSHIRE	148
Garleton Hill, near Haddington, EAST LOTHIAN	153
Geanies, ROSS-SHIRE	156
Gladhouse Reservoir, Moorfoot Hills, near EDINBURGH	158
Glamis, ANGUS	160
Glasgow	166
Glen Shira, NEAR INVERARAY, ARGYLLSHIRE	172
Glencorse, MIDLOTHIAN	175
Glenluce, WIGTOWNSHIRE	177
Glenshee, PERTHSHIRE	180
Gourock, RENFREWSHIRE	183
Granton, MIDLOTHIAN	184
Haddington, EAST LOTHIAN	186
Hermitage Castle, see Newcastleton, Roxburghshire	187
Inveraray, ARGYLLSHIRE	188
Iona, Isle of; INNER HEBRIDES	190
Jedburgh, ROXBURGHSHIRE	197
Killiecrankie, Pass of, PERTHSHIRE	199
Kilmacolm, RENFREWSHIRE	201
Kinross, KINROSS-SHIRE	202
Kintraw, at the head of Loch Craignish, ARGYLLSHIRE	204

Kirriemuir, ANGUS	205
Lasswade, NEAR DALKEITH, MIDLOTHIANSHIRE	207
Lendalfoot, AYRSHIRE	208
Linlithgow, WEST LOTHIANSHIRE	209
Lismore Island, ARGYLLSHIRE	211
Little Loch Broom, ROSS AND CROMARTY	212
Lockerbie, DUMFRIESSHIRE	214
Maxton, ROXBURGHSHIRE	216
Melrose, ROXBURGHSHIRE	221
Montrose, ANGUS	223
Morar, INVERNESS-SHIRE	227
Motherwell, LANARKSHIRE	229
Mull, Isle Of, ARGYLLSHIRE	230
Nannau, MERIONETHSHIRE	232
Newcastleton, ROXBURGHSHIRE	234
Nigg, near Fearn, ROSS AND CROMARTY	239
Oban, ARGYLLSHIRE	242
Pencaitland, EAST LOTHIANSHIRE	244
Penicuik, MIDLOTHIAN	252
Perth, PERTHSHIRE	254
Ringcroft of Stocking, Rerrick, KIRKCUDBRIGHTSHIRE	256
Roslin, MIDLOTHIANSHIRE	261
St Andrews, FIFESHIRE	262
Sanday Island, ORKNEY	263
Sandwood Bay, Cape Wrath, SUNDERLAND	265
Selkirk, SELKIRKSHIRE	270
Skye, Isle of	273
Stirling, STIRLINGSHIRE	275

Strachur, ARGYLLSHIRE	278
Stranraer, WIGTOWNSHIRE	280
Strath Conon, ROSS AND CROMARTY	281
Tain, ROSS AND CROMARTY	282
Tarbat, NEAR FEARN, ROSS AND CROMARTY	284
Tiree, Isle of, ARGYLLSHIRE	286
Watherston, MIDLOTHIANSHIRE	287
Whitburn, WEST LOTHIAN	288
IRELAND	290
Antrim, CO. ANTRIM	291
Birr, CO. OFFALY	292
Bushmills, CO. ANTRIM	296
Celbridge, CO. KILDARE	298
Cloncurry, CO. KILDARE	303
Connemara, CO. GALWAY	306
Cork, CO. CORK	309
Derrygonelly, near Enniskillen, CO. FERMANAGH	316
Dublin, CO. DUBLIN	319
Eringle Truagh, CO. MONAGHAN	328
Giant's Causeway, CO. ANTRIM	331
Kilkenny City, CO. KILKENNY	332
Killarney, CO. KERRY	333
Kinsale, CO. CORK	336
Lough Derg, ON THE BORDERS OF CO. CLARE, CO. GALWAY AND CO. TIPPERARY	340
Lough Gur, CO. LIMERICK	342
Oughterard, CO. GALWAY	345
Portlaw, CO. WATERFORD	347

Randalstown, NEAR ANTRIM, CO. ANTRIM	352
Rathfarnham, CO. DUBLIN	353
Rathlin Island, CO. ANTRIM	354
Skerries, CO. DUBLIN	355
Strabane, CO. TYRONE	356
Tuamgraney, CO. CLARE	358
Waterford, co. WATERFORD	363
Westport, CO. MAYO	367
Wexford, CO. WEXFORD	368
ACKNOWLEDGEMENTS	372
About The Author	373
Books By This Author	375

ILLUSTRATIONS

[Visit the places corresponding to each entry in the Gazetteer of Scottish and Irish Ghosts *Google Map, and find out more about Underwood's life and work at peterunderwood.org.]*

SCOTLAND

1. Meggernie Castle, Balgie
2. Ballachulish House, Argyllshire
3. The beech-lined road at Ballachulish, Argyllshire
4. Baldoon Castle, Bladnoch
5. The Binns Tower, Blackness, West Lothian
6. The Auld Wives' Lift, Craigmaddie Moor
7. Culloden Cairn, Culloden Moor, Inverness-shire
8. Auchindarroch, Duror, Argyllshire
9. Culzean Castle, Dunure, Argyllshire
10. The County Hotel, Dumfries
11. Edinburgh Castle
12. Western Infirmary, Glasgow
13. Inveraray Castle
14. Haunted Iona, Inner Hebrides (1)
15. Isle of Iona, Inner Hebrides (2)
16. St Michael's Church, Linlithgow
17. Abbotsford, Melrose, Roxburghshire
18. Hermitage Castle, Newcastleton, Roxburghshire
19. Dunstaffnage Castle Oban, Argyllshire
20. Dunvegan Castle, Isle of Skye
21. The Fairy Flag of Dunvegan
22. Ruins of Cathedral at St Andrews, Fifeshire
23. Stirling Castle, Stirlingshire

IRELAND

1. St Michan's Church, Dublin
2. The vaults of St Michan's Church, Dublin
3. Fitzwilliam Square, Dublin
4. Lake Leane, Killarney, Co. Kerry
5. Lough Derg, Co. Tipperary (1)
6. Lough Derg near Killaloe, Co. Clare (2)
7. Remains of Aughnanure Castle, Oughterard
8. Lough Gur Castle

INTRODUCTION

The stories of the haunted houses of Scotland and Ireland mirror the life that was once lived in these countries. Perhaps because many of the places are remote and isolated, they have retained for a little longer some remnants of their former history.

Both Scotland and Ireland are rich in legends and reputed ghosts; tales that have been handed down from past generations.

The ghost stories—even the legends—often have a modicum of truth in them and they should be collected and preserved before they become submerged in the cold world of computers.

Such records of a former way of life, of old beliefs and traditions, are on the verge of oblivion. These relics of the past, once so firmly rooted that they were an accepted part of reality are now all but forgotten and when some inexplicable figure is glimpsed for a moment in some ruined castle, no one knows who that form once was or what crime or suffering may have caused the shade to reappear.

I hope this book will help to remedy this state of affairs and that it will add some human element to dry histories of places and people.

I do not claim that all the entries included are factual accounts in the literal sense; but I have endeavoured to present a representative selection of traditional tales of ghostly happenings and well-authenticated instances of ghosts and hauntings, famous and little-known, arranged in alphabetical order of the place at which they are alleged to have occurred.

In December, 1970, I had occasion to write to Mr Frank W. Hansell, the factor of Drummond Castle Estates in Perthshire, and he was good enough to relate a couple of experiences which well illustrate the authenticity of ghostly happenings today:

'In the early summer of the year 1931, I was about twenty years of age, and was travelling to Perth with my father, mother, and young sister who was a teenager.

'While proceeding to Perth on what is known as the Gask Road at a point East 985, North 193 (O.S. Grid reference), I noticed at the side of the road at what used to be a watering place for cattle, a female in a most peculiar costume; as a matter of fact she was dressed in the manner of what I would take to be a witch.

'At the time I did not mention this to anyone in the car as I was the driver. However, after proceeding about a mile or two along the road, my sister passed the remark to us all, asking if I had seen the woman who was dressed as I have described at the water hole.

'Of course, I had to tell her that I did. I may say that this place is very near the "Auld House of Gask" which is famous as the home of Lady Nairne who wrote some very fine Scots poetry and songs.

'I can give you no explanation for this as I did not get out of the car to question the woman or to see if she was actually flesh and blood.

'Shortly afterwards I was describing this incident to my dentist, an exceedingly level-headed gentleman with great knowledge, and he told me that the previous week he had seen two teenage boys from Morrison's Academy (sixth formers) and they had described to him a peculiar incident they had seen on the bridge over the River Pow, while they were fishing close by.

'The location of the bridge is East 93; North 25. While they were fishing, there appeared on the bridge a lady and a small child dressed in old fashioned crinoline dresses—I should say of the period 1650-1745.

'I understand from my dentist friend that the boys had seen the two figures, separately, and they were not together when they saw the figures on the bridge and when they met this was their first topic of discussion, each one asking the other and explaining what they had seen.

'My friend spoke to the boys, separately, and he was quite sure that they had seen something very strange.'

While in a few of the legends and tales of long ago it is difficult to find much substance and reality, I have included many authentic reports of Scottish 'ghosties' and Irish hauntings in past and recent times, from the curious story of disturbances at the Edinburgh home of Sir Alexander Seton after his wife surreptitiously removed an ancient bone from a tomb in Egypt to the whispering ghosts among the mummified remains in the crypt of St Michan's Church in Dublin.

Scotland and Ireland have charms that are all their own, not least perhaps because of the magic quality of so much of those majestic and sparsely populated countries whose kindly people accept without question the possibility of visitations from the dead.

There are such individual inhabitants as Lucy Bruce who 'really did see fairies at the bottom of her garden'; Sir Shane Leslie who 'really did have a family banshee' and Captain Sir Hugh Rhys Rankin, Bart., F.S.A., who tells me that he has been followed by the ghost of Oliver Cromwell, seen a Campbell who killed a Stewart of Appin, watched a Norman headless lady carry her own severed head and observed time and time again a bent old hag on the seashore near Barcaldine Home Farm, Benderlock, Argyll, who was driven out of her holding way back after the '45.

Everyone knows that Ireland has leprechauns, often described as a dwarf or gnome in the form of an old man who can be induced only by threats of violence to disclose the hiding-place of his treasure.

Should a leprechaun be caught by human beings, he will purchase his liberty by revealing the location of his 'crock of gold', which disappears when its hiding-place is discovered.

Not everyone knows that Scotland, too, has individual ghost-like creatures: the kelpie, a ghost-horse and the water-wraith, a young woman dressed in green scowling malignantly at anyone who sees her; while the spectre of Tarbat is an example of the age-old Scottish belief that the ghost of a murdered man is earthbound for the length of time that would have been his span of life, disappearing forever on the day that he would have died had he not been murdered.

In such places as gaunt Glamis Castle and lovely Ben Macdhui it is not difficult to believe that strange things can happen; things that cannot be explained in material or scientific terms. We may all be the better for realizing that there are some things that we cannot yet explain.

I emphasize the 'yet' because I believe all these occurrences and experiences have 'normal' explanations; it is simply that we have not yet discovered the why and the wherefore.

After all none of us has seen a radio wave, yet we have all heard voices and other sounds that have travelled along these invisible waves.

It happens that I heard music in a haunted glade that I am convinced had no known origin; but there may well be some quite normal explanation, possibly on the lines of radio waves.

One day we may use telepathy, extra-sensory-perception and other 'supernormal' facilities, each and every day as our natural heritage.

When—or until—that day comes such experiences as those that are here collected are of considerable interest, whether as folk memories, as possible evidence of life after death, as wishful thinking or even as examples of the fantasy-ridden human mind; although I venture to suggest that none of these explanations will adequately cover all the material here included.

Since evidence is only as good as the witness concerned, it must be admitted that some of the witnesses for some of the accounts in this collection are shadowy and elusive; others, however, are very good.

It should be remembered by the sceptics that such keen-minded men and women as speed king Donald Campbell, television personality Fanny Cradock, Battle-of-Britain saviour Lord Dowding, author Dennis Wheatley and John, Duke of Bedford have all told me that they have seen ghosts.

I hope, too, that these accounts will add interest and give extra enjoyment to those who know the castles, mountains and lochs of Scotland and the green hills, silent lakes and majestic coastline of Ireland, as well as those for whom the pleasures of a visit to these beautiful lands is still to come.

This book would not have been possible without the understanding and encouragement of my wife and the help of many people who have brought to my attention reputed ghosts in Scotland and Ireland and many others who have helped me with up-to-date information.

I am grateful to them all and especially to my friend Donald Ross whose encyclopaedic knowledge of Scotland has been of considerable value to me.

In addition, his help in supplying source material in respect of a number of cases and his interest and advice at all stages of the book is deeply appreciated.

And if by chance you ever cross the enchanted boundary and have the good fortune to experience some strange happening or have knowledge of some legend or well-attested ghost that I have not included, I shall be most interested to hear from you.

PETER UNDERWOOD
The Savage Club
St James's Street,
London, S.W.1

SCOTLAND

ABERDEEN

The old Auchinyell district is now occupied by houses but years ago this was a bleak and barren place with an unpleasant marsh-land area known as 'The Clash'.

Bordering the south side of the marsh ran a section of the old Deeside highway to Braemar, a section where no traveller lingered on account of the eerie spectre of a cat that haunted this neighbourhood.

The several versions of the origin of the haunting all concern Menzies of Pitfodels and his cat and all have the same tragic ending.

It is said that on a particularly dark night he was riding home to Pitfodels past the marsh-land with its evil reputation, when a cat suddenly sprang at him from The Clash and, flying at the unfortunate Menzies' throat, tore at it until he was dead.

This cat is thought to have been a real one but no real cat was ever seen again in the vicinity although the ghostly form of a cat was said to haunt The Clash of Auchinyell for many many years afterwards.

ABERGELDIE, BRAEMAR

A few miles north, where the Fearder Burn joins the Dee, stood the old Mill of Inver, a haunt of the awesome spectre known as the 'Black Hand' that also appeared throughout the glen of the Fearder Burn until it was laid by miller John Davidson.

For generations the centuries-old mill (latterly serving other than its original purpose) was tenanted by a family named Davidson and one dark and wintry night in 1767 John Davidson claimed that he saw the famous 'Black Hand' while he was working in the mill.

Chancing to look upwards he saw the floating apparition of a black, sinewy and hairy hand, cut off at the wrist, which had long been reputed to terrorize the local inhabitants.

But John Davidson was made of sterner stuff. He immediately challenged the 'Black Hand' and, although he would never divulge the details of what took place, it seems that he had a fierce encounter with something.

The following morning he was seen digging deeply in a corner of the yard and eventually he unearthed a curiously wrought basket-hilt of a broadsword. This hung for many years over the fireplace at the mill and there were no reports of the 'Black Hand' being encountered thereafter.

ALVES, NEAR ELGIN, MORAYSHIRE

The dominating York Tower here, to the north-west, commemorates Frederick, Duke of York, son of King George III. It stands on the summit of the Knock of Alves, a hill long reputed to be haunted and no place to visit on dark and stormy nights when strange, indistinct shapes have been glimpsed and weird and high-pitched screeches and chuckling heard, although the Knock is indisputably devoid of human beings. This is the traditional meeting-place of Macbeth and the three 'Weird Sisters'.

ANNAN, DUMFRIESSHIRE

One night in April, 1962, on the stretch of the A75 between Dumfries and Annan, two brothers, Derek and Norman Ferguson, then aged twenty-two and fourteen respectively, had the most terrifying experience of their lives.

The two men had spent a short holiday touring Scotland, Derek driving his father's small saloon car. Now they were about to set off home and stopped for petrol in Dumfries. Then they embarked on what was to be a never-to-be-forgotten part of the journey, before they reached Annan, fifteen miles away.

It was almost midnight but they could see the white road stretching away ahead of them in the dry and moonlit spring night. Derek had just remarked that they seemed to be the only car on the road when what appeared to be a large hen suddenly flew towards them and then disappeared just when it seemed that it must hit the windscreen of the car. Derek swerved to avoid the bird and for a moment both the brothers were shaken, but much worse was to come.

They had hardly recovered from the surprise and shock when they saw the figure of an old woman rushing wildly towards the car, waving her spread arms—and then she, too, vanished into thin air, just as it seemed that the car must run into her. And she was followed by what appeared to be an unending stream of figures that loomed up out of nowhere: great cats, wild-looking dogs, goats, hens and other large fowl and strange creatures, including an old man with long hair who seemed to be screaming.

As the horrifying sights and sounds tore at the nerves of the two frightened brothers, the car zig-zagged along the road, swerving and braking and changing course repeatedly in an effort to miss the forms that tore towards them.

At first Derek, finding that the mysterious beings never made actual contact with the car, thought that it must all be his imagination but a glance at his brother, crouching wide-eyed in the seat beside him, told him that this was no hallucination: Norman was seeing the same awful phantoms.

As they proceeded through the throng of open-mouthed and wild-looking creatures, both young men noticed an appreciable drop in temperature within the car although by this time both were drenched in perspiration.

'My hands seemed to become very heavy,' Derek said afterwards, 'and it was as if some force were trying to gain control of the steering wheel; the control of the car became increasingly difficult.'

'We seemed to be suffocating and I opened the window to get some fresh air but it was bitterly cold outside and I just hung on to the wheel as screaming, high-pitched laughter and cackling noises seemed to mock our predicament. I was absolutely certain at the time that an attempt was being made to force us off the road and I was equally certain that a fatal accident would result.'

In the end Derek stopped the car. Immediately some powerful force seemed to attack them; the two young men felt the car being bounced violently up and down on the road, rocked so forcefully from side to side that they became dizzy. As Derek felt very sick, he wrenched open the car door and leaped out.

Immediately all was quiet and the road and surrounding countryside was still and utterly deserted. Yet as soon as he returned to the car and slammed shut the door, the shaking and buffeting re-commenced together with the unearthly and high-pitched laughter. A high wind seemed to blow up and there was the sensation of fists striking the sides, the front and back and top of the car to add to the terror of the unfortunate occupants.

Derek decided that the only thing to do was to press on home. He restarted the car and proceeded slowly through the night that was still full of the weird figures continually looming up suddenly out of nowhere and the frightening noises that, seemed to come from every direction.

Often the figures would stop in the path of the car, as though daring him to run them down, but although his hands and arms became almost unendurably painful with the strain, Derek kept a straight course and the figures disintegrated just as it seemed that he must slam into them. All the time Derek was conscious of his horror-stricken and strangely quiet younger brother beside him.

After a while the Ferguson brothers noticed a small red gleam ahead of them in the gathering darkness and as they drew nearer they were relieved to find that it was the tail-light of a large furniture van.

Yet no sooner was Derek pleased to find some apparently normal object on that haunted road, when he realized that he was approaching it far too quickly and that there would be a collision.

Exhausted physically and emotionally by the recent events he now discovered to his horror that he could not swerve or take any evasive action. His feet refused to move from the accelerator pedal. He screamed to his brother to prepare himself for a crash. And then they were upon the van and it vanished completely!

Shattered, buffeted and drained of strength, the brothers continued slowly on their way until Derek found the car had slowed down to a crawl. He realized that the noises and the high wind had died away and they found themselves approaching Annan.

The whole experience had lasted nearly half an hour. Afterwards Derek congratulated himself on stopping for petrol in Dumfries; had they been unable to continue along that terrible road into Annan that night, he dreads to think what the consequences might have been.

Later Derek Ferguson talked with a friend who had been stationed near Annan during his military service in the Second World War. This man had often heard tales of witchcraft being practised in the area; while another friend stated that he had read of a phantom furniture van that was reputed to have been seen in the vicinity.

Neither of the Ferguson brothers, nor any of their family had previously any kind of psychic experience nor was it ever repeated. It is interesting that Norman was an adolescent at the time, possibly the unconscious link with the strange appearances on the lonely Annan road.

ARDROSSAN, AYRSHIRE

On Castle Hill remnants can still be found of the once great castle of the Montgomerys. The spot is reputed to be haunted by Sir William Wallace, the Scottish patriot who was defeated by King Edward I at Falkirk in 1298 and executed in London in 1305.

Wallace once craftily set fire to a nearby hamlet, luring there a large detachment of the English soldiers and slaughtering them one by one as they returned to the garrison. He threw the corpses into the castle dungeon, known thereafter as 'Wallace's Larder'.

Earlier still, the castle was the home of a sorcerer, known as the 'Deil o' Ardrossan' and a stone in the yard of the local church (which was destroyed in a storm in the seventeenth century) has long been regarded as marking his burial place, although according to a different tradition he was buried on the shores of Arran in a shroud made from a bull's hide.

Legend has long linked the stone with disaster and it is said that should any portion of the earth be taken from under the stone and cast into the sea, a fearful tempest -would devastate the sea and the land.

It is only on stormy nights that Wallace's giant figure has been seen within the precincts of his old home, glimpsed momentarily as the lightning flashes.

ASSYNT, SUTHERLANDSHIRE

The wild and beautiful countryside around Loch Assynt has been haunted since a murder was committed here over a hundred-and-fifty years ago.

A pedlar by the name of Murdoch Grant amassed a considerable amount of money from trading among the lonely farmsteads; he always carried the money on his person. On the morning of March 11th, 1830, he set off to sell his wares at a wedding at Assynt.

Afterwards he announced that he was going to Drumbeg and he was last seen alive, with his pedlar's pack on his back, walking in the direction of Nedd.

A month later a courting couple on the banks of Torna-Eigin saw a body floating in the clear water and when the body had been recovered from the loch, it was found to be that of the pedlar.

There was a deep wound on the dead man's head and this injury, coupled with the fact that Grant's pack was missing, pointed to foul play.

Among the local men who had assisted in retrieving the body from the water was the village schoolmaster who watched with disdain as the superstitious villagers carried out the custom of 'touch-proof.'

All the bystanders were required to touch the dead body as proof of their innocence in causing the death: it was believed that in the case of a guilty person touching the body, blood would appear. Macleod, the school-master, refused to take any part in such superstition. He declared that in his opinion death was due to natural causes and the wound on the head was probably caused by the body striking rocks in the loch after death.

The local magistrates and minister were sent for and the latter, who arrived first, agreed with Macleod that the wound had probably occurred after death. Eventually the body of Murdoch Grant was buried.

Some time later the dead man's brother, Robert Grant, turned up at Assynt. He was not satisfied with the story of his brother's death and insisted on an exhumation.

This was done but no new light was thrown on the affair and in spite of Macleod's repeated insistence that there was no shred of evidence to suggest any other cause of death but simple drowning, Robert Grant was still unconvinced.

In particular, he was concerned that no money had been found on his brother's body. When six months passed and still there was no sign of the pedlar's pack, Robert Grant became more and more certain that his brother had been murdered.

During the course of his inquiries in the locality he talked to the village shopkeeper who told him that only that very morning school-master Macleod had dropped his purse in his shop. It had burst open and ten golden sovereigns had rolled out.

This set Robert Grant thinking afresh for he knew that school-masters were not well-paid and he had already noticed that Macleod had expensive tastes; that his fondness for feminine company was costing him much more than his salary would be likely to cover.

Furthermore, a number of Macleod's outstanding debts had been miraculously paid recently. Robert Grant saw a magistrate and Macleod was interviewed; his answers to the questions were evasive and he was arrested.

Now the police began to search for evidence but the absence

of the dead man's pack meant that they had nothing tangible to work on. It looked as though they would have to release their prisoner when a local man named Kenneth Frazer, reputed to have the gift of second sight, came forward to say that he had seen the murder in a vision.

He described the place where the deed had been done and pointed to Macleod as the murderer. In addition he told the police where the missing pack would be discovered and described its contents, including some personal items belonging to the murdered man which were found in Macleod's possession.

The police found everything exactly as the seer had foretold and before he paid for his crime Macleod confessed that he had hit Murdoch Grant over the head, robbed him of his money, hid the pack after taking some of the contents and had then thrown the body into the loch.

Thereafter for many years it was said that each March 11th, just as the watery sun sank down beyond Lochinver, at a certain spot on the mossy bank of Loch Assynt, sounds were heard of a single dreadful blow followed by a long drawn-out sigh and the noise of panting and running footsteps.

The ancient castle of Ardvreck by Loch Assynt was occupied for well over a hundred years by a wicked old dowager who, among her other peculiarities, was always meddling in affairs that did not concern her and talking scandal constantly.

A gentleman and his wife who lived nearby were lucky enough to escape her serious attention for some years but on the birth of a child the husband's jealousy was awakened by insinuations put about by the old lady. He not only taxed his wife with infidelity but even threatened to destroy the infant.

In her distress the poor woman wrote to her two brothers and within a few days they both arrived to see what they could do to help. After remonstrating unsuccessfully with the husband, they decided that their only useful course would be to visit the old lady of Ardvreck. 'I plan to confront her with a person as clever as herself,' declared the younger brother darkly. He was much travelled and a student of occult arts.

The lady at the castle received the three men hospitably enough but they decided that her candour was less than complete when they eventually broached the subject of their visit.

At length the younger brother suggested that they might seek the truth of the matter by calling in a mutual acquaintance. The old lady raised no objection and while the two men and the dowager were seated in the low-ceilinged hall of the castle, a large, rude chamber, roofed and floored with stone and furnished with a row of narrow, unglazed windows which looked out onto the loch, the younger brother rose quietly from his place and bending towards the floor proceeded to trace strange diagrams and figures, muttering at the same time in an unrecognized language.

The day was calm but as the young man proceeded in his mystifying practice, the still waters of the loch began to heave and swell. A 'fleece of vapour' seemed to rise from the surface of the waters and spread upwards like a cloud. As it disappeared, it was noticed that a tall, dark figure, as indistinct as the shadow of a man, now stood by the far wall of the room.

'Now,' said the younger brother to the husband, 'put your question and make haste.' In a timorous voice the awed man asked whether his wife had been unfaithful to him?

Back came the answer that she was completely faithful. At the same time a huge wave from the loch smashed against the wall of the castle, breaking in at the hall windows and a tremendous wind, accompanied by hail, burst upon the roof of and turrets so that the very floor seemed to rise and fall beneath their feet.

'He will not leave us without payment,' said the young man,

turning to the old lady. 'Whom can you best spare?'

She, terrified at the events that had been witnessed, tottered to the door and, as she opened it, a little orphan girl, whom she sheltered, came running into the hall, frightened by the storm. The lady pointed to the child. 'No,' said the dark stranger in the corner. 'I dare not take an orphan.'

As another enormous wave threw itself against the castle and came pouring in at the windows, the elder brother pointed to the old woman who had poisoned the trust between his sister and her husband. 'Take her,' he screamed; but the shadow replied quietly: 'She is mine already and her term is not quite run but I will take with me one whom your sister will miss more.'

The next moment the shadowy form had disappeared, the storm abated and the puzzled party looked from one to the other. Returning home they learned that the infant, whose birth had caused so much disquiet, had died at the precise time that the dark shadow had vanished in the castle hall.

It is said that for five years afterwards only black and shrivelled grain was produced at Assynt and that no fish were taken from the loch. At the end of that period the castle of Ardvreck was destroyed in a mysterious fire, the old lady perishing in the flames, and after her death things resumed their natural course once more with the wheat ripening on the corn and fat fish again swam in the quiet loch.

ATHELSTANEFORD, EAST LOTHIAN

The legend about the origin of the national emblem of Scotland tells how the Picts and the Scots under King Hungus saw a vision in the sky of an enormous white saltine. Strengthened by a belief that this was a sign that St Andrew would protect them, they won a decisive victory over the English King Athelstan.

It is interesting to note that the twelfth-century version of the legend relates how Hungus, after successful skirmishes with the British, spent the winter with his army near the English-Scottish border.

He and seven companions were nearly blinded by a 'divine light', while the voice of St Andrew was heard 'from heaven' promising them protection and telling them that the cross of Christ would precede them as they marched on their enemies. Next day the same sign is said to have moved in front of the twelve columns of Hungus's army.

A thirteenth-century version speaks of King Hungus camping at the mouth of the River Tyne with the army he gathered against the Saxon King Athelstan and of St Andrew appearing and promising him a great victory over his enemies.

A fourteenth-century version names Athelstaneford as the place where Hungus encamped and the vision of St Andrew is related as promising victory and stating that an angel would walk in front of the soldiers.

Finally a sixteenth-century version of the legend mentions a night-time vision and St Andrew's prediction of victory over the English and in addition relates that King Hungus, awakening from the dream, found his army gazing at a shining cross in the sky.

King Athelstan is reputed to have been killed in battle by a spear piercing his body. The place where he was slain and where his army was defeated was named Athelstaneford.

BALGIE, GLEN LYON, PERTHSHIRE

The Meggernie Ghost is the name given to the singular haunting associated with nearby Meggernie Castle, parts of which date back to the fifteenth century. It is an attractive French-chateau style building approached by a fine avenue of limes half-way up the longest glen in Scotland. The ghost is the upper half of a woman.

The panelled Ghost Room is high up in the baronial tower, one of the oldest parts of the castle. Among the stories of the haunting still available is one dating back to 1862 when two friends were among a number of guests at Meggernie. They were allotted a room each in the Tower. There they found a blocked-up door without even a keyhole that used to connect the rooms via a small closet.

During the darkest hours of the night one guest was awakened by what he afterwards described as an exceedingly hot kiss upon his cheek, so hot that he felt as though his face had been burned through.

He leapt out of bed and saw the upper half of a woman's body drifting away from his bedside across the room where it disappeared through the blocked-up door. Within seconds he had established that the mysterious door was still firmly fastened and although he tried to reproduce the appearance he had seen by casting shadows from a lamp and moving the curtains of the window, he was quite unsuccessful.

Eventually he returned to his bed and in the morning lost no time in calling to his friend in the next room to tell him that he had had a terrible experience during the night.

Before he could say any more his friend called back that he, too, had had a strange experience and suggested they told their respective tales individually to someone else in the first place so that it could not be said afterwards that they had worked their accounts together. This they did and when they compared notes it was found that both guests had had almost identical experiences, even to describing the look of despair on the beautiful face of the ghost.

The other guest wrote up his experience, giving the time of his awakening as two-thirty a.m. and recounting that the first thing he noticed was a strange pink light in the room which seemed to emanate from a female form standing at the foot of his bed. The figure moved to the side of his bed and leaned over him and then retreated as he raised himself up.

For the first time he then saw that the figure had no lower half. It retreated to the closet and disappeared in the vicinity of the blocked-up door. Quickly getting out of bed he, too, established to his entire satisfaction that the closet was deserted and that there was no way out of his room.

A couple of months later he met at a hotel a lady who had been to Meggernie and she told him that she too had seen a ghost there—the upper half of a woman whose appearance she described, including the look of despair on her face and the way the hair had been arranged.

Such a figure had long been said to haunt the castle rooms and corridors and in the graveyard in the park the lower half of a female figure had been seen many times walking among the gravestones and sometimes sitting on them.

While the lower trunk was clearly visible and the legs moved about unhesitatingly, the head, shoulders and arms were missing and the mutilated trunk passing briskly over the ground, picking its way among the graves in the gathering gloom must have been a weird and fearsome sight.

A week after his experience in the Tower one of the guests was sitting alone late at night writing letters when the heavy oak door of the room suddenly flew open. At the same time the temperature in the room seemed to drop to freezing-point and although he saw nothing on this occasion, the guest had an overwhelming feeling of terror.

He hastily put away his papers and could not get out of the room fast enough. On the way to his bedroom he passed along a corridor and there, looking at him through a window, he saw a face: it was the beautiful face that he and his fellow guest had seen in their respective rooms a week before! He saw it distinctly and clearly in the light from the corridor, before it faded away.

Another witness of the ghost at Meggernie was the wife of Colonel Kinloch Grant who visited the castle one autumn and awoke in the middle of the night to find a female form bending over her. She was neither frightened nor surprised for she was sleeping in the Tower part of the castle and sensed that she was seeing the ghost of a former Lady of Meggernie.

She adds in her letter detailing the experience that the churchyard at Meggernie was a lovely secluded spot and she spent many a quiet hour there, often wondering why the place had such an evil reputation after dark; for nobody at the house or at the farm or indeed any of the Glen people would go there or even pass it alone after darkness.

My friend Alasdair Alpin MacGregor told me that he had obtained evidence concerning a doctor who had visited Meggernie one October evening and had spent the night there. He found himself awake in the middle of the night with the feeling that someone or something was outside his bedroom door and while waiting for a knock to summon him, he suddenly saw a human head and shoulders with nothing below them, gliding along a wall of the bedroom, high up near the ceiling.

It stopped opposite and looked down at him. He stared back at the head without a body—and suddenly it was no longer there. Next morning he asked why he had been put in the haunted room and was told that no visitor was ever put in there and that the room he had occupied was in fact immediately below the haunted room.

His host went on to say that knocks that could not be explained were often heard in that part of the castle. Some years before, the doctor was told, when repairs were carried out in the Tower part of the castle, a skeleton head and shoulders were discovered and these bones were taken out and buried but unlike many hauntings, the half-ghost of Meggernie was seen again.

Meggernie Castle once belonged to the Clan Menzies and a former laird is said to have committed a cruel murder that gave rise to the haunting. Insanely jealous of his beautiful young wife he murdered her in the Tower, cut her body in two and concealed the portions in the closet between the two Tower rooms. Then, spreading the word that he and his wife would be abroad for some months, he left Meggernie only returning when he felt that the danger of discovery was past and he could bury the remains of his wife. Stating that his wife had met with an accident abroad, he succeeded in conveying one half of her body to the graveyard where he buried it unobserved.

He intended to do likewise with the upper part of the body but the night he chose for this task— a more dangerous one since the head would be recognizable —he was himself found dead at the entrance to the Tower in circumstances that suggested that he had been murdered; perhaps by someone who had discovered the laird's awful secret. But there was no evidence to show who murdered the murderer and the affair was allowed to rest.

Alternatively it has been suggested that the laird encountered the incomplete apparition of his young wife whom he had butchered so cruelly and met his death from shock.

And if the unfortunate lady was as free with her kisses in her life as she seems to have been in death, perhaps there was some justification for her husband's jealousy.

BALLACHULISH, ARGYLLSHIRE

Ballachulish House is haunted, as indeed it should be, for here, or rather in the house that formerly occupied the site, Captain Campbell was ordered to put to the sword every MacDonald under seventy years of age and the scene of the resulting massacre is less than five miles away.

The present house is said to be haunted by the ghost of a Stewart of Appin who gallops up to the house, dismounts and then vanishes as he reaches the doorway; while on the beech-lined road leading to the house the inexplicable clip-clop of horses' hooves has often been heard and here, too, a ghostly rider has been seen dismounting from his ghostly horse.

There is a story too of a phantom tinker seen near the gate of Ballachulish House on autumn evenings; and when the place was occupied by Sir Harold Boulton (who wrote Over the Sea to Skye) a footman complained that he had seen a ghost walk through a wall in the house.

Sir Harold always vouched for the authenticity of a very strange story. Years before he had ever heard of Ballachulish House, his mother would speak of a beautifully-situated residence about which she often thought and dreamed. So familiar did the dream-house become that she often talked about the place to the family and seemed thoroughly familiar with every corner and part of it. Imagine her surprise when she arrived at Ballachulish House to find that it was the house of her dreams!

She was able to tell Lady Beresford, the owner, about a staircase that used to be a feature of the place but was long bricked-up and out of sight. Imagine her even greater surprise when Lady Beresford told her that she, Mrs Boulton, was the little lady who had haunted Ballachulish House for years!

BALLATER, ABERDEENSHIRE

On the South Road there is a little stream still known as 'The Spinning Jenny Burn'. From time immemorial the figure of an old witch used to be seen sitting beside the stream, spinning; but when road-building altered the course of the burn she was reported to have moved higher up into the hills where she has reputedly been seen in recent years still spinning beside the stream.

BANFF, BANFFSHIRE

Not far from here, in the beautiful and wild countryside, there is a romantic valley that is almost unchanged for hundreds of years; a valley that is haunted by a Green Lady.

The wife of a local laird had been dead some six months when one of her husband's ploughmen, returning home on horseback in the twilight of an autumn evening, was accosted, as he was about to cross a small stream, by a strange lady dressed from head to foot in green.

Tall and slim, her face hidden in the mantle of her hood, she politely requested to be taken up behind the rider and carried across the stream.

There was something in the tone of her voice that chilled the hearer and, as he afterwards said, seemed to insinuate itself in the form of an icy fluid between his skull and his scalp. The request itself was odd for the stream was little more than a rivulet, small and slight, presenting no problem to the most timid traveller.

However the man offered the young woman a lift, partly on account of the odd chill that ran through him when she spoke and partly because he did not wish to appear discourteous.

She lightly sprang up behind him and he then found that she was more easily seen than touched for where she came in contact with his back it felt, he asserted afterwards, as though she was a half-filled sack of wool.

As soon as they reached the other side of the stream she leapt down as lightly as she had mounted. He turned to catch a second glimpse of her, sure now that she was a creature less of this earth than himself. She turned towards him, opening as she did so the enveloping hood of her cloak, to disclose a face, thin and pale, but apparently full of life.

'My dead mistress!' exclaimed the ploughman. 'Yes, John; your mistress,' replied the green ghost. 'But ride home quickly for it is getting late and you and I will be better acquainted before long.' John rode swiftly home and told his story.

Next evening, at about the same hour, two of the laird's servant girls were washing when they heard a light tap on the door. 'Come in,' one of the girls called out and in walked the Green Lady. She swept past the two wide-eyed girls and seated herself on a low bench which she had often used during her lifetime, as it gave her a good view of her servants.

Now she began to question them as to how their work was going as she had often done in the past but the girls were too frightened to reply. Soon she moved with a strange half-gliding motion out of the room and into another part of the house occupied by an old nurse of whom she had been very fond. She still seemed to be interested in the old woman's welfare and remarked on the emptiness of the food cupboard!

For almost a year scarcely a day passed when the Green Lady was not seen by some of the servants though never, except for one possible exception, after the sun had risen or before it set. Evening after evening she would glide into the kitchen and enquire about the girls' work and happiness.

As time passed, nearly all the people in the house became used to her presence; the servants looked upon her as a troublesome mistress they no longer needed to heed. When she arrived, they would lower their voices, thinking for a moment that it was a person of flesh and blood, then they would resume their normal chatter, remarking that it was 'only the Green Lady'.

Although shockingly pale and miserable-looking, the phantom nevertheless affected a joyous disposition and was frequently heard to chuckle and laugh—sometimes when she was not visible!

Once, provoked by the continuous silence of one of the servants, the ghost threw a pillow at the girl's head, which she caught and returned! Another time she presented her first acquaintance, the ploughman, with what appeared to be a handful of silver coins which he transferred to his pocket —only to find when he tried to spend them, that they were slivers of slate.

A horseman, passing a clump of trees, found himself repeatedly struck from behind by little pellets of turf and, riding into the thicket, discovered his assailant to be the Green Lady. She never appeared to her husband, although he frequently heard the sound of her voice echoing from the lower part of the house and sometimes also the faint peal of her cold and unnatural laugh.

Then one wet and stormy day, at noon about a year after she had first been seen, she appeared in the room of the old nurse, warning her to get help quickly to save two of the children who were in danger on the rocks by the seashore. The old woman lost no time in doing as she was directed and so impressed the father with her earnestness that he set out at once.

Reaching the top of the cliffs he saw, far below him, the two children clinging to the highest crags of a rock, with the restless and storm-tossed sea threatening to engulf them or pluck them from their perches.

Frantic with terror for their safety he nevertheless judged that he had time to get help before the waters completely swept over the rock and sure enough no sooner had the children been snatched to safety than an immense wave, twice the height of a man, broke over the topmost part of the rock.

When she returned to her room, the old nurse found the Green Lady sitting beside the fire and there she related the reason for her restlessness after death.

Ten years before, she said, a travelling pedlar broke into the fruit garden and an old ploughman was sent to drive him away, since it was a Sunday and there was no one else at home. The pedlar turned on the old servant; she went to his assistance, and in the fight that followed, the trespasser was killed.

At first it was decided to take the whole matter to the laird but when the laird's lady saw the dead man's pack with its silks and velvets and a lovely piece of green satin they hit on the plan of burying the body and dividing the goods and money between them.

The money was hidden in a little cavity under a tapestry in her bedroom and the green satin was made into a dress…

As the Green Lady's story ended the old nurse watched, aghast, as the figure slowly and sadly glided away in a gleam of light that made the old woman shield her eyes with her hand. When she looked again, the Green Lady had vanished.

A little hoard of gold coins was found concealed as the ghost had said and some mouldering remains of the pedlar; evidence of the truth of the ghost's story.

BEAULY, INVERNESS-SHIRE

The thirteenth-century remains of the Valliscaulian Priory of St John are the subject of a legend concerning a wager with the Devil that is said to be proved by the evidence of a ghostly handprint (four fingers and a thumb) on the stone doorway.

The legend became known as the 'Tailor of Beauly Priory' although in fact its origin seems to go back no more than a hundred years or so.

It probably has been confused with another from Argyllshire, at Ardchattan, where the same ingredients form part of a local legend.

BEN IME, GLENCROE, ARGYLLSHIRE

A few years ago Kenneth Richmond, a lecturer at the University of Glasgow, climbed snowy Ben Ime looking for ptarmigan, the smallest British grouse that frequents the Arctic and sub-Arctic regions of the Northern hemisphere including Scotland. Instead he found a ghost.

Richmond was eating his sandwiches near the top of the mountain when he saw, plodding towards him, the figure of an old man, dressed in a bowler hat, wearing a gold watch-chain across his waistcoat and carrying a large paper parcel under his arm. 'His face was the colour of parchment,' Richmond said, 'as if he had spent his life at a city desk, yet he did not even seem to be out of breath.'

The old man slowed down and then stopped and seemed to be fidgeting with the parcel. Richmond was intrigued as to what could have brought the man so far off the beaten track and after greeting his fellow-climber, he asked him which way he had come.

'From Arrochar' he was told, the village at the head of Loch Long, a long road and mountain walk away. Such a climb hardly seemed possible for an octogenarian, as the old man must have surely been. Richmond asked him whether he had noticed any birds on the way up. The man said he had seen four speckled water-hens and he pointed out the exact spot, downhill in the direction he had apparently climbed. 'Och, well,' he remarked, looking at his pocket watch; 'I'd best be getting along. Mustn't miss my train.'

'Train from where?' asked Richmond. 'From Glasgow: six-ten from Arrochar,' the old man replied and, with a wave of his hand, turned and set off the way he had come.

Richmond looked at his watch. It was only three-thirty, but on foot the old man could not hope to catch the train he had mentioned (especially as he seemed intent on walking via Glencroe, a long way round) and, since he had left his car down in Glencroe, the lecturer felt that he must offer his strange fellow-mountaineer a lift to his station.

He set off and soon caught up with the old man, but the latter would not hear of a lift, insisting that he had plenty of time and that the walk would do him good. With that the odd figure set off again leaving Richmond to resume his climbing. Looking back a moment later, Richmond was surprised at seeing no sign of the strange figure. The three-thousand feet of open, snowy slope below him appeared to be utterly deserted.

Thinking that perhaps the old man was resting behind a rock, Richmond sat down and scanned the slopes with his binoculars, watching for him to reappear but he did not see the figure again.

Later, on his way down the mountain, Richmond paused at the spot where the old man had seen the four water-hens and, sure enough, there they were. Then, as he was looking at the criss-cross pattern of ptarmigan trails in the snow, he realized that there were no human footprints in the snow other than his own leading down from the summit ridge.

It was twenty-to-six when he reached his car and he drove towards Arrochar. There he discovered that there was no train at six-ten. By this time Richmond was puzzled and he wondered whether the old man was still somewhere on the hills or perhaps had caught a bus—or maybe slipped and hurt himself.

Wondering whether he should notify the police, he decided to check first with the ticket collector at the station. There he was still further puzzled to learn that no man of such a description had arrived that morning, or any other morning as far as could be recollected!

'A strange business,' was Kenneth Richmond's conclusion. 'And our brief encounter will never be renewed if I can help it; since that day I have stayed away from Ben Ime.'

BEN MACDHUI, THE CAIRNGORMS

The River Spey is regarded by those who should know as one of the fastest major rivers in Britain.

The Grants have been associated with this valley (or 'strath') of the Spey since time immemorial and they even have a special snowdrift of their own on Cairngorm, the blue mountain, which is supposed to wax and wane with the fortunes of the clan.

One of the six main peaks of the Cairngorms and the highest in Ben Macdhui (4,296 feet) with its flat and bare summit; a mountain with a spectre known as the Big Grey Man of Ben Macdhui, whose 'existence' or presence has been vouched for by a considerable number of people over the years.

The appearance of the figure and the experience of the climbers vary considerably and it seems interesting to consider some of the reports chronologically.

An early report came from Norman Collie, Professor of Organic Chemistry at the University of London (1902-1928) and Fellow of the Royal Society. He stated that in 1891 he was returning from the cairn on the summit in a mist when he heard footsteps following him, but taking steps three or four times the length of his own. He stopped and listened and peered into the mist but could see nothing.

Suddenly terror seized Collie; he took to his heels and staggered blindly among the boulders for several miles until he saw the Rothiemurchus Forest ahead and realized that the mysterious footsteps were no longer following him.

In the summer of 1904 Hugh Welsh and his brother spent a fortnight camping as near the summit cairn as possible, collecting alpine plants and spiders.

During their first nights at the summit of Ben Macdhui, they both heard soft footsteps following them but they never saw anything that might account for the sounds. Later they heard distinct footsteps in daylight and were conscious of 'something' near them, an eerie sensation on a deserted mountain.

They never saw anything that could have explained the matter.

Dr A. M. Kellas, who died during the 1921-1922 Mount Everest Reconnaissance Expedition and is buried within sight of that mountain, was a very experienced mountaineer.

He claimed that one clear June night he was on the summit of Ben Macdhui with his brother; they were resting a little apart from each other. Suddenly Kellas saw a figure climb up out of the Lairig Ghru pass, wander round the cairn and then disappear again into the pass. The doctor was struck dumb in astonishment: not only by the fact that someone else was on the summit but more particularly at the enormous size of the figure for, as it passed close to the ten-foot high cairn, it seemed to be about the same height! His brother saw nothing.

George Duncan, a former Honorary Sheriff-Substitute of Aberdeen and a veteran mountaineer, told of seeing a tall figure in a black robe as he drove along the Derry road at dusk after coming off the mountain in 1914.

The figure appeared to be waving long arms in a menacing fashion and Duncan felt a cold shiver run down his spine before he turned a corner and the figure was no longer in view.

In 1928 a psychic, Joan Grant and her husband were walking in brilliant sunshine in the Rothiemurchus Forest towards the Cairngorms when she was suddenly overwhelmed with terror and turned and fled back along the path they had just traversed through the forest.

She was convinced that something 'utterly malign, four-legged and obscenely human, invisible and yet solid' (for she could hear the pounding of hooves), was trying to reach her.

A year later one of her father's professors described an almost identical experience in the same area and there was some correspondence in The Times, including a letter from a reader who claimed to have been pursued by 'something'.

In 1941 Miss Wendy Wood, a well-known Scottish naturalist, fled in terror from the Lairig Ghru pass. She had just reached the entrance to the pass at night after a dull day with slight snow on the ground, when she heard a voice 'of gigantic resonance' close beside her. It sounded like Gaelic but she was too frightened to attempt any interpretation and she was trying to convince herself that it must be an echo of a deer's bark or something of the sort when she heard the sound again, right at her feet.

There could be no doubt this time but that it was human speech. Still she tried to look at the mystery logically and she tramped round in widening circles in case someone was lying injured under the snow but once she was satisfied that she was not deserting anyone in distress, fear took over and she couldn't get away from the place fast enough.

Then she heard gigantic footfalls which seemed to follow her hurrying footsteps and she had the impression that something was walking immediately behind her.

Just as she was trying to tell herself that the footsteps were echoes of her own, she discovered that the heavy crunch-crunch behind her did not coincide with her own progress and then terror possessed her and without thought of injury to herself she stumbled down the mountain until a barking dog drew her mind back to the world of reality and she realized that she could no longer hear the footsteps following her.

In 1943 Alexander Tewnion, another experienced mountaineer, naturalist and photographer, reached the summit of Ben Macdhui one October afternoon when climbing alone, just as a dense mist spread across the Lairig Ghru and enveloped the mountain. The atmosphere became dark and gloomy and as the wind rose, Tewnion feared a storm was imminent and he retreated down the Coire Etchachan path. As he did so, he heard one loud footstep, echoing through the wind, and then another and another, spaced out at long intervals.

As he carried a revolver Tewnion stopped and peered about him into the mist that was rent here and there by eddies of wind. Suddenly a huge shape loomed up, receded and then appeared to charge straight at him! Without hesitation he pulled out his revolver and fired three times at the figure. Still it came on and Tewnion turned and ran down the path without another backward glance, reaching Glen Derry, as he put it, 'in a time I have never bettered!'

In 1942, while at the Shelter Stone of Ben Macdhui, alone at twilight, Second World War veteran Syd Scroggie suddenly saw a tall human figure appear out of the blackness at one side of the Loch Etchachan below and, clearly silhouetted against the water, walk with long and deliberate steps across the burns and disappear into the blackness at the other side of the loch.

Noticing that the figure carried no rucksack, Scroggie was quickly over the rough ground and at the spot where the figure had crossed.

No footprints were visible and there was now no sign of the mysterious figure. Scroggie began shouting but he received no reply, only the echo of his own voice. He became uneasily aware of the approaching darkness and silence surrounding him like a blanket and the brooding, watching Cairngorms. With the hair at the back of his neck beginning to bristle, Scroggie made his way back to the Shelter Stone.

These are but a few of the reports of strange experiences on the wild and stony slopes of Ben Macdhui; reports that have convinced such well-known Scotsmen as Henry Tegner that something out of the ordinary does, on occasions, take place in these Highland mountains.

BENDERLOCH, NEAR OBAN, ARGYLLSHIRE

Sir Hubert Stewart Rankine has described a figure that disappeared into the air when he encountered it in the haunted valley of the Glendhu Burn. This is a deep and unfrequented burn that runs into the sea near Barcaldine Post Office on the coast road to Appin.

A dark, dank place with little life apart from the mournful trees, and even sheep steer clear of the neighbourhood. Local people have long shunned the valley and will tell you that they 'fear something...'

On this particular winter's day his stalker was reluctant to go into the area and after Sir Hubert had shot a stag he made his way alone down the glen, in broad daylight, towards his home.

Suddenly, when he was half-way down, he noticed a dark figure standing near a forestry hut, just above a bog. As he drew nearer, Sir Hubert saw that the figure was a youngish man, large and powerfully-built, wearing a kilt and armed with a dirk.

His long hair streamed in the wind; his brogues were thick with mud and he looked puzzled and angry. It was the face of the man that impressed itself on Sir Hubert's memory for it bore a fierce and scowling expression. The figure appeared to be unaware of him. The mouth, large and cruel, was crooked in a curious way and of an unusual shape. The eyes glared as if in anger or distress but no words or indeed any sound accompanied the figure as it moved with gliding steps.

It seemed to follow Sir Hubert for perhaps half a mile down

the burn, until he reached a cottage, the only inhabited place in the area, where the figure disappeared into thin air. One moment it was there, purposefully making its way down the valley, the next there was nothing to be seen where the greyish and almost transparent apparition had been.

Sir Hubert immediately thought of Campbell (or 'Crooked Mouth' from the Gaelic words for 'crooked' and 'mouth': cam and béal). He wondered whether this was the Campbell who was the victim of the Appin murder, an historical whodunit that has attracted the attention of writers like Robert Louis Stevenson, Andrew Lang, Sir William MacArthur and Hugh Ross Williamson.

Colin Campbell of Glenure—the Red Fox—was shot dead on May 14th, 1752; an aftermath of the troubles of '45 when the clans were suppressed, the kilt forbidden and the lands of loyal Highlanders confiscated.

THE BLACK ISLE, ROSS AND CROMARTY (SEE ALSO CROMARTY)

The Devil is said to have been in the habit of appearing here in the shape of a handsome young man. mounted on a black horse, usually in the vicinity of Mount High, four miles distant from its twin peak, Mount Eagle.

Only a few years ago the older inhabitants talked of such visitations but the younger people have no time for such legends. Yet 'truth is in folklore', one historian has reminded us; 'you'll not find lies carried down the years'.

The peninsula's inhabitants included in the past Coinneach Odhar, known as the Wizard of Brahan, who had the gift of second sight and came to be regarded as an emissary of the Devil. He ended his days two hundred years ago by being burned to death in a barrel of tar at Chanonry Point, opposite Fort George on the other side of the Moray Firth.

More recently a woman known as 'Red Jock's Wife' was regarded as a witch for she had the evil eye. ft was said that she could turn butter bad at a glance or cause a cow to 'slip' her calf. Occasionally, however, she used her gift to good account.

There is a report that after he had been kind to her by carrying her basket, a youngster named Hughie lost in the harvest field a fine silver watch which he had bought with his first wages; but after he and his family and friends had spent hours searching the stubble, Red Jock's Wife led him to it, a week after it had been lost, with her eyes closed.

Another story about Red Jock's Wife concerned the Laird of Ballincailleach, a man who was inordinately proud of his high-bred white sow named Beatrice of Ballincailleach. The laird chanced to be rude to Red Jock's Wife and refused her a fill of tobacco; an action he regretted when his sow gave birth to eleven beautiful young pigs, all born dead.

A large hare was seen to dart out of the sty after the births and someone suggested that it was Red Jock's Wife in disguise since it was well known that witches could turn themselves into hares and could cause animals to be born dead.

The laird took a silver sixpence from his pocket and loaded it into his gun and he shot the hare in the leg but it ran off on three legs, through a fence and across fields, to disappear into the moor.

Red Jock's Wife was not seen for some weeks afterwards. It was rumoured that she had slipped on the stairs and hurt her leg although everyone knew how it was really hurt. When she recovered she was treated with greater respect and awe than before.

At Cromarty churchyard you can see a grave that is outside the wall of the churchyard. The reason for this is said to have been the friendly quarrel between two crofters who lived on the hillside here, Donald and Sandy. They were good neighbours on the whole but could never agree on one of their boundaries, a dividing line marked only by two large boulders several hundred yards apart.

Each winter, before ploughing began, first one of the neighbours and then the other, would get up early and push the boulders ten or twenty yards, seeking to enlarge their respective pieces of land by a strip some ten yards by three-hundred; until eventually one or the other would plough the first furrow one misty dawn and so confirm the land as belonging to him for twelve months of crops.

The following winter the same thing would happen and for years the practice continued, until one winter Sandy died, with the boulders enlarging his land. But Donald respected his old friend for there was Sandy's widow and six children to think of so he let the stones stay although he considered that they were a dozen yards inside his land.

The years passed and as he pondered on the life to come, Donald remembered that one day, so he had been taught, the trumpets would sound and the neighbors, Sandy and himself, would rise from their graves.

Donald pondered deeply about this and left instructions that he was to be buried outside the wall of the churchyard when he died for he reasoned that by doing so he would have a good start on Sandy who would have the high churchyard wall to climb while Donald would be rolling the boundary stones back to their rightful place!

From time immemorial there has been the belief that the Devil has appeared on Mount High and there is certainly an undefinable atmosphere here at midnight that makes such legends understandable.

When the moonlight shimmers on Donald's grave and the churchyard wall, it is not difficult to imagine that any minute the silence will be broken by the sound of a trumpet and that the graves will yawn and give up their undead.

Balconie House, Cromarty, has a curious and wild legendary story associated with it and the deep and narrow gorge nearby where the River Allt Grande flow's on its rocky course. It is a gloomy place that has long had a sinister reputation on account of the peculiar and strange experiences of visitors to this lonely spot.

The narrow gorge is awesome to behold with its gloomy cliffs and inaccessible caverns where the light of day never reaches, while the hoarse and hollow murmuring of waterfalls and cascades rises from the depths far below.

Back in the seventeenth century the Laird of Balconie brought home after wanderings abroad a young and beautiful wife, a reserved and quiet girl who shunned society and never talked about her life before she met the laird. For her the gorge of the Allt Grande seemed to have an overwhelming fascination and she would spend hours there each day.

Gradually a great change came over her. She became more sociable, less reserved, but she had a wild air that in some mysterious way worried those with whom she came in contact. It was almost as though she were bewitched and belonged not among mortals but to some other world.

She became particularly attached to one of the maids, a pretty and simple Highland girl. One evening the two of them went to the gorge. There a dark man in green suddenly materialized, took the young bride by the hand and led her to the brink of the gorge.

The maid stood rooted to the ground as her mistress, with a backward glance of infinite sadness, untied a bunch of household keys from her belt and threw them to the maid. They struck a granite boulder and an impression made on the stone is pointed out to this day as that made by the keys.

When she had picked up the keys and looked again for her mistress, the maid discovered that both figures had vanished. Terrified, she ran back to the house and panted out her story. The resulting search for the lady of Balconie House continued unabated but unsuccessfully for days.

Ten years later a Scottish fisherman, searching in the gorge for a basket of fish that he had lost, climbed down to a ledge and discovered an enormous cavern. Two black dogs rose as he entered but lay down again and let him pass. Beyond he saw his basket of fish on an iron table and, seated on an iron chair by the table, was the long lost lady of Balconie House!

When the fisherman offered to take her home she pointed to the chains that fastened her to the chair which was in turn fastened to the rocky wall of the cave and replied that she would never be free. She begged him to leave quickly and she threw some meat to the dogs to keep them quiet for they were becoming restive and eyeing the intruder bale-fully.

The fisherman therefore lost no time in picking up his basket of fish and leaving the cave, returning the way he had come, a difficult and dangerous scramble and climb. Once safe above ground, he lost no time in telling the local people of his adventure.

Although many tried to locate the cavern and liberate the prisoner lady of Balconie, they all failed and she was never seen again. It was generally thought that she must have broken some pact or deal with the Devil and that in the guise of a dark man in green he or one of his demon friends had captured her.

Looking down the deep and narrow gorge today it is not too difficult to visualize such a story having a profound effect on people three hundred years ago. Even in 19*70 it was possible to find inhabitants who believed that the strange noises emanating on occasions from the mysterious gorge, which produces odd acoustic effects, might be supernormal in origin.

BLACKNESS, WEST LOTHIAN

Inland, but once connected to the port on the River Forth, stands The Binns, former home of General Tam Dalyell. still looking much as he must have proudly surveyed it after its restoration.

When he was commander-in-chief of the forces in Scotland, in 1681, he formed the regiment that became known as the Royal Scots Greys and the first musters were held here. The mansion was presented to the National Trust in 1944, after being in the Dalyell family for over three hundred years.

According to those who live on the banks of this picturesque river, the countryside is peopled with native spirits. A little old man in a brown habit is to be seen gathering sticks on the hillside above Binns; a water-sprite lures the unwary to death in the dark waters of the ancient pond below the hill.

Other primitive forms are glimpsed here from time to time, perhaps survivors of the Picts who made their last stand here against the Romans.

The ghost of General Dalyell himself has been seen, mounted on a white charger, galloping across the ruined bridge over the Errack Burn; in the vicinity of the Binns tower; and up the old road to his house, where the General's riding-boots and spurs are preserved to this day.

In his lifetime, it is said, Tam Dalyell used to play cards with the Devil. Once, when Tam won, the enraged Devil threw the table they had been playing on at his head but it flew past him and dropped into Sergeant's Pond, outside the house.

This is one of many strange stories told about General Dalyell, tales of which few people took much notice until, one day during the dry summer of 1878, the water of the pond was reduced to a new low and there, stuck fast in the mud at the bottom of the pond, was a heavy carved table that must have been there for all of two hundred years.

It seems that the General had another argument with the Devil over cards, resulting in Satan threatening to blow his house down upon him. General Dalyell retorted that he would build extra thick walls to protect the house.

The Devil replied that he would blow down the house and the walls—to which the General answered that he would build a turret at every corner of the house to pin down the walls.

Today you can see turrets at each corner of the historic old house, which certainly serve no purpose—-unless they have prevented the Devil from blowing the property down!

BLADNOCH, NEAR WIGTOWN, WIGTOWNSHIRE

The one street in this riverside village leads to a bridge; a left turn and the road to Baldoon Mains leads to the ivy-covered ruins of Baldoon Castle. Opposite the castle ruins, a fine old gateway gives access to the Mains (which probably belonged to the castle years ago). Looking back, the castle ruins are framed between the picturesque pillars of the gateway.

The ruins themselves, quiet and deserted and with an air of tragedy about them, are haunted by the ghost of Janet Dalrymple who walks here in the small hours, her white garments splashed with blood.

In the middle of the seventeenth century Janet, the eldest

daughter of Sir James Dalrymple, was forced by her parents to marry David Dunbar, heir of Sir David Dunbar of Baldoon, although she loved the practically penniless Archibald, third Lord Rutherford.

Dutifully, and worn down by her parents' persistent objections to Archibald, Janet at last married David Dunbar in the kirk of Old Luce, two miles from Carsecleugh Castle, the old home of the Dalrymples. Her two brothers took her to the church and both declared later that her hands were cold as ice on that hot summer day.

There are three main versions of the events that gave rise to the haunting. In the first version the bride stabs her bridegroom in the bridal chamber and dies insane; in the second version the bridegroom stabs the bride and is found insane; and in the third version the disappointed Archibald conceals himself in the bridal chamber and escapes through the window into the garden after stabbing the bridegroom.

Whatever the facts, Sir Walter Scott immortalized the story in The Bride of Lammermoor and describes how the door of the bridal chamber was broken down after hideous shrieks were heard from within and how the bridegroom was found lying across the threshold, dreadfully wounded and streaming with blood, while the bride crouched in a chimney corner, her white nightgown splashed with blood, grinning and muttering and quite insane. She never recovered and died shortly afterwards, on September 12th, 1669.

Dunbar is said to have recovered from his wounds but refused to discuss the events of his bridal night. In due course he married a daughter of the seventh Earl of Eglinton and eventually died from a fall from his horse in 1682. Archibald, Janet's true lover, never married and died in 1685.

A macabre touch is added to the story by local tradition that it was the Devil who nearly killed Dunbar and who tormented poor Janet until she was demented. Whatever the events of the night, they seem to have left their mark here forever and there are some who claim to have seen the sad and awesome ghost of Janet wandering pathetically among the quiet ruins, most often on the anniversary of her death.

BLAIRGOWRIE, PERTHSHIRE

Lovely Ardblair Castle, built on the foundations of a Pictish stronghold, is today, after careful restoration in 1890 and 1908, much as it was back in the twelfth century. In particular, the dungeon with its six-foot thick walls is almost as it must have been eight hundred years ago.

A member of the Blair family built Ardblair Castle—probably William de Blair, a courtier to the patron of the monasteries, William the Lion. Descendants of that ancient and honoured family still live there. Blairs, with neighbouring families by the names of Herons and Drummonds, bore arms to assist Robert the Bruce. It was some differences of opinion with their neighbours that traditionally caused the haunting of Ardblair Castle.

At the time of the tragedy the Blairs of Ardblair and the Drummonds of Newton were feuding. There is a long and fanciful Scots poem that tells of the Lady Jean Drummond being whisked away by the little people immediately after her wedding, for having no wedding dress she had borrowed green finery from the water kelpies and so put herself in their power.

A more prosaic version of the fate of the Lady Jane tells of her deep love for a Blair which was not allowed to end in marriage because of opposition by the feuding families. In despair, the sad Lady Jane drowned herself in the surrounding marshes.

Whatever her end, the ghost of this gentle and lovely creature is said to haunt both Newton and Ardblair. She has most frequently been seen between five and six o'clock on sunny afternoons, sitting sadly on the window seat in the long gallery at Ardblair, gazing out of the window.

Her attitude and appearance are so sad that no one who sees her ever speaks to her. Wrapped up in her grief as she is, she never frightens anyone, either as she sits or as she passes through rooms and corridors without making a sound but opening and closing doors as she goes.

The Blair family have always regarded the Green Lady with respect and accepted her presence because of her obvious grief and unhappiness. During the 1939-1945 War some evacuees from Glasgow were billeted in the tower and long gallery where she was most often seen. She evidently disliked their presence in the castle and although her methods were not disclosed, she seems to have caused them to leave Ardblair within a very short time.

BOAT OF GARTEN, MORAYSHIRE

A little north of Boat of Garten Bridge several parts of a stone slab can be seen in a pool on the River Spey, when the water is low, embedded in the sand. Parts of an inscription are just visible, or were when I was there a few years ago.

I made enquiries and learned that the inscription related a curious 'dividing of the waters' enabling a woman's body to be carried across the river on dry ground for burial. The stone was originally erected by William Grant on March 9th, 1865.

Over the years the name of the woman has been described differently but all the stories seem to agree that she lived at Tulloch and during her last days expressed a wish to be buried in the churchyard at Duthil, across the river.

When she was told that it might not be possible if the river should be in flood, she replied, 'God will find a way,' and specified a particular part of the river where the crossing would be effected without difficulty.

After she died, the funeral party duly made for the place on the river bank that the dying woman had told them about and although the Spey was in flood, as soon as they were ready to cross the waters divided and the procession passed over with dry feet. The rector of Tulloch wrote of the 'miracle' and described the walls of water on each side of the funeral party 'like the Red Sea of old'.

It is said that salmon and other fish foundered and struggled on the wet river bed as the waters separated but when onlookers ventured forward in the wake of the procession to capture the helpless fish, the waters closed together again and no harm came to any.

Near the existing farm of Gartenbeg the mourners set up a post with an arm indicating the place where the waters had miraculously parted, although no sign of this indication of the strange happening exists today.

The 'miracle stone' north of the bridge, was consecrated for all time—like the memorial stones of the Jordan—by a sect known as The Men, of which William Grant was a leading light. After prayer and praise it was prophesied that broom would flower to the left and to the right of the stone as a sign to disbelievers. Sceptics noted that the prophecy had every chance of being fulfilled, as indeed it was, since the slab was carefully set between two bushes of the plant.

Criticism by many local people grew and resulted in the formation of an anti-stone organization whose members did all they could to discredit the alleged miracle. The local Free Church denounced the story of the crossing as an 'abominable lie' and the memorial slab as a stone that put 'lies upon God and man'. Questions were asked about the character of a woman with such apparent powers and even mutterings of witchcraft were heard.

For two years the controversy raged and then, on the morning of February 19th. 1867, the memorial stone was found broken and the pieces cast into the river. Ever since the Spey has lapped and covered and uncovered in turn the remains of the stone that was erected because of the reputed miraculous action of these waters.

Whether the stone was broken and thrown into the river by human or supernormal means was never discovered but no one attempted to restore it, although years later fragments of the stone were sought by souvenir hunters. The tenants of a nearby Knock farmhouse dug up a large portion of the stone and used it as a doorstep.

Almost immediately the house was reported to be haunted by movement of objects without human contact, unexplained appearances of articles and phantom lights.

Hailstones the size of a cricket ball are said to have plagued the occupants of the house in mid-summer; turnips and large stones are said to have hurtled down the farmhouse chimney and through closed windows without breaking the glass; furniture was moved up and down stairs at night-time; stones and straw were continually flying about the house and everyone was kept busy sweeping and cleaning up and replacing things in their correct places.

The local minister suggested the slow burning of a rowan tree outside the house, an ancient cure for witchcraft. Although this was done, it had no effect and, whether due to the mysterious happenings or not, the inhabitants of the house died within a short space of time with the solitary exception of one old woman who cured warts and other afflictions. She lived on, respected and feared and took whatever secrets she had about the house and its inhabitants, to the grave with her.

One of the first actions of the next tenant of Knock Farm was to return the slab of memorial stone to its resting place in the river—and from that day the curious happenings ceased.

From time to time the reputedly evil power of the stone comes back into the news. Some years ago five boys uncovered the stone from its sandy bed and within months they were all dead.

In 1940 a plane returning from a bombing raid on the continent crashed on the river bank not far from the stone and it was recalled that one of the crew had meddled with the stone in his youth.

Even today it is possible to find local people who regard looking at the stone as unlucky and some even believe that the stone is guarded by a giant eel which devours cattle who stray too near the mysterious Stone of Spey.

BOWLAND, VALE OF GALE, MIDLOTHIAN

In the middle of the nineteenth century a man named Rutherford, a member of the landed gentry class resident in this area, had a singular dream which intrigued Sir Walter Scott.

Mr Rutherford was being sued for a considerable sum of money, the accumulated arrears of tithes due. Rutherford himself was of the opinion that his father had procured these tithes by means of a process peculiar to the law of Scotland.

But he was unable to find any documentary evidence among his father's papers or any confirmation from those who had transacted legal business for his father or from published records. Without anything to support his defence he was about to set out for Edinburgh when, on the eve of the lawsuit, he dreamed that his late father appeared to him.

The old man, who had been dead for many years, seemed conscious of his son's troubles and told him that he had, indeed, acquired the rights of the tithes. The relevant papers were in the hands of a retired attorney, resident at Inveresk, who might well have forgotten all about the only business he ever conducted for Mr Rutherford, senior.

To bring the matter to the aged lawyer's mind, Rutherford suggested to his son to remind the old man that when the account was paid there was some difficulty in getting change and the lawyer and his client spent the balance at a nearby inn.

Next morning, the dream or vision crystal-clear in his mind, young Rutherford set off early for Edinburgh, by way of Inveresk. There he succeeded in locating the lawyer in question and after mentioning the matter of the change and the drink at the inn, the old man finally recalled the matter, made an immediate search of his papers and discovering the relevant ones, was able to send Rutherford on his way to Edinburgh with the necessary documents so that he could win the case.

BRAEMAR, ABERDEENSHIRE

Behind a shop, near the bridge over the Clunie River and not far from the cottage where Robert Louis Stevenson wrote part of Treasure Island, are the foundations and ruins of the eleventh-century castle of Kindrochit. Here, in the vaults, according to legend, a ghostly company sits forever round a table heaped with skulls, amid great treasure.

Kindrochit Castle was once the hunting seat and Highland residence of King Robert I of Scotland. It also had a more stern and wear-like purpose. Strategically situated above the gorge of the Clunie Water, the castle served to defend the ancient mountain passes of the Cairnwell and the Tol-mouth which connected the southern parts of the old kingdom with the wild and turbulent north.

As its importance increased, part of the old edifice was pulled down and in 1390 a massive stone tower (the fifth largest in Scotland) was built by Sir Malcolm Drummond, the constable of the castle. Work continued for many years, some of the stones being brought over the hills from Kildrummy, where the English had the whole garrison 'hangyt and drawyn'.

In 1402, however. Sir Malcolm was ambushed and murdered by a band of caterans who infested the surrounding hills.

For over a quarter of a century the Royal Standard flew from the battlements of the great tower and a massive bridge leading to the castle was built across the Clunie.

The castle outworks and tower rose above the woods of Mar until, suddenly and mysteriously, disaster overtook the place. Strong and flourishing in 1400, by the beginning of the sixteenth century the castle was derelict and by 1618 the place was in utter ruin.

There is a tradition that the 'Calar Mor', a terrible plague, broke out in the castle. Terrified that the pestilence might spread, the people of Braemar barricaded the gates and refused to let the garrison escape. Great cannon are said to have been dragged over the Cairnwell from Atholl and turned on the castle and so Kindrochit crashed in ruins amid the shrieks of those trapped within its walls.

When we recall that as late as the sixteenth century those suspected of carrying the plague were hanged on the nearest gallows, it is by no means impossible that there is some truth in the tradition.

For years the ruins continued to crumble, the walls disappeared, trees and bushes covered the remains. In 1746 a Hanoverian soldier was lowered into the vaults to search for the castle treasure.

When he was hauled up after frantic signals, he reported that in the dim light that seeped through to the vast vaults below, he saw an immense company of ghostly people seated around a table heaped with skulls.

In 1925, under the direction of Dr W. Douglas Simpson, serious excavation began. This time no such alarming discoveries were reported but among many interesting finds was the famous silver gilt Kindrochit brooch.

After many difficulties and much hard work the walls of the main part of the old castle were uncovered, but more is thought to exist beneath the shop. On the opposite bank of the Clunie the remains of the old bridge were unearthed which originally led to the castle, providing its name: Ceann-Drochaide or Bridgend.

One of the principal features of St Andrew's churchyard at Braemar is the massive Farquharson vault, the burial place of John Farquharson of Inverey, 'the Black Colonel'. Here he was said to have resurrected himself three times.

Farquharson's home, Inverey Castle, was demolished by Royalist troops after the Battle of Killiecrankie in 1689. Although he had often expressed the wish to be buried in the lonely graveyard near to his ruined home, he was in due course laid to rest in the Farquharson vault in Braemar kirkyard.

The very day after the funeral passers-by were shocked to see the Black Colonel's coffin above ground outside the vault. Arrangements were hastily made for it to be re-interred. Three times the coffin was found above ground and three times it was buried, until someone recalled John Farquharson's request that his remains should lie at Inverey. A raft was constructed and the body was drawn up the River Dee to his favoured place where it was buried in the spot he had loved during his lifetime.

Many years later when two young men were digging a grave at Inverey, they accidentally broke into the Black Colonel's crumbling coffin and each man took one of the Colonel's teeth as a memento. That night the ghost of the enraged Laird of Inverey appeared to both of them and signified that the teeth were to be returned. Early next morning the grisly relics were restored to the Colonel's grave and his ghost was seen no more.

BRECHIN, ANGUS-SHIRE

Kinnaird Castle, the seat of the Earls of Southesk, stands in a large deer park and is the locality of a strange legend concerning a pact with the Devil and a ghostly carriage.

It was said that the body of James, the second Earl, who died in 1669, was collected by the Devil in a coach drawn by six coal-black horses. The coach, horses and all, tore away and plunged into a well near the Carnegies' family burial-ground.

On wild and stormy nights the coach-and-six is reputed to repeat its journey, driving at break-neck speed past the Earl's former home and disappearing in the direction of the old burial-ground.

James Carnegie studied the Black Arts while a student at Padua. Legend has it that the Devil himself was among the professors there and that 'he' conducted a class for advanced students.

The predictable fee was the soul of one pupil; the unlucky one being the last to leave the classroom on a day chosen by the Devil himself. It seems that Carnegie was the last on this occasion but he had the presence of mind to tell the Devil to take his shadow which was cast behind him as he left the room. Satan, with his liking for things of darkness, took the shadow.

Consequently it is said that the second Earl of Southesk never cast a shadow after that. He used to conceal his misfortune in this respect by walking in the shade whenever possible. But the Devil seems to have won in the end.

Brechin Cathedral, now the Parish Church, was founded by King David I in 1150 and has long since been restored but the Round Tower attached to it dates from the eleventh century and is one of three such towers that survive in Scotland, probably used originally for defensive purposes.

The doorway is decorated with crude Celtic carvings of the Crucifixion and fabulous monsters. A nearby valley has long been known as 'the Devil's Den'.

CALLANDER, PERTHSHIRE

A former gamekeeper to an austere member of the Stewart family who resided here saw a ghost which caused him to mend his ways.

The keeper, James Macfarlane, was fond of the ladies in his youth and more than once he broke his master's rule that all his servants should attend family prayers each Sunday. One Sabbath night he was absent, courting a lassie beyond Doune. The head of the family, noticing his absence (and not for the first time), demanded where the 'scoundrel' was, adding vehemently:

'I wish I could give him a fright that would stop him running about courting on Sabbath nights!'

After prayers, the old man, still fuming, went to bed but soon his bedroom bell rang and when a maid-servant answered it, she found her master lying unconscious on the floor. Within minutes he was dead.

About the same time James Macfarlane, having left his sweetheart, was on his way home. As he neared Cambusmore he noticed the form of a man lying directly in his path; indeed he was almost upon it before he saw the form. At first he sprang back, startled; then, thinking it must be someone the worse for drink, he stooped to examine it, only to recoil in horror as he recognized the dead face of his master!

Knowing that his master would not be abroad at that hour on a Sunday, James's hair stood on end as he realized that the form before him was no human body. Turning away, rather than pass it, he fled from the place and took a long detour home.

Breathless and frightened, he was greeted on arrival at the

house with the news that his master was dead. Whether or not the old man had his last earthly wish fulfilled, it is a fact that for the rest of his life James Macfarlane lived a pious life and never again did his courting on a Sunday.

If he ever heard anyone expressing disbelief in ghosts he would shake his head and say: 'I ken well what I ha' seen myself.'

CASTLE DOUGLAS, KIRK-CUDBRIGHTSHIRE

A couple of miles from here, on the Kelton road, there is a little bridge that crosses a stream.

This is Cuckoo Bridge and many years ago the body of a murdered baby was buried in the stream here.

For years the sound of pitiful crying of an infant has been noticed by people crossing the bridge on moonlit nights and occasionally a pathetic little white shape, horrifying and hardly human, has been seen.

CORRIEYAIRACK PASS, INVERNESS-SHIRE

In the vicinity of a stream called the Allt Lagan a' Bhainne there is a broken bridge and here is the haunt of the Ghost of Corrieyairack.

A suspension bridge (erected by the Scottish Rights of Way Society) now spans a stretch of the dangerous stream, all too often shrouded in mist.

It is in such circumstances that a ghostly Highlander is said to loom up out of nowhere, accompanied by two great dogs, and to direct the traveller with the words: 'That way lies your road.'

The ghost only appears when the weather is misty and almost as soon as those encountering the mysterious figure become aware of the presence, the phantom figure and the silent dogs that accompany it disappear.

CRAIGMADDIE MOOR, STIRLINGSHIRE

The 'Auld Wives' Lift', three enormous drift boulders, one placed over the other two, lie at a particularly isolated spot where many visitors report a strange coldness on the warmest summer day and a sense of evil seems to overwhelm those who venture here.

The legend of the Auld Wives' Lift tells of three weird sisters, one from Baldernock, one from Strathblane and one from Campsie, who decided on a trial of strength to prove that if they were not beautiful at least they were strong.

The first hoisted a great boulder on to her shoulders, walked with it far out over the moor and there dropped it to the ground; the second did just as well and placed her boulder at the side of the first one; while the third woman picked up one as large as the other two put together and ran with it over the moor, putting it atop her rivals' pair.

On the wet and silent moor the ancient stones still stand, forming an archway for superstitious young couples to crawl through to ensure that they marry; and a constant source of argument as to which district the undoubted winner came from!

More prosaic students have pointed out that the boulders lie within a natural amphitheatre and probably formed the altar for some bleak deity eons ago. But almost everyone agrees that there is a strange atmosphere here.

One feels afraid to look round quickly for fear of finding that one has slipped back into a bygone age, facing a semi-circle of primitive watching eyes and cruel little men in the amphitheatre that probably saw much bloodshed and cruelty.

Peter G. Currie who lives at Troon tells me that he first walked over Blairskaith and Craigmaddie Moors when he was eighteen, amongst the blue mountain hares (though they were still white in a late spring). Suddenly, over a low hill, he saw the Auld Wives' Lift. Not glacial (could a glacier have perched one boulder atop of another?), Peter Currie noticed the firm foundation of the stones amongst the wet sphagnum bog and the perfect central placing of the group in a natural amphitheatre; this must surely have been design, not chance.

He continued:

'I climbed to the top stone, lay down on the sun-warm surface and fell asleep. I awoke to the worst attack of the horrors that I have ever had. The sky had darkened and thunder drum-rolled around the horizon. I was off that stone and over the moor so fast that my feet had no time to sink in wet peat! I'm not in the least superstitious but that place, to me, smells of blood.

'Talking about blood, I carefully examined the eastern edge of the top stone in September, 1972, where there is what has been described as a gutter cut to drain off sacrificial blood. The edge rises up to a lip (as does the western edge) but on the right there is a distinct depression down which liquid could run, although this depression may be due to natural weathering.'

Visiting the stones on September 2nd, 1972, Peter Currie had a good look at the base area around the stones and he told me that heather and sphagnum (peat or bog moss) sprouted everywhere else, but only grass grew around the three boulders.

He added: 'I remember once when my wife and I traced a lost drove-road through Rothiemurchus, one of the indicators was patches of good grass, where the cattle had milled around before fording a stream, or had rested with the drovers. After two hundred years the effect of the fertilizing dung still showed.

Could blood, and probably flesh and bone, show a similar difference after perhaps two thousand years? One day the surburbia of Glasgow will surround the moors, which will be drained and tamed to golf-course and building sites and the mountain hares with feet big as soup-plates will no longer be seen (there are not so many of them, even now).

A prim little park will enclose the Auld Wives' Lift, and children will scramble over it, and its story will be forgotten. Yet, occasionally, if someone with sensitive nostrils passes by, he will smell blood.'

CRAMOND, EDINBURGH, MIDLOTHIAN

There is a fine walk here along the shore and through the woods to Queensferry. It passes Barnbougle Castle which, according to legend, gets its name from the ghostly wail of a dog that has been heard for many years and reputedly dates from the time of the Crusades.

In those days a pious and lonely man lived here whose name has only come down to us as Sir Roger. He set out to fight in the Crusades.

After keeping vigil in the church of St Adamnan at Dalmeny and praying for his own safety and for the victory of the Brotherhood of the Red Cross Knights, he went to board his ship and found on the quayside his favourite hound.

The dog looked so piteous and wailed so sadly at the thought of his master leaving, that Sir Roger took it with him. For years the faithful dog accompanied the noble knight as he fought bravely.

Then, one dark night, the sound of a bugle rang out from the old tower on the shore where Sir Roger had embarked for Palestine. After a moment, a death-wail sounded on the wind, the awful baying of a ghostly hound. At that very moment Sir Roger lay dead on the battlefield in Syria, his loyal dog beside him.

Still, on dark nights a mournful and dismal wailing noise is sometimes heard that local people think is the wail of Sir Roger's hound.

This is the origin of Hound Point, farther along the shore; there does seem to be evidence to suggest that in the words of

PETER UNDERWOOD

the old ballad:

> *'And ever when Barnbougle's lords*
> *Are parting this scene below,*
> *Come hound and ghost to this haunted coast*
> *With death notes winding slow.'*

CROMARTY, ROSS-SHIRE

There is a wood and a moor near here, once haunted by grisly phantoms that would tear in and out of the trees and round the cairns on wild and stormy nights, cursing, laughing and yelling.

There are stories of ghostly knights in armour, engaged in fierce combat; of spectral old hags chuckling and chortling as they robbed dead and wounded soldiers; and of lovely young maidens who lured men to pools and swamps from which there was no escape.

One wild night a fisherman was crossing the moor and as he passed a wood he saw in the moonlight ahead of him not the distant hills and the still moor but a wild and wide storm-tossed sea, black and foam-flecked, stretching as far as he could see.

He could hear the roar of the wind and the waves; and as the moon lit up the scene, he saw a fishing boat tossed high one moment and low the next. He recognized the occupants: three were Cromarty fishermen and the fourth his own brother. Suddenly a huge wave engulfed the boat and the terrified fisherman fainted.

When he recovered consciousness, he found himself back on the lonely moor; no seas within sight or sound, only the occasional fir tree and the silent landscape, stretching away into the dim distance. Had it all been a dream? The following day there was a sudden squall off Cromarty and among the casualties was a boat containing the three Cromarty fishermen he had recognized and his brother.

Behind the old town, where the ground rises abruptly to a

height of nearly a hundred feet, there once stood the old and massive castle of Cromarty. For years before its demolition the rambling place was tenanted by a single elderly female retainer and a young girl whom she hired to stay with her.

This girl, when she was over seventy, told of the huge chimney in the kitchen; the great hall, a dark oak-lined chamber where a hundred men had more than once exercised at the pike; and the lower vaults which she had never had the temerity to explore: vast, dark and ghostly and nearly full of long, rank grass.

Years before she went there, the place had been looked after by another female who had been foolhardy enough to sleep alone. One night she was frightened nearly out of her wits and never recovered sufficiently to relate what she had seen or heard.

At times a series of mysterious noises would echo through the upper apartments, sounds resembling a heavy man pacing the floors in the deserted castle.

'If you could have heard the shrieks, moans and long, whistling sounds that used to be heard during the winter months from the chimneys and the turrets,' the old lady said, speaking of the days when she was there as a girl, 'you would have done what I did: drew the clothes over my head as I lay listening to the strange noises in the dark night; trying to get to sleep, shivering with terror.'

Once her companion was sitting in a little chamber at the foot of the great stairs when she heard a tapping against the steps and she quietly opened the door. Although the light was poor, she claimed she saw in the twilight a small white animal, something like a rabbit, rolling from step to step, head over heels and dissolving, as it bounded over the last step, into a wreath of smoke.

Another time, when a Cromarty shoemaker was passing by the front of the building one summer morning, he was astonished to see a tiny, grey-haired, grey-bearded old man, with a withered and thin face, scarcely bigger than a fist, seated at one of the windows.

Half an hour later, when he returned by the same path, the shoemaker saw the same figure, wringing his hands over a little cairn in a nearby thicket, but he did not have the courage to approach it to get a better view.

The castle has long since been demolished but two curious remnants of the old building survived until a few years ago. One piece of sculpture could be seen in a vaulted passage that leads from the modern house to the road; a stone slab about five feet in length, nearly two feet wide, that once served as a lintel to one of the two chimneys in the great hall.

There was a huntsman in the centre, attired in a sort of loose coat that reached to his knees, with a lance in one hand and a hunting-spear in the other. He sported a moustache and the peaked beard of the reign of Queen Mary Tudor. The lintel of the second chimney, just as interesting, was preserved at Kinbeakie Cottage in the parish of Resolis.

There was an excellent lithographic print of this lintel in the museum of the Northern Institute, Inverness, but Richard Milne, the Librarian and Curator at Inverness Public Library and Museum, told me in 1972 that when the Northern Institution ceased to function, some of the museum material did not survive.

What remained was acquired by the Inverness Field Club many years later but unfortunately the print of Cromarty Castle chimney lintel was not among the articles that were preserved.

When the castle was demolished in 1772 a number of earthenware urns filled with ashes and fragments of half-burned bones were dug out of the bank immediately around the building together with several stone coffins containing human skeletons, some headless, with one coffin containing a complete skeleton measuring over seven feet in length.

In 1830 a stolid and sensible Cromarty fisherman was returning home by the Inverness road after nightfall, having visited a friend in the north of the parish. It was a calm and still night with heavy clouds obscuring the moon and the fisherman walked on in a happy mood when the quiet and peaceful night was suddenly shattered by the most discordant noises that he had ever heard.

At first he supposed that a pack of hounds was in full cry in the field bordering his path and then, as the sounds faded as suddenly as they had arisen, that they were ranging the moors on the opposite side of a hill ahead of him.

Suddenly there was a fresh burst, as though the whole pack were very near at hand and baying at him through the hedge.

He thrust his hands into his pockets and, drawing out a handful of crumbs, offered them to the supposed hounds but instead of open mouths and gleaming eyes he only saw a man a little ahead of him. The sounds ceased at the same time.

Thinking that the man must be the keeper of the pack, the fisherman resumed his walk homewards, noting as he did so that the silent figure ahead kept pace with him—until, reaching a gap in the hedge, he saw the man turn towards the path that he was on.

Increasing the pace of his walk in the expectation of company for the rest of his journey, the fisherman was astounded, as he drew nearer to the figure, to see it grow taller and taller and then, dropping on all fours, it assumed the form of a horse!

Hurrying on his way, the horse hurried too. When the fisherman stopped, the horse also stopped. Resuming an ordinary pace, the horse walked also, step for step with him, without either passing or falling behind. He now saw that it was an ugly and misshapen beast, bristling all over with black shaggy hair and lame in one foot.

The form accompanied him until he reached the gate of a cemetery, then just outside the town, where he was momentarily blinded by what seemed to be an intensely bright flash of lightning and as soon as he recovered, he found himself alone.

There is a much older story told of a man who encountered the Devil in five different shapes during a night-time journey in this part of Scotland. A few hours afterwards he lost his senses through fright; sceptics always say he lost his senses a few hours before his night walk!

Navity Wood, nearby, used to be haunted by the ghost of a murdered miller. A few days after the body was found on a bleak moor nearby, a postman named Munro was passing through Navity Wood one evening on the way to his home at Cromarty when he heard footsteps behind him. In the failing light he saw a tall figure which he at first thought to be a farmer friend but as the figure drew nearer, he was horrified to recognize the dead miller!

Turning tail, he fled home as fast as he could. The ghostly miller kept pace with him as he could see whenever he glanced over his shoulder. However, when he reached Cromarty churchyard, Munro was relieved to find that the frightening figure had disappeared.

The next night Munro made his way home by a different route, crossing a succession of fields instead of going through Navity Wood. As he entered a hollow that was part of the Cromarty House estate, he again saw the ghost of the dead miller, this time emerging from a clump of bushes and once more the figure followed the terrified postman.

This time, reaching the low wall separating the old parish churchyard, Munro turned and faced the apparition; whereupon it spoke to him: 'Stop, stop, I must speak to you.' But Munro had had more than enough. 'I have neither the faith nor the strength to speak to the like of you,' he replied, and hurried home without another backward glance.

Next day he related his experiences to the local minister who decided that Munro was having delusions, probably due to nerves or indigestion, and poor man was told to see a doctor.

Instead, he went to see an old Udoll farmer he knew who listened with interest to the story and then offered to accompany Munro through Navity Wood the following evening.

They met a few miles from Munro's home before sunset and made their way into Navity Wood. What befell them before they reached Cromarty town they would never tell anyone, but after that night Munro made his own way through Navity Wood a score of times and never saw the apparition again.

However, both Munro and his farmer friend came to regard with suspicion an inhabitant of Cromarty who had travelled with the miller on his last journey. Both were known to have been drinking and to be somewhat quarrelsome.

After the miller's body was found this last man to see him alive changed from a social and genial, if unpredictable, man to a dejected, spiritless and taciturn individual, avoiding company and seldom speaking to anyone. After a lingering illness, he died a few years later, still a young man.

CULLODEN MOOR, INVERNESS-SHIRE

Here the fate of the house of Stewart was sealed, in a setting that has changed little since the last pitched battle in Britain was fought here on April 16th, 1746.

Bonnie Prince Charlie's nine thousand tired and hungry Highlanders met nine thousand government troops under the Duke of Cumberland, third son of King George II, and it was all over in sixty-eight minutes. The Highlanders' losses were enormous, the victors cruelly massacring their wounded enemies; the English dead only numbered fifty.

A cairn and green mounds mark the soldiers' burial-places and from time to time visitors to this sorrowful place report strange happenings.

On occasions, the dim form of a battle-worn Highlander has been seen at dusk in the vicinity of the impressive cairn and one visitor, while looking closely at the Highlanders' graves here, lifted a square of Stewart tartan which had blown down from the stone on the grave-mound and distinctly saw the body of a handsome, dark-haired Highlander lying, at ease it seemed, full length on top of the mound.

The visitor sensed that the figure she was looking at was dead. His clothes were dirty, muddy and of old-fashioned cut and material. His tartan was the red Stewart. As she fully realized that she was seeing something of a supernormal character, she turned and fled from the field of memories.

DINGWALL, ROSS-SHIRE

This county town and royal burgh derives its name from the Norse 'Thingvollr', translated as the 'Field of the Thing' or 'Council'. In the area where once a celebrated prophet, the Brahan Seer, roamed, now the Brahan Estate, Maryburgh, there has long been an outdoor case of mysterious breathing which has never been satisfactorily explained.

As recently as October, 1968, local papers recounted that at the foot of the imposing Brahan Rock, the two-hundred foot high rock-face at the end of a narrow and twisting cul-de-sac, up to fifty cars could usually be found each night around midnight, their occupants intent on hearing the strange noises that have variously been described as resembling snoring, whispering, breathing, panting and gasping.

A farm worker was quoted as saying that he had heard the noise regularly since coming to Brahan Lodge (a hundred yards from the cliff) five years earlier. 'We can even hear it in the house on a calm night with the windows open,' he stated.

Another man in the same house, blacksmith Alan Macleod, reported: 'Along with two friends we went up the rock face one night while the breathing was being heard but each time we reached the spot we thought it was coming from, it seemed to move further up the face.'

One possible explanation would be warm air escaping from underground caverns through crevices, a theory that needs exploring. At all events the noise has been heard for many years; schoolmaster Mr J. A. Mitchell claims that a postman told him it was heard as long as eighty years ago.

DORNOCH, SUTHERLANDSHIRE

This royal burgh and county town of Sutherland was once the seat of the Bishop of Caithness. It has a magnificent golf course and the prim appearance of a small cathedral town but it is distinguished as the scene, in 1772, of the last judicial execution for witchcraft to take place in Scotland.

The witch was an old woman named Janet Horne who was charged with having changed her daughter into a pony to ride to the witches' meeting place, where the 'animal' was shod by the Devil. She was burnt to death and the Witches Stone, in a garden close by the golf course, recalls the event. The simple slab of rough bluish whinstone bears the date '1772' and marks the spot where the burning took place.

There are those who claim that the old woman is still seen on occasions, struggling and cursing against the rising flames and smothering smoke on autumn evenings, when the moon is on the wane.

DRUMELZIER, NEAR PEEBLES, PEEBLES-SHIRE

Just below the churchyard here, at the side of the burn that runs through the village, lies the grave of Merlin, the wizard who worked many wonders at the court of King Arthur.

He is said to have been the offspring of a Welsh maiden and a demon. Saved from evil by baptism, he retained throughout his life his father's gift of divination and the power to work magic.

One day, long ago, the stream that used to be known as Powsail Burn, overflowed violently, leaving its course and pouring into the River Tweed beside the Merlin grave. This was the day that Queen Elizabeth I died and James VI of Scotland became James I of England. Thus one of Thomas the Rhymer's prophecies was fulfilled:

> 'When Tweed and Powsail meet at Merlin's grave, England and Scotland shall one monarch have.'

In this quiet, secluded village, shrouded with huge trees and full of shadows, ringed with brown hills and with an air of enchantment, it is not difficult to believe in Merlin and the fulfilment of the Rhymer's prophecies.

DRYMEN, STIRLINGSHIRE

The partly demolished nineteenth-century Buchanan Castle once housed Rudolf Hess, Hitler's deputy leader. Today it is derelict and haunted by a strange moaning or gasping sound that is heard during the summer months. It usually begins about eleven o'clock and continues until dawn, especially on clear, still nights.

The noises, which are reported to be much too regular and loud to originate from birds or animals, have been heard many times by scores of impartial witnesses, including people in houses two hundred yards away; and they have even been recorded on tape.

One witness, Mrs Ann Ostrau of Stirling Road, reported in August 1968, that she had heard the noise many times. She was emphatic that it could not be caused by birds or animals because of the loudness, 'besides it is far too regular and precise', she added, 'and the sound comes from one side, then moves round to another side.'

One possible explanation is escaping air from the many holes in the ground that may lead to underground caverns but this is only a theory which no one has yet troubled to prove or disprove.

But other, apparently inexplicable incidents have been reported here; for example there is the evidence of Mr Norman McAuley who maintains that he climbed to the second floor of the castle with a friend, carrying a powerful electric torch which would not work at all on the second floor. All connections were checked and found to be in working order. On returning to the ground floor, the torch functioned perfectly.

DRYNACHAN, NEAR FORT AUGUSTUS, INVERNESS-SHIRE

A cottage on the shores of Loch Oich, five miles from Fort Augustus, was haunted by a man in a top-hat a few years ago. At that time the place, once the home of a laird of the Clan MacDonell, was occupied by a retired gamekeeper, Andrew Ross and his family.

At first Ross was sceptical when his wife told him she had seen the figure of the previous occupier, Angus Maclean, a jobbing carpenter who had died some forty years previously. Mrs Ross saw[r] the ghost whom she and her husband had known, standing beside the cottage one evening. He was dressed in an old-fashioned suit and a 'lum' hat. Soon afterwards the Ross's son sate the ghost.

All the family heard unexplained sounds resembling an old person groaning as though in great pain. During his lifetime they had always found Maclean to be a kindly man and although not unduly alarmed by the disturbances, they began to think that perhaps he might have hidden something in the cottage and wanted it to be discovered.

They never found anything and the noises were never explained.

Bonnie Prince Charlie rested at the same cottage during his flight from the Battle of Culloden.

DUMFRIES, DUMFRIESSHIRE

The County Hotel is reputed to be haunted by the ghost of Bonnie Prince Charlie.

In 1936 a visitor in the upper lounge saw a male figure, attired as a Jacobite, emerge from a doorway and stand for a few moments, deep in thought and looking very worried. He then turned and went away through the same door which, incidentally, is no longer used and now has heavy furniture barring it.

Only next day did the visitor learn that the upper lounge is known as Prince Charlie's Room; that he had been there in 1745 and slept in the room on the other side of the now-disused door.

Appropriately the floor of Prince Charlie's Room is carpeted in Royal Stewart tartan and the original panelling that Prince Charlie saw is still there.

DUNBLANE, PERTHSHIRE

Nearby Braco Castle seems always to have enjoyed the reputation of being haunted, but details are scarce and as far as I can establish no real evidence exists.

The present owner, Commander G. R. Muir, R.N., tells me that his family have owned Braco Castle for some fifty-five years.

Although many years ago some guests reported that their bedroom doors opened unaccountably, and some thirty years ago Commander Muir himself recalls noticing the dogs apparently observe something on the front stair 'with great fear', he neither saw nor felt anything unusual.

He has no details of any other inexplicable happenings and no idea as to exactly who, or what, is supposed to haunt the castle.

The incident concerning the dogs did not take place in the oldest part of the property, which is traditionally supposed to be the part that is haunted.

DUNURE, AYRSHIRE

Picturesque Culzean Castle perches on the cliff edge and was the scene of the roasting of a Stewart in 1570. Echoes of this gruesome operation have been reported in recent years.

From the fourteenth century the castle was the home of the Kennedys. It was Gilbert Kennedy, fourth Earl of Cassillis, who arranged for Allan Stewart, Commendator of Crossraguel Abbey, to be seized when he visited the property which became Crown territory after the Reformation.

The unfortunate Stewart was taken to the Black Vault in the castle where he was stripped naked, bound to a spit and roasted before a great fire, being liberally basted with oil every few minutes to ensure that he did not burn.

After he had prayed to be delivered from the torment by

death, he signed a document surrendering the lands of the Abbey to the Earl. Six days later, however, he refused to sign a confirmatory document and the Earl ordered him to be roasted again.

When near death, he signed the land away. Kennedy was fined £2,000 by the Privy Council and bound to keep the peace with Stewart, but he kept the lands and paid Stewart a life pension.

Occasionally—and particularly it seems on the quiet of a Sunday morning—the crackling and roaring sounds of a great fire have been heard from within these ancient walls, accompanied by faint, smoke-smothered screams and agonized sighs that soon fade away into silence.

The castle was rebuilt in 1777-1792 by Robert Adam. The late President Dwight D. Eisenhower used an apartment that was put at his disposal as a token of Scotland's thanks for his services as Supreme Commander of the Allied Forces in the Second World War on three occasions.

In 1972 three servants at the castle stated that they had independently seen an indistinct and inexplicable shape, on different occasions, in one of the passages in the dungeons of the castle.

Nearby is the freak hill known as 'Electric Brae'. As you travel south, you imagine your car is climbing when in fact it is going downhill.

DUNVEGAN, ISLE OF SKYE

Dunvegan Castle dominates this village at the head of Loch Dunvegan. The castle was formerly accessible only from the sea by a small gateway with a portcullis opening on the rocks. The present entrance is by means of a bridge thrown across a ravine which used to serve as a moat.

The Fairy Bridge has long had an evil reputation and for years it was said that no horse would cross the bridge without shying. Horses and dogs are, of course, notoriously super-sensitive.

Parts of the castle, including the Tower, date back to the fifteenth century. The walls are ten-foot thick and the dungeon entered from the second floor near the drawing-room.

It contains a host of interesting objects, including an Irish cup of bog-oak, the drinking horn of Rory More (Sir Roderick Macleod, the twelfth-century chief, knighted by King James VI), relics of Bonnie Prince Charlie and letters from Dr Samuel Johnson dated 1773 and Sir Walter Scott dated 1815 referring to their respective visits.

In the early sixteenth-century South Tower of this long-standing seat of the Macleod of Macleod you can see the fascinating Fairy Room containing the priceless Fairy Flag of Dunvegan.

Scottish fairies, brownies and kelpies are supposed to be more malignant than their Irish brothers and are creatures of storms and tempests. The castle stands in a delightful old-fashioned garden, in charming contrast to the wilderness and wild countryside around. A waterfall in the nearby woods is known as 'Rorv More's Nurse'.

The Fairy Flag of Dunvegan

DUROR, NEAR BALLACHULISH, ARGYLLSHIRE

In the steep, short and lonely valley of Glen Duror, with Ben Vair rising in the background, stands Auchindarroch, one of the oldest buildings in the district. It is a rambling mansion-like property with a ghost known as 'the Maid of Glen Duror' and a low-ceilinged Haunted Room that opens off the dining-room on the ground floor and is now used as a bedroom.

The Maid of Glen Duror has often been seen hereabouts, a little woman peering through the windows on the ground floor; glimpsed for a moment inside the Haunted Room or the adjoining premises, or gliding sadly along the lower slopes of Ben Vair just behind the house.

Occasionally she is seen for a moment in a lonely part of secluded Glen Duror. She is thought to be a dairymaid employed long ago by the original Stewart owner of Auchindarroch who during a great storm was swept down the glen, together with the cattle she was tending, and out into Loch Linnhe.

When I was in the vicinity a few years ago Mrs Jean Cameron told me that when she lived at Auchindarroch she had often seen the grey form of the Maid, usually at dusk.

Many are the strange happenings at this old farmhouse: doors and windows that have been left open bang to with great violence and those that have been shut continually open by themselves and then slam shut. Yet in the morning the doors and windows are always found exactly as they have been left at night.

Faces peer into the house through the old windows. A peculiar chill is often noticed in the dining-room. Articles are moved and even strewn about, particularly in the Haunted Room. A ghostly old woman stands by a side door and moves across the lawn to vanish in the gloom while an unidentified hooded figure has been seen both in the dining room and at the foot of the staircase.

Once four people heard three distinct bumps followed by three loud crashing noises. The sounds seemed to originate from the direction of the staircase but nothing could be found to account for them except perhaps three heavy paperweights that seemed to have jumped off a window sill by themselves in a bedroom where a little girl lay fast asleep.

A few weeks later a party of nine people, including a couple of Air Force officers, were guests at the farmhouse and every one of them heard three loud bumps from the room above, as if someone had dropped something deliberately three times. Yet on investigation nothing was discovered out of place. No living person was upstairs at the time.

No sooner had everyone returned downstairs than another

three bumps were heard and again immediate investigation produced no explanation. Yet a third time three loud bumps were heard and by now the whole party was terrified as to what was in store for them. When a final and complete tour of the property still provided no possible explanation, the guests, one after the other, made excuses and left haunted Auchindarroch.

Not long afterwards a French Air Force officer spent several nights in the Flaunted Room. One night the whole household was awakened by a tremendous crashing noise as though all the crockery in the house had been broken. A few moments later the occupants heard another loud sound, similar to the first.

It was thought that the guest had got up in the night and stumbled into the dresser loaded with crockery and brought it crashing down and that he had banged into it again on his return journey to his room. But in the morning there was no trace of anything to account for the very loud noises and the guest reported that he had enjoyed an excellent and undisturbed night!

Similar crashing noises have been heard by the occupants and by visitors to Auchindarroch on many other occasions and nothing was ever found that might account for them.

Occasionally, too, a peculiar but not unpleasant perfume pervades the oldest part of the house. Alasdair Alpin MacGregor told me that when he stayed there he and the only other occupant heard what sounded like an express train roar along the back of the house, which literally shook with the deafening sound.

Yet when it had passed, there was no trace of anything that might have caused such a thunderous noise and in fact haunted Glen Duror seemed incredibly still and silent.

EARLSTON, BERWICKSHIRE

A small spur of the Eildon Hills known as Lucken Hare, the ruined grey tower, the Bogle Burn, and Eildon Tree have all ghostly associations with Thomas the Rhymer and King Arthur and his Knights.

There is a strange mark on the hillside resembling a galloping horse and rider that some people regard as a warning to those who are rash enough to intrude into the land of mystics and magicians. Thomas the Rhymer's Glen, where Thomas of Ercildoune met the Fairy Queen, is on the Abbotsford estate, in the vicinity.

The peculiar shape of the commanding Eildon Hills is said to have been caused by an evil spirit who split what had been one big hill into three at the command of Michael Scot (c. 1175-1234), a celebrated magician known as the 'Wizard of the North'.

Many Roman remains have been found and before the Romans the priests of Baal sacrificed here to the sun-god, while on these slopes Thomas the Rhymer 'conceived and delivered' the prophecies that gave him his name.

Some two hundred years ago a horse-trader named Dick Canonbie used to bring horses to the market at Melrose. Several times a year he would ride over from his home beyond Hawick.

Dick was popular with the ladies of the Melrose district and on one occasion, looking forward to a successful market next day, he persuaded an old friend, Maggie, to meet him that evening although she was now married to Sandy, a fierce and jealous man.

Sandy followed Maggie that night and set about Dick who returned blow for blow and it was a bruised and battered husband who took his wife home.

That night, as Dick was settling his horses in preparation for selling them next day, Maggie burst in to warn him that Sandy and a dozen of his friends were out looking for him.

Deciding that discretion was the better part of valour, Dick lost no time in leaving Melrose and set off with his horses at speed towards Bowden Moor.

It was a pitch-black night and as he reached the western spur of the Eildons, known as Lucken Hare, he dismounted and was about to look for a spot to spend the rest of the night when the horses whinnied and shied violently at the form of an old man which had suddenly appeared close at hand.

The long-haired and white-bearded figure wore a cloak that covered clothes strangely out of date; so much Dick observed as he tried to quieten the horses. Then he asked the stranger what he wanted. It seemed that the stranger wanted black horses and was prepared to pay a good price for them.

Without further ado Dick sold his horses and was surprised to receive in payment gold coins bearing unicorns and bonnets, long superseded; but of their value there was no doubt and Dick was well pleased. When the stranger offered to purchase more horses one month hence Dick readily agreed.

Subsequently Dick returned several times and sold black horses to the old man, always receiving generous payment in the same old but valuable gold coins. His own horse always became terrified in the presence of the stranger and tore madly from the place as soon as the transaction was completed.

Then one midsummer night Dick asked the old man where he lived for he could see no habitation within miles. When his customer tried to put him off Dick persisted and asked whether he could not see the man's home. At length the old man agreed but warned Dick that he might see things that would test him to the utmost; should his courage fail, the consequences might be disastrous.

Dick followed the strange old man as he led the way through the deep heather and up the steep slope of Lucken Hare. Eventually they arrived at the hidden entrance to a cave which led deep into the heart of the hills, its vast interior lit by flickering lights in iron brackets fixed into the wall of the cavern.

As they advanced into the depths of the enormous cave Dick was astounded to see stall upon stall fixed into the rock and stretching as far as the eye could see, each containing a coal-black horse and at the foot of each quiet beast there lay a knight in black armour with a drawn sword in his hand. Horses and knights did not appear to be breathing although they had the appearance of life.

Deep in the heart of the cave Dick found that he had been ushered in to a vast torch-lit area, still, cold and deathly quiet. The old man led Dick forward to a great heavily carved oaken table with strange and mystic signs and symbols. Then the stranger took him firmly by the arm and pointed to a hunting horn and a sword that lay on the table.

Drawing himself up to his full height the old man spoke fiercely: 'Since you have been rash enough to intrude upon the realm of mystery and knowledge long forgotten and forsaken by the world of men, a choice is forced upon you. Either draw the sword or blow the horn. One or the other you must do. Choose well and you reign here as king; choose badly and you forfeit your life. Trifle not with me for I am Thomas of Ercildoune.'

The name of the great wizard, Thomas the Rhymer, struck terror into Dick's heart and he tried to reason which choice to make. What if the sleeping knights awakened to find him wielding a sword? Would it not be wiser to awaken them with a blow on the horn?

He took up the horn and blew. Immediately there was a tremendous roaring sound, like thunder, that filled the cave and echoing cavern; the very earth seemed to tremble; a torrent of wind rose in the depths of the subterranean caves and came rushing and shrieking upon them.

In a moment horses and knights were awake and Dick hastily dropped the horn and drew the sword to defend himself as the cave became full of armed knights seemingly about to hurl themselves upon him. As he lifted the sword he became aware that the old man had disappeared but his voice echoed round the cave:

'Woe to the coward, that ever was born; Who did not draw the sword before he blew the horn.'

Suddenly Dick felt the hordes of knights upon him and he was carried off his feet, swept back through the long passages and dashed senseless on the hillside.

Next morning he was found by two shepherds and although they did all they could for him, he was past human aid. In answer to their questions he gasped out his story and expired.

No trace of the entry to the cave has ever been found but a strange mark appeared on the hillside where Dick died; it resembled a galloping horse and rider and centuries of men have looked on the mark and wondered whether it is indeed evidence of a mystic realm beyond the everyday life of mankind.

There are those who claim to have seen the shape of an old man by Eildon Tree on midsummer nights, while others maintain that they have either seen black-armoured knights on black horses in the vicinity of the ruined tower, or heard a screaming wind when the night is still as death on Lucken Hare.

EDINBURGH

When number 15, Learmonth Gardens was occupied by Sir Alexander Hay Seton, tenth Baronet of Abercorn and Armour bearer to the Queen, it was the scene of many strange happenings that seemed to centre on the bone of an ancient Egyptian. Certainly Sir Alexander believed that he was the subject of an Egyptian curse.

The story begins when Sir Alexander and his first wife, Zeyla, visited Egypt in 1936. They were duly impressed by such places as the Temple at Luxor and the tomb of Tutankhamun but rather disappointed with a visit to the Valley of the Kings which they undertook riding, as Sir Alexander afterwards put it, 'on a rather unpleasant camel'.

However they enjoyed the bathing and good cuisine at the Mena Hotel in Cairo, close to the Sphinx and the Great Pyramid, and it was while they were there that a local guide, Abdul, offered to take the Setons to visit a tomb that was then being excavated.

This was too good an opportunity to be missed and the visit was arranged without delay. On the appointed day Abdul led them down some thirty rough-hewn steps into a chamber where a crumbling skeleton lay on a stone slab.

Sir Alexander was told that the remains were those of a high-class girl, one of hundreds unearthed in the area of the Pyramids. After a look round the party made its way back up the steps and into the sunshine, but Zeyla was fascinated by the place and she slipped back to have a second look by herself.

Later that night, back at the hotel, Lady Seton showed her husband a bone that she had taken from the tomb. 'It looked like a digestive biscuit, slightly convex and shaped like a heart,' wrote Sir Alexander in an unpublished manuscript. It was in fact a sacrum, the triangular bone at the base of the spine linking it with the pelvis.

Later, home in Edinburgh, Sir Alexander and Lady Seton showed the bone to some friends when they were talking about Egypt and its mysteries.

Afterwards Sir Alexander, with mock dignity, deposited the bone in a glass case and ceremoniously placed it, temporarily, on a small table in the dining-room. Almost immediately strange things happened until Sir Alexander came to believe firmly that he was cursed for having the bone in his possession.

The same evening that he had handled the bone, just as his guests were leaving, there was a resounding crash and a huge piece of roof parapet smashed to the ground within two feet of where he stood. Next morning a chimney pot was found to have fallen to the ground, but Sir Alexander admits that it was a windy night.

A few nights later the Seton's nanny burst into their bedroom to tell them that she had heard someone moving about in the dining-room. Sir Alexander immediately went downstairs but could find nothing to account for the sounds and nothing out of place. Later the same night he heard a heavy-crash himself and next day his wife accused him of upsetting the corner table, which she had found on its side, with the glass case containing the bone on the floor. The practical Sir Alexander decided that he must have set the table unevenly against the wall and that it had toppled over from vibration caused by passing traffic.

In the weeks that followed any number of odd and inexplicable noises were heard at 15 Learmonth Gardens and when a nephew, young Alasdair Black, came to stay for a few days he calmly announced one morning that when he had gone to the lower lavatory during the night he had seen 'a funny-dressed person going up the stairs.'

Other visitors and servants soon claimed that they, too, saw a spectral robed figure wandering about the house at night and before long domestic help began to be a problem.

One night Sir Alexander decided to keep watch on the Bone (he spells it with a capital B throughout his manuscript), which now resided in the upstairs drawing-room where there were also some valuable snuff-boxes. Sir Alexander carefully locked the doors and windows and kept watch from the balcony.

Nothing happened for several hours and at length he decided to go to bed, only to be rudely awakened by a shout from his wife to say that someone was moving about in the room containing the Bone. Quickly picking up his revolver Sir Alexander investigated, meeting on his way a very scared Nanny who had also heard sounds of movement from the locked room. When the door was unlocked, for Sir Alexander had taken the key with him to his bedroom, they found the room looking, in his words, 'as if a battle royal had taken place!'

Chairs were upset, books thrown about, furniture moved, a vase upset—and in the middle of it all the Egyptian relic alone remained untouched. Sir Alexander ascertained that the windows were still securely fastened and there seemed no possible way for any human being to have entered the room.

After a few weeks of quiet, apart from two unaccountable fires, bangings, crashes and other unexplained noises re-commenced, and they always seemed to come from the direction of the drawing-room.

Eventually the Setons decided to move downstairs to the sitting-room most of the articles that had been flung about, leaving just the heavy furniture in the drawing-room. The Bone in the glass case and the small table on which it stood were also moved to the sitting-room.

A week later this room was found one day in a complete shambles, articles thrown about, furniture tipped over, ornaments broken, glassware smashed inside a cabinet and hardly anything in its right place. Even the table on which the Bone stood seemed to have been subjected to some kind of severe pressure for one leg was cracked.

The newspapers got hold of the story and there were headlines in Scottish papers such as 'baronet fears pharaoh curse ox family'. One reporter asked whether he could borrow the Bone for a few days. He returned it after a week, saying that nothing had happened while it had been in his possession but a couple of weeks later he became ill and had an emergency operation for peritonitis.

Shortly afterwards the Setons left their Edinburgh home. Sir Alexander explains: 'I suppose our nerves were frayed. We had a domestic scene and I went off to live at my club while Zeyla took Egidia (their five-year-old daughter) and went to stay with her family.'

Meanwhile the Bone had been returned to the upstairs drawing-room. While the family nanny was alone in the house one night she heard a terrific crash from the direction of the drawing-room; she was too frightened to go upstairs.

When she told Sir Alexander, he went up to explore, but the room was undisturbed, except for the Bone and the small table on which it had stood. It lay on its side, smashed and the Bone lay beside it, broken into five pieces.

Now there was talk of how the Setons should dispose of the Bone, although Lady Seton would not hear of it. One report stated that Sir Alexander had arranged for Lady Seton to make a special trip to Egypt to replace the Bone in the tomb from which she had removed it; other suggestions were that the Bone should be buried or disposed of in deep water.

Sir Alexander refused many offers to purchase the relic for he was determined that no one else should endure similar experiences.

Lady Seton took the Bone to a doctor friend and asked him to mend it as well as he could. Afterwards it was placed on a table in the hall outside the dining-room. One report stated that the doctor's maid broke her leg running in terror from a mysterious robed figure while it was in her master's possession.

One evening the Setons held a dinner party and as the cheerful guests were talking and drinking merrily, the Bone and the table on which it stood suddenly hurtled across the hall and hit the opposite wall with a tremendous thump.

No one was anywhere near it at the time but, perhaps understandably, something like chaos followed. The maid fainted, a cousin swooned and the party broke up in a somewhat hysterical fashion.

Now Sir Alexander decided that he must get rid of the Bone and he thought it best to do this while his wife was away from home. Accordingly he arranged for his uncle, Father Benedict of the Abbey at Fort Augustus, to come and exorcise the evil object.

The solemn ceremony duly took place in Lady Seton's absence and the Bone, having been blessed, was destroyed in the presence of Sir Alexander by burning. He made sure that no part of it escaped.

The nanny, Miss Janet Clark, confirmed the end of the bone. 'I was glad when Sir Alexander decided to get rid of it,' she said in 1965. 'He brought it into the kitchen and we put it on the fire and watched it burn. It took a long time and what was left was put into a bucket with the ashes.' Egidia is now Mrs Norman Haynes and it is to her husband, director of a printing and publishing group, that I am indebted for much of the information about this story.

Mrs Haynes, as we have seen, was only five years old at the

time of the curious happenings and naturally she does not remember much about it but she recalls that she never liked the Bone. 'It was an evil thing and 1 always believed that there was something in the curse.'

On the other hand Sir Alexander's brother, the late Sir Bruce Seton, the eleventh Baronet, never accepted the story of the curse; before his tragic death he always felt that the various troubles that beset Sir Alexander: ill-health, financial and family difficulties, had nothing whatever to do with the Egyptian relic.

In his own narrative Sir Alexander states emphatically: 'The curse did not end with the destruction of the Bone. From 1936 onwards trouble always seemed to beset me. Zeyla never forgave me for destroying the Bone and it did not help our already rocky marriage.'

Sir Alexander and Lady Seton were in fact divorced in June 1939 and although Zeyla re-married, she had a lot of misfortune, unhappiness, poor health and eventually died while still quite young.

Sir Alexander married Flavia, granddaughter of the Earl of Rosslyn in 1939 but they separated in 1953 and were divorced in 1958. Flavia, Lady Seton, died in 1959 and in 1962 Sir Alexander married Julia Clements, the lecturer and author of books on flower-arrangement. She recalls that during their honeymoon they visited the family seat at Seton Place, Longniddry, where her husband showed her the family coat of arms and the space on the chapel plaque for his own epitaph.

He was, she says, outwardly always cheerful but inwardly he was deeply affected by his misfortune. He often talked about the Bone and believed that it had an evil and uncanny influence on his life. 'I was born during an earthquake,' he states in his manuscript, 'and my life has been a tremor ever since.'

Sir Alexander Seton had a premonition while on his honeymoon and he told Julia, Lady Seton that they would probably be married for only six months. In fact, he died seven months later. No one could ever convince him that there was nothing in the well-known belief that robbing a tomb brought bad luck, especially an Egyptian tomb.

There is still much of the nearby village of Colinton that the boy Robert Louis Stevenson must have known. The manse, the garden, the churchyard, even the room in which his grandfather wrote his sermons, although no longer a 'dark and cold room, with a library of bloodless books'.

Parts of the place are unaltered and on the sides of what is now a doorway, one can trace the scars left by the former shelves of the cupboards of Stevenson's grandfather.

Above this room is the window from which at night the novelist as a boy would gaze hopefully into the graveyard below, looking for 'spunkies' playing among the graves. The so-called 'Witches' Walk' is a narrow passage between the garden bordered by shrubbery on one side and on the other by the wall of the kirkyard. Nearby stands an enormous yew Stevenson knew and wrote about.

It is here that his ghost is reported to be seen on occasions: a pale, long-haired figure, glimpsed for a moment in the shade of the great tree, sheltering perhaps from the brilliance of the sunlit lawn. A macabre relic of the past can be seen in the churchyard. It is a massive 'mort-safe', used to cover the newly-buried until the bodies were of no use to grave-robbers.

The Grassmarket, Edinburgh has a ghost, too. The notorious murderers Burke and Hare lured their victims to Tanners' Close and provided fresh bodies for dissection. Major Thomas Weir, the eloquent Presbyterian and Commander of the Town Guard, the man who led Montrose to the scaffold lived in West Bow.

Weir himself was burned to death in 1670 after confessing to witchcraft and to consorting with the Devil. For over a hundred years after his death his ghost terrified the inhabitants of West Bow, for his phantom form was repeatedly seen flitting about the streets and sometimes 'fiendish laughter' would be heard coming from the locked and empty house that he had occupied until, it is said, Satan himself came to Edinburgh and carried him off in a black coach.

Once towards the end of the eighteenth-century a William Patullo was delighted to rent the fine property but he only spent one night there. He recounted that as he and his wife lay in bed a strange apparition, something like a calf, came to the bedside, then set its front feet upon the bed and gazed steadfastly at the occupants. Terrified, the next day they left the house.

Edinburgh life revolved for centuries around the ancient Mercat Cross. The restored cross incorporates the original age-old shaft, supporting the unicorn and hundreds of years ago citizens heard the laws of the city proclaimed from here.

On the eve of the Battle of Flodden, on September 9th, 1513, when cannon were being removed from the castle for the use of the army, ghostly heralds are said to have appeared on the platform of the historic Mercat Cross and recited the names of those who would die in the battle where England was to lose five thousand men and Scotland their king, some ten thousand men and the flower of all the noble families of Scotland.

Pitscottie, in his Summons of Pluto, relates that at midnight, while the artillery was rumbling out of the castle, a cry was heard at the Mercat Cross, proclaiming a summons, named and called by the proclaimer thereof, 'the summons of Pluto', which desired 'all men to compear, both earl and lord and baron and all honest gentlemen within the town, every man specified by his own name, within the space of forty days, before his Maker'.

Pitscottie maintains that no man called in the summons escaped death at Flodden, except one: a certain Richard Lawson who, hearing the summons from his gallery in the High Street, called in reply: 'I appeal me from your justice, judgment and sentence, and betake me all hail to the mercy of God.' He was at Flodden and returned alive.

Among the many narrow and quaint passages or 'closes' in the old part of the city that have the reputation of harbouring ghosts, Mary King's Close was, until it disappeared during reconstruction, significant for the number of terrifying apparitions that were seen there.

Among the inhabitants at one time was a respectable law agent, Thomas Coltheart, who moved to a large property in the Close despite warnings that the house was haunted. Soon after he moved in, the maid left and finding themselves unable to procure another willing to reside in the house, the Colthearts managed as well as they could on their own.

One Sunday afternoon Coltheart, who had been unwell and was resting, was listening to his wife's reading of the Scriptures. Suddenly something caught her eye and as she looked up she was horrified to see an old man's head, with a long and straggling beard, floating without a body in the air at the other side of the bed; his piercing eyes were fixed intently upon her.

She fainted with shock and fright and remained unconscious until friends called in on their way home from church. Thomas tried to convince her that she had imagined the whole thing and the rest of the evening passed without further incident.

Shortly afterwards however Coltheart awakened one night to see the same phantom head floating in mid-air over the bed and surveying him with unblinking and frightening gaze. Coltheart rose from the bed, lit a candle, awakened his wife, and began to pray. Still the apparition stayed in the room and after about an hour was joined by the head of a child, also suspended in the air, followed by an arm naked from the elbow which, despite their revulsion and reluctance, seemed anxious to shake hands with Mr and Mrs Coltheart!

Coltheart called again and again on the phantoms to relate the reason for their appearances but the hovering faces continued silently and solidly to stare at him and his wife as though they were intruders and wished them to go away.

Soon other phantoms came, including a dog which curled itself up in a chair and seemed to go to sleep. Others, more frightening, appeared until the whole room swarmed with them and then when the unfortunate couple were at their wits' end, they heard a deep and awful groan, whereupon all the apparitions vanished.

Not surprisingly the Colthearts began to make plans to leave the house but during the whole of the extended period of negotiations for moving they saw no more apparitions and when the projected move fell through, they decided to postpone moving and in fact continued to live at the house for many years, undisturbed in any psychic sense.

Some years later, after Coltheart had died, a strange story was told concerning a client of his who lived at Tranent, ten miles from Edinburgh. This man was awakened one night by a nurse who was frightened by 'something like a child moving about the house'. Starting up and instinctively reaching for a weapon to defend the nurse and himself, he was amazed to recognize in the middle of a weird, cloud-like substance that had appeared in the bedroom, the features of his friend and legal adviser Thomas Coltheart.

He had the presence of mind to ask what the trouble was and could this mean that Coltheart was dead? The apparition only shook its head twice and then melted completely away. The gentleman was much mystified and in the morning lost no time in proceeding to his friend's house in Mary King's Close, Edinburgh, where he found Mrs Coltheart mourning the recent death of her husband.

Edinburgh was also the scene of an interesting and well-attested case of premonition in the seventeenth century; an account kept both by Robert Chambers (author and co-founder with his brother of publishers W. Sc R. Chambers) and by Sir Walter Scott.

Lady Eleanor Campbell, youngest daughter of James, second Earl of Loudoun, was married at an early age to James, first Viscount Primrose, a man of ill-temper, dissolute habits and considerable brutality.

Things came to such a pass that the gentle Lady Eleanor began to fear for her life—and not without good cause for one morning, as she was dressing, she saw, reflected in the mirror, her husband creeping stealthily towards her, knife in hand and a look of murder on his face.

Terrified. Lady Eleanor, thinking only of escape, promptly jumped through the first-floor window into the street below. Fortunately she received no serious injury and she was soon in the care of relations. After such an episode any hope of reconciliation seemed doomed to failure and the ill-matched couple agreed to live apart.

Lord Primrose went abroad and for a long time the Lady Eleanor had no news of him. It was during this extended period of separation that she chanced to meet a necromancer visiting Edinburgh who declared that he was able to locate the present whereabouts of absent friends and relatives, irrespective of the distance involved.

Perhaps out of curiosity (it could hardly be from love) Lady Eleanor, together with a friend, went to the fortune-teller's lodgings in Canongate to enquire about her husband, where he was and what he was doing.

She was led to a large mirror and looking into it she distinctly saw the inside of a church where a marriage ceremony was in progress. On looking at the chief characters in the vision she was astonished to recognize her husband as the bridegroom, although the bride was a stranger to her.

The ceremony had apparently just begun when a man hurried towards the bridal pair, a man whom Lady Eleanor recognized with a start as one of her brothers. He seemed, at first, to be a friend who had arrived late but, as he drew nearer to the couple about to be married, his expression changed to one of extreme anger. He drew his sword and attacked the waiting bridegroom who speedily sought to defend himself, whereupon the mirror-scene became cloudy and finally disappeared completely.

Back home, Lady Eleanor carefully wrote out a minute account of the whole affair, dated, signed and sealed it—all in the presence of a witness—and deposited it in a place of safety.

Some time later her brother visited her on his return from abroad and she enquired, during the course of conversation, whether he had happened to hear any news of her husband while he was on the continent. Her brother replied that he never wished to hear the man's name again and then, at her request, disclosed that he had in fact met Lord Primrose under somewhat strange circumstances.

While staying in Amsterdam, he became acquainted with a wealthy family whose beautiful daughter was heiress to a fortune. He learned that this girl was engaged to a Scotsman of good position who had quite recently come to live in Holland. Later he was invited to the wedding. He did, in fact, attend the ceremony, arriving late, but just in time to prevent the marriage of the Dutch girl to his own brother-in-law!

Recalling her mirror-vision and the fact that it was signed and dated, Lady Eleanor asked her brother the date of his encounter with her husband. Then she fetched a copy of her account of the vision and showed it to him; not only did it correspond in every particular with the actual experience but the date of the attempted marriage was the same as that of the vision.

The earl died in 1709 and despite many good offers, the Lady Eleanor, more than a little disillusioned with marriage, rejected them all including the well-known John Dalrymple, second Earl of Stair—though she preferred him to all the others. The earl, determined to break her resolution not to re-marry, hit upon a plan that, as one writer puts it 'marks the age as one of little delicacy'.

Having bribed one of Lady Eleanor's servants to admit him to her dressing-room which overlooked the High Street, the earl, when the morning 'was somewhat advanced' showed himself en deshabille to the passers-by!

The effect of such an exhibition upon the lady's reputation induced her to accept him as her second husband and as Countess of Stair she lived happily, outliving the earl who died in 1747. The Lady Eleanor died in Edinburgh at an advanced age in 1759.

Edinburgh Castle is reputed to harbour several ghosts, including a headless drummer who has been seen as recently as 1960.

During their residence at the castle Major Griffiths and his wife were visited by their young nephew Joseph D'Acre from Kirklinton in Cumberland.

One afternoon he mentioned that the following day he planned to join some other youngsters on a fishing expedition. No objection was made to this but during the night Mrs Griffiths found herself suddenly waking from a troubled dream, calling out in terror: 'The boat is sinking—oh! save them...'

Her husband attributed the dream to apprehension about their nephew's planned fishing trip but she insisted that she had no uneasiness on that score and indeed, had thought no more about it. She was soon asleep again, only to be awakened with the same dream; the feeling of terror repeated itself no less than three times during the course of that night.

On the last occasion Mrs Griffiths saw the image of a boat sinking and the whole party drowned. By this time she was thoroughly alarmed and rising from her bed, she put on a dressing-gown and, not content to wait for morning, went to her nephew's bedroom persuading him with some difficulty to abandon his plans.

The next day broke fair and clear and the fishing party duly set off consisting of a Mr Patrick Cumming, Mr Colin Campbell, a boy named Cleland and two sailors. Mrs Griffiths and her nephew felt rather silly at their decision that he should not accompany the party but their minds were made up and they let things stand.

At three o'clock in the afternoon a sudden squall arose from the south-east, the boat foundered and all the occupants were drowned except Campbell who was picked up after being in the water for five hours. The accident took place on August 7th, 1734 and is narrated in the Caledonian Mercury dated August 12th.

EDROM, NEAR DUNS, BERWICKSHIRE

Where the waters of the Whiteadder and those of the Blackadder join, stands the village of Allanton. Nearby, on the north bank of the Blackadder stood haunted Allanbank with its pathetic ghost of 'Pearlin Jean'.

In the seventeenth century Allanbank was owned by the Stuart family and one Sir Robert Stuart wooed and won Jean or Jeanne, a lovely French girl. He took her to France with him but one morning in Paris Sir Robert abruptly left the trusting girl, striding out of the house and seating himself in his coach without a backward glance.

In her silks and 'pearlin' lace poor Jean ran after her lover and tried to get into the carriage, but the postillion drove on. She was thrown to the ground and the heavy wheels of the carriage passed over her head.

Back at Allanbank, where the heartless Sir Robert arrived one autumn evening at dusk, the first thing he saw, sitting on the archway high above the entrance gateway, was the figure of his murdered Jean, gazing down at him with her crushed and bloody head.

From then on, it is said, the sad ghost of Pearlin Jean walked the corridors of Allanbank. Sometimes only the rustling of her silks and lace would be heard; at other times her sad figure would be seen and no sound heard.

Once seven ministers attempted to exorcise the ghost but they were unsuccessful. Local people were proud of the sad but sweet Jean and when the house was demolished in the nineteenth century, many of the villagers were worried as to what would happen to 'Pearlin Jean'. They need not have worried for her ghost has been seen and heard long after all traces of the old house have disappeared; especially at dusk on autumn evenings.

'Pearlin Jean' was for years the most remarkable and best-known ghost in Scotland and it is still possible to find old inhabitants who will relate stories of eerie experiences: the rustling of silk along empty passages and up and down deserted stairways; the sound of footsteps walking backwards and forwards in certain bedrooms.

The occupants became so used to the disturbances at one period that they calmly accepted and all but ignored the strange noises and continual reports of a female figure seen in the house and grounds.

For a time a picture of 'Pearlin Jean', hanging between portraits of Sir Robert and Lady Stuart, seemed to keep the ghost comparatively quiet. Then the stories started again. There was a childrens' nurse at Allanbank who arranged to meet her boy-friend in the orchard at moonlight.

He arrived first and seeing a female figure wearing a light-coloured dress he hurried forward with open arms to embrace his Jenny but as he almost reached the spot, the figure vanished, to reappear again far off at the edge of the orchard. The would-be lover took to his heels but Jenny, when she did arrive, saw nothing; however she forgave her Thomas and they were eventually married.

ELGIN, MORAYSHIRE

This ancient royal burgh has a history going back to 1190 and was much favoured as a royal residence, especially by James II. Part of the town was burned by the Wolf of Badenoch in 1390 and half of it sixty years later in the struggle between Huntley and Douglas.

Bonnie Prince Charlie spent eleven days here at Thunderton House, later Gordon's Temperance Hotel, before fateful Culloden. Johnson and Boswell described a 'vile dinner' they had here in 1773 at the old Red Lion, still standing in the High Street.

When Thunderton House Hotel was for sale in April, 1970, the proprietress, Mrs Agnes Brown, stated that she had heard the sound of bagpipes on more than one occasion in one of the second-floor bedrooms; music for which there seemed to be no normal explanation. A former member of the hotel staff whose room had been near the top of the rambling old building claimed that she heard a voice a number of times say 'Come in' as she walked along the corridor to her room, although no one was there.

The wife of the previous proprietor, Mrs Lessels, said she had no doubt that the place was haunted and she and her son David saw a standard lamp rise over a foot into the air one evening; it moved across the room entirely of its own accord and landed with a thump at the opposite side undamaged, apart from the shade being dislodged.

ETHIE CASTLE, ANGUS

In 1178 a fortified farmhouse stood here where today a fine pink castle stands, full of fine furniture—and traditional ghosts. It is unlikely that Cardinal David Beaton, Abbot of Arbroath in 1524, built Ethie Castle although he has long been credited with that honour, for there was a great house here long before the prelate was born.

It is certain, though, that he loved the place. He brought his beautiful young wife to Ethie Castle and they had seven children before he was brutally murdered at St Andrews Castle on May 29th, 1546.

Soon the Cardinal's ghost was seen at Ethie and there are still occasional reports of appearances of his stately figure in the vicinity of the secret passage in the wall of the Cardinal's Chamber.

There are also frequent, unexplained footsteps and a dragging noise has been heard for some minutes in an otherwise silent night. A contemporary portrait of Cardinal Beaton hangs in the dining room.

A more sinister story concerns the older portion of the house, part of which had been unoccupied at night for many years until a new governess arrived and spent her first night there.

In the morning she complained that she had been awakened by the patter of children's feet, by heart-breaking sobs and the rattle of a wheeled toy somewhere over her head.

All this happened not once but many times and when eventually some effort was made to discover the cause and locality of the disturbances, it was found that the only entrance to the room above that occupied by the new governess had long ago been bricked-up and panelled over.

When the wall was broken down the skeleton of a child was discovered close to the remains of a little wooden cart. After the bones had been buried the distressing sounds were heard no more.

FEARN, ROSS AND CROMARTY

There are a few green mounds and traces of an old hawthorn hedge at a spot where the parish of Nigg borders that of Fearn; the last reminders of a ghost that walked here for years and perhaps still walks.

King Charles II, during his exile in France, procured a contribution of £ 10,000 from the Scots who at that time wandered as itinerant traders throughout Poland. One of these men returned to his native land in his old age, possessed it is said, of such considerable wealth that he was known locally as 'the rich Polander'.

He died suddenly and in his will, the only thing in his strongbox, he bequeathed large sums to various relatives whose whereabouts were unknown. Some people thought that he had loaned money in the neighbourhood; others that he had a brother in Poland to whom he had entrusted the greater part of his money but who had been robbed and murdered by bandits on the continent.

In the midst of such speculation the 'rich Polander' himself, it seems, returned to try to settle the matter. The rough pasture, near the green mounds that were formerly part of his house, was then a lawn with a gate in the eastern corner and another in the west corner.

Between them a road ran passing in front of the old man's house. For years the apparition of the 'rich Polander' was seen, evening after evening, walking along this road. It always approached from the east, lingered for a while in front of the building that stood empty and silent and then glided away to the west, disappearing as it passed through the western gate.

Dozens of people saw the figure; scores more heard about it, but no one had the courage to approach the ghost and perhaps try to find out about the legacies which it is said, remain unpaid to this day.

One witness saw the apparition in bright moonlight and described the richly-embroidered waistcoat, the white cravat and the 'small clothes' of crimson velvet, together with the laced hat and broad shoe-buckles. The thin, withered hands were clearly distinguishable but the features 'wholly invisible'.

Also in Fearn there used to be a cottage half-way up the hill with an old elm tree beside it, a cottage that was once occupied by a farmer and his wife, a bad-tempered, one-eyed woman.

The farmer had been married before and his son of five years and a daughter of seven found their stepmother hard and unkind; the little girl was shrewd enough to remark on one occasion, when she was beaten by her stepmother for tasting a piece of cake straight from the oven, that her second mother could see better with one eye than her first mother could with two!

The dead children's mother, an industrious and devoted housewife, had left behind her a large store of blankets and bed linen; yet the children's bed, for the summer and autumn after the second marriage of their father, was only covered with a few worn-out rags. When winter set in, the little ones would lie in each others arms for the early part of each night, shivering with cold.

Then, for a week, they found when they awakened each morning that they were closely wrapped up in some of their mother's best blankets.

The stepmother stormed and raged and replaced the blankets in the big store chest, furnished with lock and key, but it was all in vain and each morning the blankets were regularly back on the children's bed.

The poor children were threatened and beaten but they could give no account of the matter other than they were very cold when they fell asleep but were warm and comfortable when they awoke.

Then one night the girl was able to explain the mystery. Her brother had fallen asleep but she was cold, bitterly cold and lay awake deep into the night. Suddenly the bedroom door opened and there entered a lady clothed in a long white dress.

As she went to the chest, the lock sprang open and she withdrew some blankets, wrapped them around the children, kissed the boy and was about to kiss the girl when the child recognized her mother's features. Turning, the figure vanished into the darkness and thereafter the children were allowed to have warm bedclothes on their beds.

There is yet another ghost story associated with Fearn concerning a farmer who had buried his wife one day and the same evening called on a young woman with whom he had become friendly. She lived in a cottage almost adjoining Fearn burial ground.

The couple were getting along famously and soon after midnight the young woman was seated on the farmer's knee close to a window that opened to the burial ground. When the mother of the girl came upon them unexpectedly, she was shocked by their levity and reminded the farmer that the corpse of his recently deceased wife lay not forty yards from where they sat, 'in its entireness and almost still warm with life'.

'No' replied the farmer, 'entire she may be but cold she certainly is for she was cold enough long before we laid her there.' As he spoke he turned towards the window and there, looking at him through the panes of glass, he saw the face of his dead and recently buried wife!

Hurrying home the farmer became ill and died of a brain fever only a fortnight later—after which widowers in these parts were noticeably less hasty in courting their second wives for years afterwards!

FETTERCAIRN, KINCARDINESHIRE

An old hostelry used to stand on the south side of a nearby summit and many years ago when the Reverend Dr Rule was Chancellor of Edinburgh University, he and his entourage sought shelter there while on their way to Aberdeen.

As the hostelry happened to be full, the landlord suggested that Dr Rule might care to accommodate himself in an empty house close by where the landlord said he would gladly light fires and ensure that bedclothes, candles and other necessities were available. 'But,' he added, 'I must warn you, sir, that the house is haunted!'

Dr Rule was not in the least perturbed by this information but his servants were loath to accompany him and they found lodgings among the hospitable local people, leaving the Chancellor to spend the night alone. Being weary from his journey, he retired as soon as the rooms were ready, undressed, blew out the candle and went to bed.

But an hour or so later he awakened to find a ghostly figure in the room. It approached the bed-side table, took up the candle, lit it from the embers of the fire and then turned to leave the room, beckoning to Dr Rule to follow! Instead the doctor, deciding with Falstaff that discretion was the better part of valour, remained in his bed and 'commended himself to God's keeping'.

The ghost seemed to realize that Dr Rule was reluctant to leave his bed and evidently resolved on more positive action for as Dr Rule watched, with wide eyes, the apparition placed a poker in the fire and, when it was red-hot, withdrew it and laid it on the floor pointing towards the bed.

At this Dr Rule decided that he had no choice in the matter. He rose and followed the ghost which led him out of the bedroom and down a flight of stairs; at the foot of which it placed the candle on the floor—and vanished!

Dr Rule, with commendable calmness, picked up the candle and returned to his room where he pondered on the matter and decided that his spectral visitor had tried to convey some message to him. He thought it might concern murder. He spent the rest of the night undisturbed.

In the morning he enquired of the landlord as to whether he knew of any unsolved crimes in the district and although the good doctor was reassured on this point, he nevertheless felt sure that he was right.

Determined to see whether he could discover anything about the matter himself, he made arrangements to spend the weekend in the area and announced that he would preach at the church on the Sunday. He added that he hoped the landlord would do all he could to ensure a good attendance.

Word quickly spread that the well-known divine was to be heard at church and when Sunday arrived, Dr Rule, to his satisfaction, found a large congregation.

He took for his sermon the subject of conscience and must have been most impressive and lucid for at the end of the service an old man came to him and said, with tears in his eyes, that he could keep silent no longer.

He told Dr Rule that as a young man he had assisted in the building of a house (the house in which the Chancellor had spent his disturbed night); that he and another man had quarrelled and fought and, more by accident than intention, the other man had been killed. Terrified of the consequences, he had quickly dug a hole at the foot of the stairs in the house and there buried his victim.

A skeleton was later unearthed at the foot of the stairs in

the haunted house and after the bones had been buried in the churchyard, the ghost was never reported again.

An account of the affair is preserved among the old church records at Fettercairn.

FORFAR, ANGUS-SHIRE

A grove in the beautiful Vale of Strathmore is haunted by the ghost of a penitent girl.

One day she had met in this grove Edmund Graeme, the only son of a laird. He had fallen in love with her and they would often keep their trysts in this romantic grove on the laird's estate. Soon they became engaged to be married but then, one evening, when he went there for a pre-arranged meeting, it was to learn that she had been unfaithful to him.

The shock nearly broke his heart. Before long, the ghostly sounds that are always heard before the death of a Graeme terrified the family and servants and soon Edmund Graeme was dead.

Hardly had he breathed his last before the girl he loved so much came to him, full of remorse. Distraught at being too late, she kissed the still lips and bade the attendants meet her in the grove that night to receive instructions about the burial of her beloved.

On the stroke of midnight Edmund Graeme's servants met the girl in the grove. She persuaded them to promise to bring the next night to the same grove the body of Edmund, in a double coffin. As they arrived with the coffin, again at midnight, the girl emerged from the trees clad in a white shroud. She told the attendants that it was here that she had first met Edmund Graeme, here that he had learned of her unfaithfulness, and here that he and she would be buried.

So saying she stepped into the coffin, lay down by the side of her dead lover and bade the servants put on the lid and bury them both on the spot. Too terrified to disobey, the servants carried out her instructions and the deed was done.

Ever since that day the glade has been haunted and whenever a girl passes through it at night, the ghost of the penitent betrothed of Edmund Graeme appears and warns her never to be unfaithful to the man she loves.

FYVIE, ABERDEENSHIRE

The magnificent fourteenth-century Fyvie Castle, formerly the seat of the Lord and Lady Leith of Fyvie, is probably built on the site of an even earlier castle. It is haunted by a weeping stone and a phantom trumpeter and it has a ghost room, a murder room and a secret chamber.

Beautifully situated near the river Ythan in a wooded valley, the impressive castle was given by King Richard III to Sir James Lindsay from whose family it passed to Sir Henry Preston of Craigmillar who distinguished himself at the battle of Otterburn in 1388.

While Sir Henry Preston was demolishing a nearby monastery and using the stones to construct what is now known as the Preston Tower, he had no less a visitor than Thomas the Rhymer, Scotland's prolific prophet, poet and bard, whose abilities are said to date from his contact with the Queen of the Fairies in the Eildon Hills.

It chanced that during the transference of many weighty stones three fell into the river and were lost; a circumstance that did not put Sir Henry in a good mood. When Thomas the Rhymer appeared at the castle at this inopportune moment to request a night's shelter, he was not admitted and the great gate was shut in his face.

Always quick to take offence, Thomas proceeded to pronounce a curse in front of the awed spectators who had hurriedly gathered to catch a glimpse of the famous wizard. He declared that until the three stones had been recovered, the Fyvie property would never descend in direct line for more than two generations.

As he spoke a violent storm burst over the castle; the wind and rain drenching the watchers who noticed, with amazement, that the spot where the Rhymer stood was calm and dry.

Two of the lost stones were eventually recovered but the third was never found. Of the two retrieved one was found to have moisture on it and so it remained ever after no matter how dry and warm the weather might be. Thus the name 'Castle of the Weeping Stone' became attached to Fyvie: weeping perhaps on account of the missing stone and the curse.

Sir Henry Preston had only a daughter and she married into the Meldrum family to whom the castle passed on his death. Later it was sold to Alexander Seton, third son of the sixth Lord. He was created Lord Fyvie and Earl of Dunfermline.

It was a Seton who rescued Bruce from the English but they always considered that the family was blighted as long as they remained at Fyvie because of Thomas the Rhymer's curse. Indeed, the estate was forfeited when the fourth Lord Fyvie espoused the Jacobite cause.

William, second Earl of Aberdeen, became the owner in 1726 and he bequeathed it to his son by his third wife. The direct line died out, I understand, after two generations.

It was during the eighteenth century that the Phantom Trumpeter first made his appearance. Among the several stories in circulation to account for this famous ghost perhaps the most commonly accepted concerns Andrew Lammie, a trumpeter in the service of the castle who fell in love with Agnes Smith, the daughter of a prosperous local miller. Agnes's parents did not approve of the match and so the couple used to meet in secret.

There is no telling how the affair would have ended had not the Laird of Fyvie himself desired Agnes for a mistress. Learning of the clandestine meetings, he arranged for Andrew to be seized and transported to the West Indies. However, after a few years in slavery, he managed to escape and returned to Scotland to look for his beloved Agnes, only to learn that she had died of a broken heart.

The shock took its toll on Andrew's weakened frame and soon he, too, died. On his deathbed he cursed the Laird of Fyvie and swore that the sound of a trumpet would henceforth foretell the death of every Laird of Fyvie and would be heard both within and outside the castle walls.

It is said that shortly after the death of Andrew Lammie the haunting of Fyvie began and for many years afterwards the harrowing blast of a trumpet would be heard at dead of night before the death of a laird. Sometimes a tall and menacing figure, a shadowy man clad in a picturesque tartan, would be seen in the vicinity of the castle walls; a figure that had no reality and which disappeared into thin air when approached.

A variant of this story tells of the parents of Agnes Smith, angry with her for loving Andrew Lammie and rejecting the powerful Laird of Fyvie, actually being responsible for her death. In any case, the story of the love between Agnes and Andrew is immortalized in an Aberdeenshire ballad entitled 'Mill O'Tifty's Annie'; the poet substituting fictional names for the real characters.

On the summit of one of the castle's turrets is a stone effigy thought to represent Andrew Lammie and the trumpet in his hand points in the direction of a monument erected in Fyvie churchyard to the memory of his beloved Agnes Smith.

Another ghost at Fyvie Castle is the Green Lady who, Elliott O'Donnell told me a few years ago, is still seen from time to time. She emerges from the room known as the 'Haunted Chamber' and, gliding noiselessly through the winding stairways and panelled rooms, descending and ascending stairways, she returns at length to the Haunted Chamber, to disappear until the next time.

Some years ago a monster fungus developed in the old gun room and when the giant growth was eventually removed the masons and carpenters discovered a complete skeleton. After these bones were unearthed a number of disturbances were reported, including re-appearances of the ghostly Green Lady.

One of the maids at the castle (who had stoutly maintained that she did not believe in ghosts) lay in bed one night and saw a 'white object' step out of the wall of her room near the head of the bed. Too terrified even to cry out, she saw that the figure resembled a lady dressed in a wide and flowing whitish-green gown. The apparition 'sailed' rather than walked across the chamber, turned once and seemed to look sadly at the terrified occupant of the room, then disappeared through a closed door.

Other witnesses told of meeting the Green Lady wandering through the corridors of the castle, a lonely and silent figure, disappearing into solid walls of panelling. After the Lord of the time gave instructions for the skeleton to be replaced in the wall where it had been discovered, there were fewer reported appearances of the mysterious Green Lady.

No one seems to know who the Green Lady might be; perhaps she is connected with another mystery here, a secret room which, according to rumour, has been kept locked for many years.

It is believed that should the room be opened, grave misfortune will befall the inhabitants of Fyvie Castle. Some people think that the room contains ill-gotten treasure; others that it holds the bones of victims of some dreadful family tragedy; yet others that it is the entrance to dungeons where dark and awful deeds were committed long, long ago.

GALASHIELS, SELKIRKSHIRE

Ancient Buckholm Tower stands in this deserted landscape, a sentinel looking out over the valley of the Gala, a silent reminder of dreadful deeds.

The Laird of Buckholm, nearly two-hundred years ago, was named Pringle. He was a dark, evil man who had so ill-treated his wife and young son that they had left him. No woman was safe in the house and his cruelty was a byword for miles around. There was nothing he enjoyed more than employing his two ferocious hounds in hunting down Covenanters, outlawed religious dissenters.

One June day a troop of dragoons were in the vicinity in order to surprise an assembly of Covenanters who were due to hold one of their clandestine meetings on nearby Ladhope Moor. Pringle was known as a loyal supporter of the Government so the dragoon captain came to Buckholm Tower for his help and advice as to the most likely spot on the wide moor that the Covenanters would choose.

Pringle was delighted. He had little doubt as to the place and after the troops were refreshed, he eagerly led them to Ladhope Moor. His guess was right but the Covenanters must have received warning for they had fled, leaving behind one old man, Geordie Elliot, whose wife had served Mrs Pringle at the Tower in happier days, and whose son, Willie, had stayed to help his father when the old man had fallen from his horse. Both were known Covenanters.

The wicked laird of Buckholm was in favour of dispatching the two men without argument but Captain Bruce of the Dragoons suspected that the men might be persuaded to disclose information about their fellow-Covenanters and he persuaded Pringle to keep them prisoner at Buckholm for the night. Next day an escort would collect them.

After the captain and his dragoons had departed, Pringle had the two men thrown into the tower dungeons which exist to this day, gloomy and damp with an ominous row of iron hooks suspended from the roof where hams and salted beef would hang in Pringle's happier days. There is also (or was) a blood-stained beam nothing would clean, a grim reminder of dreadful happenings.

With his prisoners safe Pringle sat down to celebrate the capture of the two Covenanters. His secret supply of French brandy dwindled alarmingly as he treated himself to glass after glass. The hours passed and Pringle still drank his brandy alone and became more ill-tempered with each glass.

At length he lurched to his feet and made for the dungeons. At the massive doorway he encountered several of his servants who had been disturbed by calls for 'Help' from the dark dungeons. It sounded, they said, as though old Geordie was in a bad way and his son was calling for assistance.

Pringle pushed his men to one side, opened the dungeon door and pulling it close after him, disappeared, cursing and staggering, into the gloomy interior. Quaking with apprehension the loyal servants listened to the raised voices, then the sounds of heavy blows, a dragging noise and strangled screams before silence and the reappearance of the laird, panting, wide-eyed and cursing all and sundry.

He stumbled out of the dungeon and was about to return to his study for more brandy when a knock sounded on the entrance door of the tower. Pringle stopped in his tracks and one of his servants hurriedly opened the great door. Outside stood an old woman, dignified and accusing. Pringle recognized Geordie's wife, Isobel. She had come in search of her husband and her son.

'Ye want to see your menfolk, do ye?' snarled Pringle, pointing to the dungeons. 'Come with me, then. By God, ye shall see them!'

He dragged the old woman with him and they disappeared through the dungeon doorway. Again he slammed the door shut behind him. A moment later a piercing scream broke from old Isobel's lips, for there, suspended on the cruel hooks, were the bodies of her husband and her son.

Scream after scream echoed from the dungeon as the distraught woman stumbled out and collapsed, sobbing at the tower doorway. Now Pringle emerged from the dungeon, laughing hideously and shouting something about 'Swine should be treated as swine

He paused as he saw Isobel, a pathetic heap, sobbing and shuddering in her sorrow. He stood over her, remorseless, calling her an old witch. For a moment the watching servants thought he was going to strike her but after a moment the sobbing ceased and the old woman slowly dragged herself to her feet.

Her eyes burned with hatred. She faced the drunken laird fearlessly and cursed him quietly, invoking the vengeance of God for what he had done. 'May the memory of yer evil deeds haunt ye for ever, like the hounds of hell,' she said. 'May they pursue ye waking and sleeping and may ye find no rest in this life or through eternity.' The next moment she was gone.

Thereafter the laird of Buckholm was a haunted man. Whatever potency the curse may have had, Pringle certainly believed that he was hunted by ghostly hounds, not perpetually but at any time of the day or night the horror would be upon him. He would suddenly turn in his chair, eyes staring, and lash out at some invisible presence; he would wake from his sleep screaming that dogs were at his throat.

Time after time his servants would burst in on him after hearing his screams and cries for help, to find him beating about himself with his arms in all directions as though warding off attacks from all sides.

Often he would return to the tower, hat ing obviously ridden long and hard, flung himself from his panting horse and clamour for protection from the fearful things that he said had chased him.

Before long he died, wretched in mind and body, full of haunting horror and his last moments saw his body racked by convulsions, for all the world as though he were worried and badgered to death.

The months passed and as the anniversary of the laird's death approached, the atmosphere at Buckholm Tower seemed charged with expectation.

Three days before the date on which he had died one of the servants swore that he had heard the baying of hounds and the cries of a man fleeing for his life, a mile or so from the tower. The pursuit seemed to pass close to him and faded away in the direction of Buckholm although he saw nothing to account for the fearsome noises.

The next night everyone at the tower heard the baying of hounds and a voice calling for help. The sounds drew nearer and nearer until the chase seemed to arrive at the very door of Buckholm and then came the noise of loud beating on the door and a man's voice imploring refuge; a strange, hollow voice that sounded like the late laird of Buckholm.

Yet, when the door was opened the sounds ceased and the courtyard was seen to be totally deserted.

On the night of the anniversary of Pringle's death the baying of hounds and the piteous cries for help were heard yet again and this time they seemed to come from the dungeon.

They grew louder and more terrible until finally someone was brave enough to open the dungeon door. Still the awful sounds came from within, although nothing was visible in the darkness. The door was shut again and then lingering footsteps were heard, heavy crashing noises and sudden thuds sounded from within the dungeon; then the tower seemed to vibrate with repeated heavy blows on the dungeon door as though someone wanted desperately to get out.

The awful noise continued for hours with no one daring to open the dungeon door again. At the time that Pringle had breathed his last, the battering noise ceased, a long-drawn-out sobbing sigh was heard and then silence.

Each year on the anniversary of the death of the laird of Buckholm noises resembling the baying of hounds, cries for help, heavy footsteps and thuds on the dungeon door are said to be heard, in varying intensity, by those who venture here after darkness has fallen.

GARLETON HILL, NEAR HADDINGTON, EAST LOTHIAN

The mansion-house called Garleton was said to be haunted by a mysterious tall man who walked about the old house with heavy footsteps, trying to persuade someone to listen to his long tale of woe. Foundations of the haunted house that took a long time to die can still be traced.

Towards the end of the eighteenth century one of the still-habitable wings of the decaying house was occupied by the eccentric Miss Janet Hepburn, a tall, thin woman who walked the countryside at all times of the day and night, dressed in black from head to foot and invariably carrying a cane with a gold chain and tassel.

One night, or rather morning, for it was just before sunrise, she had seated herself on a grassy knoll not far from her home when she was approached by a strange man whose looks she did not like at all. He was tall and pale with piercing eyes and he seemed most anxious to convey something to Miss Hepburn.

But such a dislike had she taken to the odd figure which she had neither seen nor heard approach but suddenly found close to her, that she waved her cane at him and set off home. Looking back a moment later she discovered that the man was nowhere in sight.

That night Janet Hepburn took care to lock and bolt all her doors and windows and even put the key of the front door under her pillow for she found herself unable to forget the strange man. Living alone with only a maid, she feared that he might have followed her in some way and found out where she lived.

In the middle of the night she awakened to hear the sound of the front door opening, followed by heavy footsteps climbing the stairs towards her room.

The footsteps ceased and she then heard the sounds of movement within her bedroom. 'Who's that?' she called out, with as much defiance in her voice as she could muster. And the man who had accosted her the day before stood by her bed! 'This is my home,' he said in deep and hollow tones, and there was an indescribable sadness about his presence and his voice. 'I have a long story to tell you.'

Janet Hepburn felt sure that her visitor was a burglar. She pointed to her jewel box and told the man to take what he wanted and be gone. He shook his head and said that he only wanted to talk to her.

Frightened and uneasy beyond words, Miss Hepburn told him that she would never listen to his story and waved him away. Without another word the strange figure turned and left the room. She heard heavy footsteps echo through the old house as he slowly made his way downstairs and out of the house. She only breathed again when she heard the front door slam shut.

For the rest of the night she tossed and turned, dreading that she would again hear the heavy footsteps and see the tall, sad man at her bedside. Yet she decided not to disturb her maid.

In the morning however she told her about the night's events and learned that the maid also had heard footsteps at the dead of night and also a man's voice; but thinking she must be dreaming, she had gone back to sleep.

Now both women hurriedly looked everywhere to see what was missing but all the valuables were untouched, the front door was still locked and bolted and all the windows fastened.

In the years that followed heavy footsteps were heard from time to time at dead of night or very early in the morning but no trace of any intruder was ever found; locked doors and windows were never tampered with but, perhaps because Miss Hepburn had been so insistent that she would not listen to the visitor's story, the figure was never seen again.

GEANIES, ROSS-SHIRE

Some years ago a cottage a mile away from the estate lodge, occupied by a labourer and his wife, their two boys and elderly grandparents, was haunted by an invisible presence that knocked, threw things about and pinched people in bed.

The disturbances were investigated by Professor George J. Romanes, F.R.S., Professor of Physiology and a friend of Charles Darwin. An element of intelligence was observed for some strange scratchings were heard on an outside wall.

When Professor Romanes asked whether his height could be indicated, a long scratch was heard; and when a similar question was asked regarding Mrs Romanes, a short scratch came—thus crudely but correctly asserting that while the Professor was tall, his wife was short! These noises and the knockings were heard when the boys were at school.

The movement in the beds seemed to be perceptible under the ticking of the mattress, almost as though a small animal were trapped there. There was gentle heaving and faint movement.

Many times occupants of the cottage maintained that their sleep was disturbed by the pinching of invisible fingers. Incessant knocking accompanied this manifestation and sometimes the old man's night-cap would be snatched from his head and tossed to the floor.

Rabbit-traps placed on the bed were found flung to the floor with the wires broken and when the mattress was taken out of doors, split open and the stuffing removed and carefully examined, nothing untoward was discovered. Yet when it was re-stuffed and replaced on the bedstead, the movements returned exactly as before.

Professor Romanes and a friend spent a night at the cottage but nothing of a mysterious nature occurred during their visit and later the disturbances ceased. No explanation was ever discovered.

GLADHOUSE RESERVOIR, MOORFOOT HILLS, NEAR EDINBURGH

The reservoir covers land where once Hoolet House stood, a small farmstead long occupied by a miserable middle-aged man who had no known relatives and few friends. His widely separated neighbours who knew him by sight, were surprised beyond words when he returned from a visit to Falkirk with a young bride.

Now Hoolet House had servants and for a time there was light and gaiety but within a few months the fifty-year-old bridegroom was once again morose, irritable and unsociable.

The servants left one after the other and fresh ones stayed only a short time, except for a young Irishman. He alone seemed to remain faithful and the farmer only awoke to the young man's real reason for staying at the lonely old house when, after a long day at market he returned to his farmhouse to find his wife missing, together with the young Irishman and some £200.

The disgruntled farmer organized searches high and low for the guilty pair but without success. It began to be generally assumed that they had left Britain for one of the colonies, although curious stories began to circulate about the couple being seen in the vicinity of the old farmhouse and of the figures disappearing when they were approached.

Such reports grew more and more numerous until the phantoms of Hoolet House were well-known in the neighbourhood and no one ventured that way after dark, if they could help it.

Soon the animals on the farm were stricken with a strange and deadly malady so that the farmer was hard put to it to bury the animals single-handed and he was forced to hire men to help him with the unpleasant work.

It was as they were about to bury the last horse, having moved to another part of the farm from that to which they had been directed, that a shout from the farmer ordered them to stop digging. But it was too late; already a human hand was unearthed and before long the mutilated bodies of the farmer's wife and the Irish servant were uncovered.

Suspicion soon fell on the sullen and unpopular farmer but before the law could take its course he fled and was never seen again in the locality.

Hoolet House remained empty. The land was divided between neighbouring farms and as time passed, the very stones of the house were used for dykes and dividing walls. By the time the reservoir was constructed, hardly anything of the former house remained. And after the bodies of the young couple were uncovered and re-interned in consecrated ground there were no further reports of the phantoms of Hoolet House.

GLAMIS, ANGUS

It is an unforgettable experience to approach Glamis Castle along the tree-lined drive on a shimmering summer's day. The haunted castle, solid and silent in the sunshine, has about it an air of mystery even under these conditions.

This splendid seat of the Earls of Strathmore is mentioned in thirteenth-century records; Shakespeare refers to it in Macbeth', and it was the birthplace of Princess Margaret.

What a place Glamis is for those who love mysteries!

There is the Haunted Chamber; ringed stones in several of the bedroom floors now cleverly covered with built-in cupboards which are always full; the unexplained noises and strange nocturnal visitors that occupants have heard and seen; the fearsome appearance of huge and bearded 'Earl Beardie' who is reputed to have played cards with the Devil, and lost; the mysterious rooms that seem to have no doors; the everlasting blood-stain in King Malcolm's room where Malcolm II was murdered in the eleventh century (no amount of scrubbing and cleaning would remove it so in the end the whole floor was boarded over!); the pathetic and shy Grey or White Lady who is still seen quite often in the vicinity of the chapel dedicated to St Michael; the unrecognized tall figure in a long coat, fastened at the neck, which always enters a locked door halfway up a certain winding stair; the shadowy figures that are always being seen flitting about the castle; the bedroom door that opened every night whether it was locked, bolted or had furniture piled against it... eventually the wall was taken down and the door removed.

There is the Queen Mother's bathroom where no one could sleep soundly when it was a bedroom; the tongueless woman who looks out of a barred window or runs across the park pointing to her bleeding mouth; and the ghostly little Black Boy who sits on a stone seat by the door into the Queen Mother's sitting-room and is supposed to be a Negro servant who was unkindly treated over two hundred years ago.

There is even a vampire legend at Glamis. A woman servant who was caught in the act of sucking the blood from one of her victims was hustled into a secret room and left to die—but that is not one of the ways to rid the world of a vampire; and legend has it that her secret tomb is still open somewhere in Glamis and her menace still potent.

Then there is the mystery of the number of rooms at Glamis and the story that house guests once hung towels out of every window from within the castle but when they went outside they discovered that no towel fluttered from any of the dark windows in one very old square tower, nor could they find a way into that particular tower.

The Haunted Chamber, sealed for years by walling, its position known only to a few, is thought to have got its name in the feuding days when a number of the Ogilvy clan, fleeing from the Lindsays, sought shelter at Glamis Castle. Although the owner at the time admitted them, he had no sympathy for their feud and on the pretence of hiding them, he secured them in a remote chamber of the rambling castle and there left them to starve.

The chamber, it is said, still contains the remains of the unfortunate men and when many years ago, the earl of the day was much disturbed by strange night-time noises, Lord Strathmore and some companions went to the Haunted Chamber. He collapsed, however, when he encountered the contents of the unventilated chamber. Today the white-walled, bare chamber has a sense of brooding uneasiness.

A Dr Lee records that when a woman and her young son were staying at the castle and the child was asleep in an adjoining dressing-room, the woman suddenly felt a blast of cold air which extinguished a night-light at her bedside but did not disturb the light in the room where the child was sleeping.

The woman saw a tall figure in armour pass silently from her room into the dressing-room where the child awoke with a shriek. When the lady comforted her child, she learned that he had seen what he described as 'a giant' who came into the room and leaned over the bed, peering closely at him.

High up in the uninhabited tower is the room where the ghost of 'Earl Beardie' gambles with the Devil. Earl Beardie was an ancient Lord Crawford who quarrelled with the Lord Glamis of the day as they gambled. Beardie, a huge man, was thrown down the stone staircase, only to return, according to legend, stamping his feet and roaring with rage, bellowing that if no man would play with him, he'd play with the Devil himself. Instantly a tall, dark man in a cloak strode in and play began. No one knows what happened but the man was never seen again and Earl Beardie died shortly afterwards.

Ever after the ghost of Earl Beardie gambled, stamped and swore with 'something' in the empty room with two doors and an ominous trap door. Even today servants at the castle maintain that they hear at night the rattle of dice, heavy stamping noises and the sound of men cursing from the direction of the empty room.

A former Lord Castletown's daughter awoke during a night she was spending at Glamis to see the figure of a huge old man seated in front of the fire in her bedroom and when he turned to look at her, she saw that his face was that of a dead man. Dr Nicholson, a Dean of Brechin, occupying a room off the central staircase, awoke to see a tall figure in a cloak standing by his bed. The figure disappeared through a wall—a ghost that the Bishop of Brechin, Dr Forbes, was to encounter the very next night.

Once three sets of rooms on the Clock Landing were allotted

respectively to Lady Strathmore's sister, Mrs John Streatfeild and her husband; the Trevanions, Lord Strathmore's sister; and Mr and Mrs Munro from Lindertis who occupied the Red Room with their young son sleeping in an adjoining room.

During the night Mrs Munro was awakened by someone bending over her, and a beard brushing her face. She awoke her husband and they both plainly saw a figure pass into their son's room; he immediately shrieked with terror and rushed into his parent's chamber, declaring that he had seen a giant.

The time was four o'clock. In the morning Mrs Trevanion related that she and her husband had been awakened during the night by the restlessness of her little dog and they had both heard a tremendous crashing noise followed by the sound of a clock striking four times.

The following night the three couples sat up to watch and although they saw nothing on that occasion they all heard a loud crashing noise from the direction of the landing and as they were examining the area with its great old clock, the hour of four boomed out.

Lady Granville, elder sister of the Queen Mother, told my friend James Wentworth Day that when she lived at Glamis, children often woke up at night in the upper rooms, screaming that a huge, bearded man had leaned over their beds and looked at them.

All furniture has long been taken out of these rooms and they are never used in these days; nor is the Hangman's Chamber which is said to be haunted by a butler who hanged himself there. Sir Shane Leslie told me that the ghost of Earl Beardie had been seen by his Aunt Mary when she was a visitor at Glamis.

There are many accounts of a White or Grey Lady being seen at Glamis Castle; one account relates that the figure was seen by three people at the same time, from different vantage points;

and there are persistent accounts of a strange, elusive, racing figure nicknamed 'Jack the Runner' who speeds across the park on moonlit nights.

I was told more about the Grey Lady when my wife and I were at Glamis. Lady Granville was in the chapel one sunny day when she saw a grey figure kneeling in one of the pews and although the detail of the dress the figure was wearing was quite clear. Lady Granville noticed that the sun shone through the figure and made a pattern on the floor.

The last Lord Strathmore saw the Grey Lady in similar circumstances. He was checking the details of some of the interesting de Wint pictures in the chapel one afternoon when he turned round and saw the figure in grey, kneeling in one of the pews. Not wishing to disturb her, Lord Strathmore tiptoed quietly away. My wife and I silently examined the pictures in this quiet little chapel when we were there but we saw no ghost.

And then there is the famous 'monster' legend. It is said that nearly two hundred years ago a 'monster' or frightfully deformed child was born within the family, a grotesque and bloated being that grew up in a hidden room to a large size and possessed enormous strength; a closely guarded secret known only to successive heirs and the faithful factors of the estate.

The creature is said to have lived to an incredible age; one person who should know maintains that he died in 1921. That some such secret lies buried in the hundred-odd rooms and incredibly thick walls of Glamis, seems certain. Listen to Lady Granville again: 'We were never allowed to talk about it when we were children... my father and grandfather refused absolutely to discuss it.'

The last Lord Strathmore felt sure that a corpse or coffin was buried somewhere in the walls and the walk, high up on the roof, is still known as the Mad Earl's Walk, perpetuating the legend and dating perhaps from an escape attempt or the place where the poor monster was exercised.

Haunted and romantic Glamis Castle has many secrets and many ghosts.

GLASGOW

The second largest city in Great Britain with over a fifth of the total population of Scotland; its name is derived from the Celtic meaning 'dear, green spot'.

In the high-standing thirteenth-century cathedral a rare fifteenth-century rood-screen depicts the seven deadly sins; the tomb of St Mungo who founded a bishopric here in ad 543 (the saint's well is nearby) and the strange 'Rob Roy's Pillar' from behind which a mysterious stranger conveyed a warning to Frank Osbaldistone in Scott's romantic tale. The city has also a haunted infirmary and a number of haunted houses.

The ghost at Glasgow's Western Infirmary is said to be Sir William MacEwen, the brain surgeon who died some fifty years ago. Shortly before his death at the age of seventy-six, Sir William declined to perform an operation for severe headaches on a young artist.

After he left the surgeon, the artist, suffering from one of his violent headaches, fell to his death down four flights of stairs at the Infirmary. The ghost that has been seen here from time to time in the corridors of the hospital is thought to be the remorse-filled spirit of Sir William, returning to the scene of the tragedy.

Quite recently a young nurse reported seeing a white-coated figure coming towards her one night along one of the dimly-lit passage-ways. When the form almost reached the door of the operating theatre, it vanished.

Many hospitals have ghosts. The authorities are invariably sceptical and say that such stories are put about as a joke to frighten new night-staff. The nurses hope that the officials are right but evidence, such as that for the ghost of Sir William, mounts steadily and is not easily explained away.

Elliott O'Donnell once told me of a visit he made at a haunted house in Duke Street, Glasgow, which he first heard about from a solicitor who had visited the property with the idea of renting it, until he encountered something unexpected.

Almost as soon as he let himself into the empty house he heard footsteps that seemed to follow him as he climbed the stairs and explored the various rooms. At first he thought the sounds must be some peculiar acoustic result of the deserted house.

But when he stamped his foot there was no answering echo although the footsteps continued to follow him when he resumed his exploration.

Gradually, as a level-headed man, he began to feel that there was something strange about the place for although it was a warm and sunny summer's day he felt icy cold.

As he walked along a passage with a large uncurtained window behind him letting in the summer sun, he suddenly saw on the wall ahead of him the shadow of a man—not his own! This figure had its arms outstretched and, with a shudder, the solicitor noticed that while the right hand seemed normal, there was no left hand at all!

Thoroughly frightened now, he turned and ran out of the house. But during the days that followed he found himself thinking more and more about it, reminding himself of its advantages, its low price and its sense of mystery. Within a few weeks he had taken the property and moved in with his wife and family.

For a while all went well. Then one morning the children's nursemaid burst into his study looking distressed. It seemed that the children were playing with something in the nursery that looked like a dog, and yet wasn't one! As he entered the nursery, the solicitor saw the blurred outline of a large dog come out of the room where the children were.

Far from being frightened they were delighted with their new-found 'play-thing' although they told their father that it was a 'funny dog' because it never wagged its tail and they could never get near enough to touch it.

That same night, as he went to switch off the light after working late, he found his outstretched hand caught by something large and soft which had no fingers. The light went off as he screamed in surprise; his hand was released and he heard a tremendous crashing sound from the room above where his wife was already in bed.

Rushing upstairs he found his wife sitting up in bed, apparently still fast asleep but talking to a vague dark shape that crouched on the floor at the foot of the bed. As he approached, it seemed to disappear into the wall.

The sleeping woman now awoke and implored her husband to

take her away from the house. She had dreamed of a murder being committed in the room and she described the murderer approaching her with outstretched hands. Next day the solicitor and his family moved out of the haunted house.

Elliott O'Donnell told me of the short time he spent there one night. Soon after arriving at the house a loud knock sounded at the front door and he found a policeman who was suspicious at seeing a light moving about in the empty house.

O'Donnell soon reassured him that he was no intruder and when he explained that he intended to spend a night at the place the police officer commented that he had little to fear with a dog 'like that one' to keep him company, pointing towards the stairs. O'Donnell looked up and saw a huge, shadowy, dog-like shape half-way up the stairs. As they watched, it seemed to retreat and disappear into the wall.

At the same time O'Donnell told me that he sensed an overwhelming air of evil. Acting on the spur of the moment, he explained to the policeman that there was no physical dog in the house and he hurriedly left with him.

The distinguished writer on the occult told me he always regretted leaving the house that night although at the time he felt that he just could not stay a moment longer. He never had the opportunity of visiting the house again.

A correspondent has related peculiar happenings experienced some years ago in a council flat where she and her husband moved with their six-month-old baby, having looked forward for a long time to a home of their own.

Their happiness was, however, short-lived, for before long they both began to notice strange bumps and knocks at night-time which could not be accounted for; furniture and other articles apparently moving of their own accord.

The constant knowledge that something inexplicable might happen at anytime of the day or night began to tell on their nerves and soon they fled to live with relatives.

A party of investigators sat all night in the deserted flat, hearing and seeing nothing unusual. They tried again and this time they certainly had a most extraordinary experience. Inexplicable bangs and crashing noises echoed through the flat at irregular times and for irregular periods; articles moved of their own volition, including a pair of iron fire-tongs which behaved as though propelled by invisible hands.

A medium was invited to join the next all-night sitting and in a dark room, while in trance, he spoke in what sounded like the croaking voice of an old woman.

The communicating entity seemed agitated, her words were jumbled and disjointed but at length the sitters established the fact that she was worried about a baby; the child had something wrong with its throat and must be taken to hospital immediately, 'she' insisted, or it would die.

'She' identified herself as a relative of the young couple who had been driven from the flat and claimed that 'she' had caused the disturbances in an effort to attract their attention.

When the couple heard about the warning they were sceptical, for their child seemed perfectly fit. but they arranged for an X-ray examination and the same day surgeons removed a small obstruction from the baby's throat which, had it moved towards the windpipe, could have caused suffocation.

The vicinity of George Street was, it seems, haunted a few years ago by two ghosts, dressed in the fashion of the eighteenth century. They were seen by a man at two o'clock one morning as he walked home from late shift-work.

He said afterwards that he heard no sound but suddenly became aware of two men, dressed in the clothes of two hundred years ago. walking beside him; 'going about their own amicable business' as he put it, obviously chatting pleasantly to each other although no sound of any kind reached the witness.

Within a few seconds the ghosts faded and vanished.

Far from being frightened or upset the down-to-earth workman stated that he had enjoyed the experience and rather hoped that it might be repeated!

GLEN SHIRA, NEAR INVER-
ARAY, ARGYLLSHIRE

One warm and sunny day in 1765 a man accompanied his father, a farmer from Glen Aray, to nearby Glen Shira, where both had business to attend to. They had walked there by crossing the hill between the two places and having finished by mid-day, they decided to return by way of Inveraray.

They reached the Gairan Bridge and turned north, when they were astonished to see a great number of men under arms marching on foot towards them.

The men marched in regular order from the Quay, along the shore and high road, crossing the River Apav near the town, at the spot where a bridge was later constructed—and still there appeared to be no end to the column.

Father and son stood and watched the vast army for a considerable time and, as far as they could see, the column of men came marching towards them from the distance.

At last the two men walked on. stopping now and again, with the marching men constantly in their view. They counted sixteen or seventeen pairs of colours. They clearly saw the soldiers, six or seven abreast, with children and women on each side, some carrying pots and pans.

The soldiers were clothed in red and the bright sun of the summer day gleamed on the muskets and bayonets. At one point the two men noticed an animal that looked like a deer or possibly a horse, in the middle of a circle of soldiers who seemed to be forcing the animal forward with their bayonets which they used to stab and prod the tired beast.

The older man had served with Argyll's Highlanders in the rising of 1745 and in answer to his son's questions he said that he supposed the army 'had come from Ireland and had landed in Kintyre and that it was proceeding to England'. He considered the number of men to be greater than all the combatants at the battle of Culloden.

The two men had now reached the Thorn Bush, between the Gairan Bridge and the gate of the Deer Park and were able to observe the marching men minutely. There was an officer on a grey horse (the only mounted man they saw) and from his appearance they considered that he must be the commander-in-chief. He wore a gold-laced hat and a blue hussar-cloak with wide and loose open sleeves, all lined with red; and boots and spurs.

The younger man now began to fear that the army might possibly attempt to take him along with them if they noticed him so he climbed over a stone dyke that fenced the Deer Park from the road. His father, being an older man, had no such fears and he continued on his way, by now untroubled by the marching men.

After walking behind the dyke for a time, the younger man reached a clump of bushes. There he stopped and looked back to see how far the army had progressed when, to his utter astonishment, he found that they had all vanished and not a soul was to be seen! Rushing back to his father he asked what had become of the army of marching men.

Only then, it seemed, did the older man become aware that the army was no longer there. He could offer no explanation and, like his son, was utterly astounded at the disappearance of the vast army.

So the two men proceeded to Inveraray, meeting on their way an old acquaintance from Glen Shira. He was driving a horse before him and both father and son thought that this was the same animal that they had seen being driven along by the army.

The son asked the old man, whose name was Stewart, what had become of the marching men who had recently travelled along the road. Stewart seemed puzzled by the question and replied that he had seen no one since leaving Inveraray but it was such a warm day, the air so close and sultry, that he felt hardly able to breathe. His horse too had become so feeble that he had felt obliged to dismount and drive the animal before him.

It seemed that only the two men in this remote part of Scotland had seen the phantom army but they were both honest and upright men, seemingly incapable of inventing such a pointless story. They often recounted their experience and no one to whom they told it ever doubted that they were telling the truth.

GLENCORSE, MIDLOTHIAN

A little over a century and a half ago, on the site of the present barracks, stood Greenlaw House, a fine mansion set among fir trees; a property that was used to house French prisoners during the later years of the Napoleonic War.

The prisoners enjoyed considerable freedom and were permitted to wander without escort throughout the house and grounds. One young officer, strolling through the peaceful glades of nearby Frith Woods, met one day the daughter of a local farmer. Their friendship developed rapidly and soon they were meeting and walking together in the privacy of the woods.

But one evening, as they walked hand-in-hand, they were suddenly confronted by the girl's father and a young man who was his choice for his daughter's hand.

Without a word they set about the startled Frenchman who defended himself bravely but was no match for the two enraged Scots. Before long the luckless man lay dead at the feet of the grief-stricken girl, who sobbed and struggled as she was dragged home and locked in her room.

Late at night, however, she escaped and fled from the house. In the morning when her absence was discovered an immediate search was instituted. Before long the dead body of the broken-hearted girl was found at the foot of a rocky gorge on the North Esk, a spot known to this day as Lover's Leap.

On numerous occasions, since the tragic death of the unhappy maid, the sad figure of a girl has been reported in the Frith Woods; sometimes standing as if waiting for her lover from France, but more often glimpsed running wildly, her hair dishevelled and blown by the wind, towards the place where her lover was killed before her eyes.

Occasionally, too, she is seen sobbing silently and sorrowfully beneath a tree near this haunted spot.

GLENLUCE, WIGTOWNSHIRE

For four long years, during the seventeenth century, a ghost plagued the cottage of weaver Gilbert Campbell. The visitant earned the name of the 'Deil of Glenluce' and became the talk of all Scotland when exorcism by Presbyterian ministers had no effect.

The disturbances seem to date from the time that a wandering beggar named Alexander Agnew called at the Campbell cottage and was sent away empty-handed. Agnew had long enjoyed an evil reputation and on this occasion he loudly abused the family and threatened them with ill-fortune.

Gilbert Campbell's son, Tom, on vacation from Glasgow University at the time, soon complained that he was followed by a 'spirit' that made loud noises and shrill whistlings whenever he moved about the house or yard. His sister Jennet, too, complained that she was troubled by an invisible 'demon' that had threatened to 'cast her into the well'.

Through the long winter nights the family became increasingly plagued by what they called 'restless spirits' who hurled stones at doors and through windows, destroyed materials and property, tore to shreds clothing that members of the family were wearing and interfered with Gilbert Campbell's work, severing the warps and threads as he laboured at his loom.

Bedclothes were repeatedly dragged off the cots of the smaller children; chests and trunks were opened and their contents thrown out and scattered about the rooms; loud and mysterious noises were reported at all times of the day and night.

The disturbances became so troublesome and frightening for

the younger members of the family that the Campbells were at last compelled to send their children away and it is reported that when only adults occupied the house, all was quiet.

But soon Tom returned from Glasgow on another vacation; almost immediately the 'haunting' re-commenced and reached a hitherto unparalleled intensity including one occasion when the cottage was set alight and narrowly escaped complete destruction.

Having come to the conclusion that their son Tom was the main object of the 'spirit's' malice, Campbell and his wife asked the local minister to take the lad into his house. This was done but the disturbances at Campbell's cottage continued unabated and at length several ministers convened a solemn meeting at the haunted house.

Tom was brought along and there followed a long and complicated series of alleged conversations with the haunting 'spirit' (which claimed to have a commission from Heaven to vex the family).

During the course of these communications several witches of Glenluce were named and the 'ghost' requested a spade to dig a grave for itself! One minister suggested that the 'voice spoke out of the children of the family': an insinuation which the haunting entity much resented. Soon afterwards this particular clergymen fell to loud praying when he claimed to see the apparition of a hand and arm.

Still the trouble continued and a meeting of the local presbytery at Glenluce to free the weaver's cottage from the 'evil spirit' had no effect. Soon the children claimed that they were thrashed daily 'with heavy staves' and their parents were also assaulted and knocked about.

More stones were thrown and considerable damage caused, including some small fires, before the manifestations suddenly ceased; after which the family lived on in the house for many years without further trouble.

It was later discovered that Agnew, the tramp who had predicted the whole affair, was hanged at Dumfries on a charge of atheism and as he died, the disturbances ceased.

GLENSHEE, PERTHSHIRE

In this desolate and wild stretch of mountain and bog the ghost of a murdered English soldier used to walk.

In 1749 Sergeant Arthur Davies of General Guise's Regiment of Foot was in charge of a patrol of eight men sent from Aberdeen twice-weekly to meet another patrol at Glenshee.

With memories of the '45 still vivid in everyone's memories, their duties were to ensure that Perthshire inhabitants did not carry arms or wear the kilt.

Sergeant Davies was a keen sportsman and known to be in the habit of wandering away from his men in pursuit of game although he had been warned that this part of the country could be dangerous for lone Englishmen. At all events, when Davies' patrol reached Glenshee, Davies himself was missing and he was never seen again.

The fact that his wife, then staying near Braemar, asserted that he had on him over fifteen guineas in gold, some silver, a silver watch, two gold rings and other valuables, soon gave rise to suspicions that he had been murdered.

But where was the body? And what connection, if any, was there between the missing English sergeant and the naked ghost seen occasionally in a wild and lonely spot, a ghost that vanished when it was approached?

Nine months after the disappearance a Glen Dee man, Donald Farquharson, received a visit from someone named Alexander MacPherson who told him that he was 'much troubled' by the ghost of Sergeant Davies.

He stated that one night when he was in bed, the missing sergeant had appeared in his room, dressed in a blue coat and declared who 'he' was. Later the ghost returned, this time naked, and asked for its bones to be buried. It told MacPherson to visit Farquharson and said it would show them both where they were.

Farquharson was sceptical but agreed to go with MacPherson. They were led to a local spot known as 'the Hill of Christie' where they found, half-hidden, the much-decayed remains of the murdered man with remnants of his blue coat and other clothes but no valuables. They buried the bones on the spot.

Suspicion in respect of the missing Sergeant Davies fell on a man of questionable character named Duncan Terig who, although previously penniless, had been known in recent months to have money to spend. In addition he had married and Farquharson testified that one of the gold rings on Mrs Terig's fingers was similar to one worn by Sergeant Davies.

Five years after Davies disappeared the authorities arrested Terig and also a man named Alexander MacDonald. They were sent to the Tolbooth in Edinburgh and tried for murder. Things looked black for the two men in the dock. It was quickly shown that accounts of their movements at the time of Davies' disappearance disagreed and was at variance with other evidence.

Terig was shown to have attempted to silence one witness and altogether so damning was the case against the men that even their own counsels believed them to be guilty.

When the matter of the ghost was discussed, however, the affair took a totally unexpected course. Isobel MacHardie, a former employee of Alexander MacPherson, testified that she too had seen the ghost when she was in bed at one end of the room and MacPherson in bed at the other end.

She saw 'something naked come in at the door' which frightened her so much that she drew the clothes over her head. Next morning she asked MacPherson what it was that she had seen and he told her not to worry for it would not trouble them any more. Whereupon the jury, without exception, found the two men 'not guilty'.

GOUROCK, RENFREWSHIRE

Where the Clyde swerves sharply south, heading for the open sea, there stands on a grassy plot a seven-foot high block of grey mica schist, known as Granny Kempock. It is a stone which has long been held in superstitious awe, heightened by the fact that the plot of ground has a condition of tenure attached forbidding any building there in perpetuity.

The Granny Kempock stone may mark the site of a Druidi-cal altar and among local seafaring folk there seems to have been always a belief that Granny Kempock ruled the seas and controlled the weather. Years ago the fishermen would bring gifts and a basket of sand from the river shore to sprinkle at the foot of the stone as they circled it several times, imploring calm seas, good weather and big catches.

Newlyweds besought Granny Kempock's help as they set out on the voyage of matrimony; they, too, asked for a calm and fruitful expedition as they walked round and round the stone, hand in hand.

In 1662 Mary Lamont confessed to having danced round the talisman with the Devil as her partner. She said they had plotted to cast the stone into the sea to bring harm and bad fortune to the fishing boats and fishing folk. There are those who maintain that dim and silent figures still ceremoniously circle the mute stone on nights of the full moon.

GRANTON, MIDLOTHIAN

On the shore road between Granton and Cramond rise a pair of quaint and ornately-topped stone pillars with a wooden gate between them. This is the old sea-gate of Caroline Park, the well-preserved house that was built by George Mackenzie, Viscount Tarbat, first Earl of Cromartie.

He called the place Royston. John, second Duke of Argyll, bought it with its priest's hiding-hole and secret passage and renamed it Caroline Park, after the reigning queen.

About a hundred years ago the resident was Lady John Scott of Spottiswoode. It is said that she left behind a green ghost and a mysterious bumping sound like a cannon-ball bouncing along the white-panelled Aurora drawing-room.

Here she would sit, the portraits of exiled Stewart kings lining the walls, playing her harp and singing fine Scots songs she wrote and composed herself: 'Ettrick' and 'Duris-deer'. It was her genius that transformed 'Annie Laurie' into the present well-known song.

One still night at about eleven o'clock Lady John was sitting in the Aurora Room when the unearthly noise was heard for the first time. A window suddenly burst open and a cannon-ball came bouncing into the room. In three leaps it bumped across the floor and came to rest at the foot of a draught-screen. Lady John rang the bell and her servants answered her summons but by the time they arrived the window was shut fast and there was no sign of any cannonball.

In 1879 a governess heard the same sounds and witnessed precisely the same sight when she was alone in the same room, which has no apartment above it. She would never sit alone in the Aurora drawing-room afterwards.

After that date the noise became almost commonplace and resident servants grew quite accustomed to the strange sounds that emanated from the empty room.

When Lady John Scott was at Caroline Park there was an old moss-covered well on the east side of the house and in the little square courtyard there used to be a wrought-iron bell pull.

At midnight on certain dates the green ghost of a former Lady Royston is said to emerge slowly from the well in emerald robes covered with mystic designs and float to the front door of the house. There she disappears, only to reappear in the little courtyard and ring the old bell.

Lady John's grand-niece, Margaret Warrender, always maintained that when she stayed at the old house she used to lie awake night after night and hear the tolling of the bell, when everyone else in the house was in bed and asleep and when there was no breath of wind. The Green Lady may still walk occasionally and the bell may still toll without being pulled by human hand.

HADDINGTON, EAST LOTHIAN

The parish church of St Mary, formerly a fourteenth-century abbey, stands on the riverbank. It is also known as Lucerna Laudoniae, the Lamp of Lothian, a title that originally belonged to the now-vanished church of Haddington's Franciscan monastery, sacked in 1355.

The hereditary burial chapel of the Maitlands, earls of Lauderdale, is behind the iron-studded door in the south wall and the coffins of these famous statesmen lie in the vault beneath.

There is John, the seventeenth-century Lord Maitland of Thirlestone, Lord High Chancellor of Scotland; his son John, the second Lord Maitland and first earl; James, the eighth earl.

Baronet of Nova Scotia and Standard Bearer of Scotland; a later John, Duke of Lauderdale, the most learned and powerful minister of his age, whose funeral cost £2,800 and was attended by over 2,000 horsemen. A large leaden urn, containing the brain and intestines of the Duke, was placed near the coffin.

This coffin was found in different positions whenever the vault was visited. This fact fed other stories suggesting that the duke did not rest and that his ghost was often abroad, until it was discovered that the flood-waters had probably moved the coffin. The figure of the grim-faced duke, still reported to be seen from time to time in the vicinity of the chapel, has never been explained.

HERMITAGE CASTLE, SEE NEW-CASTLETON, ROXBURGHSHIRE

INVERARAY, ARGYLLSHIRE

Passing through Inveraray a couple of years ago my wife and I called at Inveraray Castle, the home of the Dukes of Argyll, and the haunt of the strange little 'Harper of Inveraray'. Rob Roy MacGregor's dirk handle and sporran are among the relics displayed at Inveraray Castle; the ruins of Rob Roy's house are five miles away at the Falls of Aray.

The part of turreted Inveraray Castle in the area of the Green Library has long been said to be haunted by a loud crashing sound.

One Sunday evening, according to a former duke of Argyll, a tremendous commotion, like books being thrown violently to the floor, continued for over an hour. Nothing was found to account for the disturbance.

Usually only the family hear the sounds even when other people are present, although friends and visitors shared the experience on occasions.

Nothing is ever moved and nothing has ever been discovered that might account for the loud sounds that have been reported from time to time for nearly a hundred years. The sound of harp music used to be heard in the area of the Blue Room, although no harp was in the castle at the time.

The Harper is said to be the ghost of a man who was hanged at Inveraray when Montrose's men were hunting the first marquess of Argyll. In fact, Argyll lived to see Montrose hanged in the Grassmarket at Edinburgh.

Occasionally the Harper is also seen. It has been noticed that he always wears the Campbell tartan and never harms or frightens anyone; he has most frequently been seen by the successive duchesses of Argyll and only rarely by the dukes. A number of women visitors have seen and heard 'the Harper', noticeably at the time of a duke's death and during a ducal funeral.

IONA, ISLE OF; INNER HEBRIDES

This holy island with its mellow ruins and burial-ground containing the tombs of some sixty Scottish, Irish and Norwegian kings, and the ancient monastery founded by Saint Columba who came here in the year 563, has plenty of ghosts from the silent Viking longboats and the massacred monks on the White Sands to phantom bells, ghostly music and twinkling blue lights.

The strange and sometimes terrible enchantment and 'call' of this strange and irresistible island persists.

I have been receiving first-hand accounts of the ghosts of Iona for over twenty years, since I first heard about the strange happenings from my friend Tommy Frankland, a former Royal Air Force officer.

I recall that we discussed Iona and its mysteries for hours in such varied surroundings as a haunted church on the Essex marshes, Tommy's Cadogan Square flat and my home, at that time not far from the river at Richmond.

Many are the reports of ghostly monks seen here over the years, often at certain spots where the local people will not venture at night-time, such as the Angels' Hill, almost in the centre of the island, where many odd things have happened. Miss Lucy Bruce, who had a home on Iona, told me that she had seen ghostly monks on several occasions on the island, both indoors and outside.

She said that they were always Columban monks, with brown robes and a hempen rope about the waist; they never spoke or made any sound, appearing to be unconscious of the presence of human beings.

The ghost monks of Iona have only appeared since the time of the Reformation when great numbers of the sacred crosses marking the monks' graves were cast into the sea. Twinkling blue lights have often been reported when the ghostly monks have been seen.

Tommy told me about a sighting of the famous fleet of ghost Viking longboats at the well-known White Sands, a spot popular with artists. John MacMillan, at that time like Tommy, a member of the Iona Community (the brotherhood of ministers and laymen whose summer work consists of restoring the early Columban buildings on Iona) was walking one evening in midsummer along the road from the old abbey towards the north end of the island.

(He rarely went towards the south end which has an evil reputation locally: Lucy Bruce used to refer to crowds of elementals in the south of the island and John MacMillan always said that he could smell death there.)

As he walked John saw a croft, perhaps half a mile from the

abbey, and thought he would call on Mrs Ferguson, an elderly and blind lady whom he had come to know during his six years' association with the Iona Community. To his astonishment, he couldn't find her croft.

He realized with growing apprehension that he could not locate the croft of his friend John Campbell either. Surely it stood down there on that deserted grassy plain. He continued on his way towards the White Sands, becoming more and more puzzled at the apparent disappearance of familiar landmarks. Had he stepped back in time, before the crofts were there?

Suddenly as he approached the White Sands, sparkling in the bright moonlight, he saw a fleet of Viking longboats emerge from behind a islet off the north of Iona, Eilean Annraidh, and make for the north shore. He counted the ships, fourteen of them and he watched the oars swoop gracefully through the water.

He saw the Viking emblems on the great square sails and the fierce-looking men, who seemed to be shouting and gesticulating as they neared the shore where a group of monks stood apprehensively. John MacMillan heard no sound himself.

Aghast, he watched as the invaders flung themselves upon the defenceless monks, slaughtered them and then set off over the hill towards the abbey. Time had no reality for the spellbound watcher and he could never say whether a moment or an hour elapsed before he saw the Vikings reappear with the monks' cattle and precious possessions, while the sky behind them turned to a red glow as the abbey went up in flames.

Still John MacMillan watched as the cattle and valuables were loaded on to the longboats and, the silent invaders aboard, the ships pushed off into the dark sea and the White Sands were again deserted.

That evening John MacMillan sketched the coloured emblems

that he had seen decorating the mysterious longboats. Subsequent consultation with the appropriate authority at the British Museum dated the designs as belonging to the late tenth century.

As a matter of historical fact on Christmas Eve in the year 986 a party of marauding Danes did descend on the island at the place now known as the White Sands and there slew the abbot and fifteen of his brethren, afterwards plundering and setting fire to the abbey.

Among other witnesses who claim to have seen the ghostly Viking invasion at the White Sands there is the Edinburgh artist F. C. B. Cadell and a party of three visitors who watched what they thought must be a rehearsal for a pageant or a film.

Tommy Frankland had two experiences on Iona which he is totally unable to explain. One afternoon he encountered an invisible presence half-way up the original old wooden stairs in the abbey buildings; something that made it impossible to proceed, a force the like of which he had never met before—and hopes never to meet again.

Tommy is no lightweight but whatever it was on the stairway that bright and sunny afternoon, it stopped him in his tracks and he had no choice but to retreat and make his way out into the grounds. After a time he felt able to attempt the stairs again and this time no presence, visible or invisible, barred his way.

Another afternoon, in the company of two nuns, Tommy walked to Columba Bay where they found some of the lovely green Iona stones. On the way back to the Bishop's House they halted for a moment on a high headland that separates Larachan Bay from the Bay of Coracles. Looking back towards Larachan all of them saw three columns of smoke apparently emanating from a deserted spot some distance away.

The smoke rose straight upwards to a height of some twenty

feet. With typical curiosity Tommy made extensive investigations and enquiries but he was totally unable to find any explanation for the three distinct columns of smoke that day. One of the nuns said that it was the most extraordinary thing she had ever seen.

One other incident always puzzled Tommy. He was among a group of students, young and old, in the library at the Bishop's House one evening when he and others present noticed an elderly clergyman standing by the open window that looks out towards the Sound of Iona. The man stood absolutely still, his whole being focused on the quiet bay.

After a while he left the room and Tommy saw him walking quickly towards the ebbing sea. There, without a moment's hesitation, he walked straight into the water and he was waist-deep before Tommy reached the shore, shouting and calling to the man to come back.

After what seemed an eternity the man turned; at last he seemed to hear the calling and shouting and he slowly made his way back.

Afterwards he said that he had seen the abbey as it had been a thousand years ago and he had thought he would walk along the causeway. which has long since disappeared. Until he heard his name being called, he had no idea that he was in the water.

And what about the famous 'call' of Iona? The enchantment that can be fatal? Perhaps it is best described in the true story, told to me by Lucy Bruce, concerning a young Italian lady, Marie Emily Fornario, who came here because, far away in her Mediterranean home, she heard a 'call', the Call of the Island.

For a while she enjoyed the peace and tranquillity of this unforgettable place. She wrote poetry with a strange, mystical quality about it; she interested herself in the legends and folklore of the island.

This beautiful and gentle soul soon became absorbed by the eerie and mysterious places of Iona; especially a bleak and lonely spot which has no real track leading to it where, it is said, the spirits of the dead hold sway.

One day the lady said that she must leave the island at once. Her bags were packed and her belongings were taken down to the pier but it was a Sunday and there was no way of leaving the island until the following day. Marie returned to her room and some hours later opened her door to say that her departure was no longer necessary. Her things were brought back into the house and unpacked.

Next morning Marie had disappeared. She was found two days later, naked and quite dead. A silver chain she wore had turned black. There was a knife in one of her hands and her head rested on the other. She had died of exposure and exhaustion in the place where the spirits of the dead are said to roam: perhaps she had answered their call that moonlit night when she had walked out, unseen and unheard, to die on their ancient ground.

Haunting and haunted Iona has ghostly monks in procession and solitary; faery music; evil elementals; invisible presences; mysterious twinkling lights; ghostly music; phantom Viking longboats; and the uncanny 'call' that will not be denied.

JEDBURGH, ROXBURGHSHIRE

All traces of Jedburgh Castle have now disappeared and its site has been occupied by a succession of buildings (including the old prison) but none of them can boast an apparition as fearful as that which interrupted a ball many, many years ago.

Time was when Jedburgh enjoyed an important place in Scottish history and, after it was surrendered to England by the treaty of Falaise in 1174 as security for the ransom of William the Lion, was a favourite residence of royalty. Malcolm IV died here in 1165.

Alexander II and Alexander III were often here and it was during the second wedding feast of the childless Alexander III in October, 1285, that the grisly and singular spectre is said to have appeared—an occurrence that may have given Edgar Allan Poe the idea for his macabre story The Masque of the Red Death.

The wedding festivities were at their height when a strange figure was noticed by the startled guests, an awesome form that seemed to glide through the throng of guests, tall and gaunt and shrouded from head to foot in grave-clothes, while a mask resembling the face of a corpse concealed the identity of the wearer.

Soon the king noticed the weird figure that dampened the festive air. He gave orders for the person to be seized and unmasked and hanged at sunrise from the battlements for insulting him with such blasphemous mockery on his wedding day. At his words the group of pale courtiers made movements in the direction of the intruder but some nameless horror held them back.

None laid a hand on the mysterious figure; indeed, the entire assembly shrank back to the walls of the room and the grim figure made' its solemn way with unhurried steps in the direction of the king. At last his immediate guards flung themselves forward only to gasp in unutterable horror at finding the grave-clothes and corpse-like mask which they seized, 'untenanted by any tangible form'.

Nothing further is known of the strange spectre but it was, perhaps not unnaturally, regarded as portending some great calamity. The seer and prophet, Thomas the Rhymer, informed the Earl of March, in the presence of some of the earl's relations and household, that March 16th would be 'the stormiest day that ever was witnessed in Scotland'.

In fact the day dawned clear and bright and many scoffed at the prophecy, when news came that the king was dead. 'That was the storm I meant,' said the Rhymer, 'and there was never a tempest which will bring more ill luck to Scotland.' Indeed, the news caused distraction among the people and civil war between the claimants to the throne of Scotland.

Alexander III, riding between Burntisland and Kinghorn in failing light, was thrown from his horse over a cliff and killed in his forty-fifth year, a few months after his second marriage. Many people recalled the ominous presence at the king's wedding and felt that it had foretold his early death.

KILLIECRANKIE, PASS OF, PERTHSHIRE

The battle of Killiecrankie took place on July 27th. 1689, when William Ill's troops under General Mackay were routed by three thousand Highlanders under John Graham of Claverhouse, Viscount Dundee, for James II; 'Bonnie Dundee' himself fell mortally wounded almost at the moment of victory.

The battle itself was fought on the hillside above the main road a mile north of the pass through which King William's men advanced to engage the Jacobites and shortly afterwards returned in retreat as they fled from the torrent of barefooted red coats and tartans that swept down the valley.

Each July 27th, I have been told, a red glow hangs over the scene of the conflict; a phantom light that many people, but not everyone, can see in the valley through which the Highlanders charged. The mysterious glow is thought by local people to have its origin in a vision seen by Viscount Dundee on the eve of the battle.

As he slept, Dundee saw a man whose head poured with blood standing at his bedside, bidding him to get up and follow where he led. Dundee awoke but seeing no one, interpreted the vision as a dream and returned to sleep. But again he was awakened by the same voice and the same figure; this time the form pointed to its bloody head and seemed to implore Dundee to rise and follow. Now Dundee did get up and ascertained from the guard that no one had entered his tent.

Satisfied, he once more returned to his bed but for the third time the same form appeared to him, bidding him arise and pointing towards the plain of Killiecrankie, seeming to indicate that he would meet Dundee there.

When the figure had disappeared Dundee got up, dressed and discussed the strange vision with a Highland chief who agreed never to speak of the matter if the coming battle should prove successful for the Highlanders.

On the day of the battle Dundee was reluctant to descend from the high ground. Perhaps he had a premonition of his own death or maybe he wished to wait until darkness before coming to close quarters with the enemy so that his troops could find shelter in the mountains if they were defeated.

At all events, it was sunset before he gave the order to charge. Within minutes King William's forces were defeated and beginning to flee when, almost as if by accident, a fatal shot struck Dundee in the side.

KILMACOLM, RENFREWSHIRE

A ruined wall is all that now remains of haunted Duchal Castle in Strathgryfe. Once it stood, proud and invincible, at the junction of two burns, the Green Water and the Blacketty Water.

The ghost was an excommunicated monk who would be seen sitting on the castle outbuildings, jeering at inhabitants. The form, described as 'foul and gross', was seen, heard and even touched by scores of people in the thirteenth century.

Arrows that found their mark melted as they struck home and only the eldest son of the Knight of Duchal Castle, an exceptionally pure-hearted individual, was able to defy the troublesome ghost with any success.

One night he lay in wait for the foul fiend and wrestled with 'him' as soon as he appeared but the following morning the brave young knight's body was found in the wrecked hall. The ghost was never seen thereafter.

It was at Duchal Castle that a son of King James IV was born to Marian Boyd; a man who became Archbishop of St Andrews at eighteen, founded St Leonard's College there and died with his father at the Battle of Flodden.

KINROSS, KINROSS-SHIRE

The minister's house at this country town on the shore of Loch Leven (Mary Queen of Scots was imprisoned in the fifteenth-century castle) was infested by a typical poltergeist in the year 1718 when the parish minister, a Mr McGill, was plagued almost beyond endurance.

Initially some missing silver spoons were located in a barn, buried among straw, and although McGill readily admitted that this incident could have had a normal explanation, the disturbances quickly took a more serious turn.

(It is interesting to note that in poltergeist cases it is often the first incidents that are the easiest to explain.)

Before long McGill discovered that at every meal pins of various sizes were mixed in his food! Even boiled eggs bristled with them!

His wife decided to supervise the cooking of her husband's food herself but to her consternation she found a dish that she had most carefully prepared with her own hands—full of pins!

Soon there were other inconveniences and difficulties to contend with. Linen hung out to dry was found to be torn to shreds and before long clothes, even as they lay in cupboards where they were stored, were found rent and in some cases destroyed beyond repair.

Visitors complained that their clothes suddenly developed cuts and clips. Everyone noticed that this spiteful and annoying occurrence happened most frequently in the parlour of the house; either as they sat there or as they passed through the room.

Once the minister's Bible was thrown on to the fire but it was recovered unharmed. On the other hand when some silver spoons were inexplicably thrown into the fire, they melted instantly. As with most poltergeist cases, the affair ceased as inexplicably as it began.

KINTRAW, AT THE HEAD OF LOCH CRAIGNISH, ARGYLLSHIRE

In the valley of the River Barbreck in this delightful and thinly populated district of heathery rocks and low hills between Ardfern and Ford, a mysterious figure known as the 'hooded maiden' has long been reported by local people and, occasionally, by visitors.

The area where the figure has been seen lies within the Barbreck estate with its Georgian house and vast acreage of moor and river and loch fishing (Craignish is a sea-loch with wooded islets). Consequently it is fishermen, shepherds and ghillies who have seen 'her' most often.

The 'hooded maiden' invariably wears a plaid of dark but unidentified tartan. Her hair is long and seems to cling to her face, framing the pale, sad features of the young girl. Who she is or what she waits for, nobody knows. She is always seen seated on a rock and she always disappears as soon as she is approached.

KIRRIEMUIR, ANGUS

Cortachy Castle, seat of the earls of Airlie, is haunted by a drummer. The sound of his drumming has long been regarded as heralding the death of a member of the Ogilvy family.

The tradition is thought to have its origin in a drummer-boy who angered a former Lord Airlie. He was put to death by being thrust into his own drum and thrown from the window of the castle tower.

Here is the chamber where the ghostly music most often seems to originate. Before his death the drummer is said to have threatened to haunt the family if his life was taken.

He seems to have been as good as his word for the drum is reported to have been heard before the deaths of members of the family on a number of occasions over many years.

One account tells of a visitor to Cortachy Castle hearing, while she dressed for dinner on the evening of her arrival, a strain of music which seemed to originate below her window and which finally resolved into the well-defined sound of a drum.

She mentioned the matter at dinner and made enquiries about a drummer playing near the castle. She noticed that Lord Airlie turned pale at her words while Lady Airlie looked distressed and several of the other guests seemed embarrassed. She therefore changed the subject, but later that evening she asked a member of the family about the mysterious music and the effect it seemed to have on Lord and Lady Airlie.

She was then told about the legend of the drummer-boy who is reputed to play a drum about the house whenever a death is impending in the family; and that it had been heard before the death of the previous Countess.

The visitor was much concerned at having unintentionally caused distress to her hosts. When she again heard the ghostly drummer the next day, she made her apologies and left Cortachy, stopping on her way back to Dundee to call on some friends to whom she related her experiences.

Within a short time Lady Airlie with whom she had stayed was dead, leaving a note referring to the drummer having been heard by a guest and adding that she knew the drum had sounded for her.

Five years later a member of the Earl of Airlie's shooting party heard a swell of faint music accompanied by a distant drum; sounds which were totally inexplicable as far as he could establish. The following day the Earl of Airlie died.

Thirty years later Lady Dalkeith and Lady Skelmersdale heard drumming music which sounded like the traditional Airlie Drummer. The death of Lord Airlie took place the same night in America and it was established that the drumming sound was heard approximately an hour before his death.

After the death of the twelfth earl in 1968, his widow, whose son Mr Angus Ogilvy is married to the Princess Alexandra, informed me that she did not know of anyone who had heard the drum on that occasion.

LASSWADE, NEAR DALKEITH, MIDLOTHIANSHIRE

Romantically situated on the river bank Lasswade lies below you from whatever direction you approach. The old and now disused parish church overlooks the little town.

Here lie buried Henry Dundas, first Viscount Melville, whose lofty column graces St Andrew Square, Edinburgh: a man known as the uncrowned king of Scotland.

A much enlarged cottage, opposite the gates of Dunesk House, was the first married home of Sir Walter Scott. He lived very happily here for six years and it is not difficult to place some of the scenes from his famous books.

A mile away, De Quincey Cottage was the home of Thomas De Quincey for the last nineteen years of his life.

It is said that his ghost is often to be seen wandering about in the vicinity of his cottage and along the banks of the River Esk as far as Lasswade, usually in the small, dark hours, wildly flourishing a lantern he used to carry during his long and treasured night walks.

LENDALFOOT, AYRSHIRE

The tall fragments of a grey building perched high on a hill overlooking the cleft of Lendal Water is all that now remains of Carleton Castle.

The area is haunted from time to time by mysterious shrill cries and strangely fading screams. This is the castle, immortalized in a ballad, where a baron lived who disposed of seven wives by throwing them over the cliff; but his eighth, May Cullean, was more than a match for him and pushed him to his death.

LINLITHGOW, WEST LOTHIANSHIRE

The parish church of St Michael's was the scene of one of the best-authenticated instances of a purposeful apparition.

A ghostly old man, dressed in a long, blue gown, is said to have appeared here to King James IV of Scotland while the monarch was at evening worship, warning the king of his defeat and death at Flodden in 1513.

The bare-headed figure, carrying a pikestaff, told the king not to march into England and then disappeared. Those who were with the king at the time included David Lindsay, the Scottish poet, a man of complete integrity, who vouched for the story.

The odd figure appeared and disappeared in circumstances that cannot be explained in any rational way. The prophecy was fulfilled exactly for James was not to be dissuaded; the great army marched south and into the tragedy of Flodden Field.

There is a room in the fine loch-side fifteenth-century palace known as Queen Margaret's Bower where the queen waited in vain for the king's return from Flodden. Here, too, you can see the room where Mary Queen of Scots was born on December 7th, 1542.

LISMORE ISLAND, ARGYLLSHIRE

The picturesque ruins of Caifen Castle, on the west coast of the island, just across from Clachan, was named after a prince.

Caifen was the son of a Norse king and he lived at the castle with his beautiful sister Beothail. who was as gentle as her brother was warlike.

While he never seemed to allow his galleys to rest and was known as a hard master but a fair one, Beothail became betrothed to a son of Lochlann. When her beloved was killed in battle, the fair princess died of a broken heart and she was buried at nearby Eirebal.

But death did not bring her peace and her voice was often to be heard crying in the wind. She wanted to be buried in Norway beside her lover.

At length a ship came to Caifen Castle, Beothail's body was disinterred, washed in the holy well, taken on the long voyage to Lochlann and there the bodies of the lovers were laid beside one another.

Still Beothail did not rest and her form was seen pointing to a missing bone in her left foot. Again the ship went to Caifen and in the holy well where the body had been washed, poor Beothail's small toe bone was found and was at length buried in the lovers' grave in far away Norway. Thereafter there was peace for Beothail.

In Lismore there is still a well known as the Well of the Bones of Beothail.

LITTLE LOCH BROOM, ROSS AND CROMARTY

On the wild, northern shore, not far from the mouth of the loch, a solitary cottage once sheltered George, first earl of Cromartie, when he was Sir George Mackenzie. The croft was the scene of a prophetic vision.

Sir George, a loyal Royalist, was engaged in raising troops for the king shortly before the Restoration of the Monarchy and, with some friends, chanced to find themselves stormbound on the north shore of Little Loch Broom.

They sought shelter in a lonely loch-side cottage and after a while spent in chatting among themselves and the residents, Sir George's servant, an old Highlander, went out to attend to the horses.

On his return, he hurried to his master's side as soon as he entered the room and urged him to rise from the chair he was occupying, saying that he could see a dead man seated on the vacant chair beside him. Everyone present rose to their feet at the words but they only saw the empty chair.

The vision of a dead man was visible only to the old Highlander who described the figure as a pitiful sight, his head bound with a blood-stained bandage, his ashen face streaked with dried blood and one of his arms hanging broken at his side.

Next day a party of horsemen passed along the steep side of a hill in the neighbourhood when one of the horses stumbled and threw its rider. The man, grievously injured by the fall, was carried unconscious to the cottage.

On being brought into the primitive dwelling in a death like condition, he was placed in the identical chair which the Highlander had seen occupied by a dead man in his vision.

The man's head was found to be deeply gashed and one of his arms was broken but he did eventually recover. Contemporary evidence includes a letter from Sir George Mackenzie relating the story to the celebrated Robert Boyle.

LOCKERBIE, DUMFRIESSHIRE

Five miles north, west of the Glasgow road, beside a loop in the River Annan stands Jardine Hall, seat of the Jardine family. Opposite stands Spedlin's Tower, haunted for centuries by an unpleasant ghost that terrified the countryfolk hereabouts.

Many years ago the laird of Applegarth was Sir Alexander Jardine, the first baronet, who had occasion to punish a miller named Porteous. He confined him in the dungeon of the Tower, after the miller had, for some unknown reason, set his cottage alight.

One day Sir Alexander had to go to Edinburgh on urgent business and in his haste he took with him the key of the dungeon. As soon as he discovered what he had done, he sent the key back post-haste but it was too late; the unlucky miller had died of starvation.

Indeed, it is said that the dying man was so ravaged by hunger that he had gnawed at his own hands and feet in the last throes of torment.

Soon after the miller's death Sir Alexander's household was plagued by his ghost. A loud battering noise would be heard at the door to the dungeon, late at night, and a hollow voice would call piteously: 'Let me out... let me out... I'm dying of hunger...'

When mischievous children of the household inserted a stick through the keyhole, it is said that the hungry ghost stripped the bark in an instant.

It was discovered that if an ancient 'black letter' Bible was left in a niche by the dungeon doorway, all was quiet; but when it was removed for re-binding, the ghost, it seems, returned. By this time the Jardine family had moved to the new residence on the other side of the River Annan.

The ghost is reported to have followed them, entering the baronet's bedroom and creating such a noise and disturbance that no time was lost in restoring the Bible to its place. As soon as this was done, peace was restored.

MAXTON, ROXBURGHSHIRE

Near here, on the banks of the River Tweed, stand the ruins of Littledean Tower, the scene of strange happenings long ago that are echoed here on certain stormy nights.

One of the last lairds of a once proud and powerful family was a dark and handsome but wicked man whose gentle wife Margaret sought solace in quiet prayer. Her cruel husband was hated by his servants, suffered by his friends and feared by the young maids of the locality.

As time passed and stories of his cruelty grew and spread, especially after he had caused the death of a stable boy in a fit of anger, his former associates kept away and his wild parties began to be peopled with the lowest and worst characters in the area. Margaret, much distressed, began to leave him to his own devices and her absence was often the cause of ribald jokes.

One evening a certain 'gentleman' who was commonly believed to be the black sheep of a famous family, a man who had an eye for the ladies, taunted the laird about his wife's absence at the 'dinner party' whereupon the host, more drunk than sober, fetched his frightened wife and commanded her to greet his motley collection of friends.

Terrified but proud, Margaret refused and the guests, mustering together such dignity as they could, left embarrassed as the laird swore and screamed at his wife. He raved and cursed at her after they had left, calling her everything from unfaithful to useless. 'I'd rather be wedded to a fiend from Hell than to you,' he screamed, 'She'd have more warmth about her, at any rate...'

This was too much for the gentle Margaret. She raised herself from the floor where she had slumped in despair and looked her husband straight in the eyes. 'You will live to regret those words', she said and walked to her room with dignity, leaving him to fume and curse to himself.

The laird called for more brandy but his wife's words and her sober looks troubled him. Before long he called for a horse and, drunk as he was, he rode off into the night not caring which direction he took. Soon it began to rain in torrents and looking for some shelter he turned into a small wood where he found himself in a clearing, with a wretched and crumbling cottage at the far end.

As he approached, figures seemed to recede into the shadows leaving one woman sitting on a stool, spinning, just inside the cottage. When the woman turned towards him the laird thought that never had he seen such a lovely face. He struggled to speak as the beautiful woman smiled at him in the shadows.

Then, lifting the thread that she was spinning, the woman held it high towards him and snapped it in two, laughing in his face. For the first time the laird noticed the restive snorting and stamping of his horse; at the same time he felt some strange force beginning to hold him captive in the glade. With an effort he tore himself away, mounted his horse and rode out of the wood.

In the days that followed he could not forget the beautiful woman he had seen and in a sort of sickness he searched again and again for the wood into which he had strayed that stormy night.

Then one evening, after spending hours in fruitless search for the mysterious place, he was almost home when he noticed a movement beside a cluster of trees by the river bank, only a few hundred yards from Littledean Tower. He looked again; it was the same woman. Quickly he dismounted, went into her open arms and together they walked into the silent trees.

Thereafter he would meet the mysterious woman almost daily for she was ready and eager to satisfy his every desire, almost under the windows of the Tower, although she would never agree to meet him elsewhere.

Soon the inevitable happened. The pair were seen and seen again. The scandal spread and the story reached Margaret's ears. She faced her husband and threw the rings he had given her at his feet. She had decided to leave him but two of her friends from the old days counselled her to wait until they had trapped the woman to discover who she was.

One evening, having seen her enter the little knot of trees, they circled the plantation and then met in the middle—but the only living thing that came out of the trees was a hare that scampered away across the fields.

Hours passed and the laird returned home, later than he had ever been before. He looked shaken to the core, frightened out of his wits. He bade the servants withdraw in a hushed voice and whispered to Margaret: 'Devils, Devils, Devils everywhere...' His wife shrank away from him and after she had led him silently into the great hall, he told her his story.

He said that he had been riding home in the twilight when he had passed a hare which, to his surprise, followed him. Presently another joined it and then another and another, until a whole flock surrounded him as he rode on, his horse sweating with fear. After a time he tried to trample on them but he never succeeded in touching one.

He found that however fast he travelled, the hares kept pace with him and soon some began to leap across his saddle bow. Drawing his sword he slashed at them but they were hard to hit.

At length he did strike one, more daring than the rest and severed its paw which fell into his empty pistol holder. At this the whole pack suddenly made off and looking about him, he discovered that he was in the vicinity of Midlem, reputed home of many witches and miles from Littledean Tower.

As he concluded his story, Margaret asked to see the hare's paw and a moment later her husband withdrew his hand sharply from the gun holster where the paw had fallen, exclaiming that it had bitten him! When tipped from the holder it was found to be a woman's hand, wearing a ring that Margaret recognized.

The laird drew his sword and speared the hand that seemed to squirm as he pierced it, then he sped with it to the nearby river where he scrambled down the bank and swung the hand off his sword with all his strength far out into the deep water, hearing it splash in the darkness.

Hurrying back up the steep bank of the river side, he was making his way home in the darkness when he realized that he was close to the little cluster of trees where he used to meet the mysterious woman. Something led him in among the trees and he saw the woman, huddled on the ground with her back towards him.

As he approached she turned to face him and to his horror he saw that she was no longer young and beautiful; instead, he found himself looking into the face of a hag: bitter, ugly and ghastly in the moonlight.

Her eyes glowed with hatred and she held up her right arm to show him a raw and bleeding stump. He sensed rather than heard her tell him that he had taken her hand and he would never be parted from it.

Somehow he stumbled back to Littledean Tower, a silent, broken man. He slowly made his way to his bed-chamber and, refusing food or drink, sat slumped in front of the fire, puzzling over the events that had befallen him.

After an hour or so he chanced to notice a lump in the pocket of the riding jacket that he still wore and thrusting his hand inside drew out the hand that he had thrown far out into the river! Rushing to the window, he tore it open and threw it out into the darkness.

Dreading the dreams that would mar his sleep, he put off going to bed until dawn streaked the sky. When he eventually stretched out on the bedstead, he reached beneath the pillow —and encountered the hand again! He snatched up the awful thing and threw it into the fire, watching as it crackled and burnt to a cinder.

Next morning the laird did not appear for breakfast and when eventually Margaret had servants break down the door of his chamber, they found the bedclothes dragged off the bed in the direction of the hearth and in front of the cold fire lay his dead body with marks on his throat that suggested that a hand had choked the life out of him.

On stormy nights the ghostly figure of the laird is still to be seen sometimes, mounted on a phantom horse, plunging madly through the wind and rain.

MELROSE, ROXBURGHSHIRE

Nearby Abbotsford House is the large and turreted mansion built by Sir Walter Scott between 1817 and 1825. If concentrated thought and excessive single-mindedness coupled with love and death, can bring about ghosts and hauntings then Abbotsford should be haunted.

The silent figure that has been seen on rare occasions in the dining-room (where Scott died) may be the ghost of the great novelist who built his life's dream in the baronial style—and out of his hard-earned savings.

A year after the house was completed, financial ruin overtook poor Scott and although the house and estate were restored to him by his creditors in 1830, he died on September 21st, 1830, on a bed placed near the window in the dining-room, where he could view the fast-flowing River Tweed.

The property was formerly a small farm which Scott bought in 1811 and it was during the alterations, in 1818, that Sir Walter reported a 'violent noise, like drawing heavy boards along the new part of the house.' Next night he heard the noise again, at the same time, two o'clock in the morning.

He quietly reached for 'Beardie's broadsword' and thoroughly investigated the rooms and half-built passages where the noise seemed to originate; but he could discover nothing that might account for the sounds.

It is interesting to record that George Bullock, Scott's agent who was responsible for the early alterations at Abbotsford, died suddenly when the mysterious disturbances were at their height.

Today the house is owned by Mrs J. Maxwell-Scott, a descendant in the female line, and parts of the large and picturesque house, including the haunted dining-room, are open to the public. In addition to many fascinating mementoes of the famous novelist, historian and poet, there is a fine collection of Scottish historical relics.

MONTROSE, ANGUS

The old aerodrome here has long been reputed to be haunted by two ghosts, one a pilot from an aircraft that crashed in 1913 and the other a wartime officer of the Second World War who was also killed in a crash here.

A fighter pilot whose squadron was sent to Montrose during the winter of 1940 to rest after the Battle of Britain, related his experiences which are said to have their origin in the earlier crash which took place at the perimeter of the airfield, the plane bursting into flames and leaving practically no wreckage or remains, except for the ghost of the pilot, a figure in flying kit that disappears near the Old Mess.

Men of the squadron stationed here in 1940 said that they saw the ghost and the figure was seen five times by Major Cyril Foggin in August 1916 and by the Commanding Officer and several instructors during the autumn of that year. Once he seems to have flown his ghostly biplane to the danger of a Hurricane, witnessed by scores of airmen.

It happened that one night the squadron were summoned from their beds by the warning that a marauding Heinkel was somewhere over the aerodrome. A Hurricane taxied out in an attempt to intercept it. Half-an-hour later the pilot reported 'No joy' and was instructed to return to base. No chances were taken by lighting up the airfield in case another enemy aircraft was somewhere aloft and only a twin row of glim-lights were laid along the grass to guide the Hurricane in.

The pilot was experienced, a regular service sergeant-pilot; hard-headed, unimaginative and very reliable, who should have had no difficulty in landing in these conditions. Scores of the airmen watched the glow of the Hurricane's exhaust as the plane crossed the boundary.

The pilot touched down—and then, with a roar, he opened up the engine and disappeared again into the night. The ground crew decided he must have thought that he was not aligned correctly with the flarepath and, sure enough, he approached again, this time with his navigation lights on; but again, just as he was about to land, he opened his throttle wide and roared away, climbing over the sea.

The ground crew decided that they must take a risk and put on the Chance light, a type of horizontal searchlight, bathing the whole path of the landing-ground in a wide ray of yellow-white light.

This time the Hurricane made a perfect landing, taxied in and shut off the engine as ground-crew and airmen gathered round. The hood slid back and the pilot tore off his helmet in annoyance and shouted: 'The fool! Who was the fool who cut me out?' Someone said that no one had cut him out. 'Of course someone did,' replied the angry pilot. 'Why do you think I went round again?

Some madman in a biplane baulked me just as I was touching down—a thing like a Tiger Moth.' 'There's no one else flying' replied the flight commander quietly. 'Besides, there isn't a biplane on the station.' Only the wind blew in the darkness of the night and in silence pilot and airmen returned to the crew-room. The only explanation seemed to be that the phantom airman was keeping his hand in.

One morning in the summer of 1942 an unpopular flight-lieutenant took off from this airfield and crashed within seconds, being killed instantly. He had earned for himself a reputation as a stickler for discipline and was disliked by the ground staff because he seemed to find fault whenever he could.

About a week before the fatal flight he had been involved in a scene with a fitter working on the aircraft he was about to fly, shouting at the man for some trivial offence and putting him on a charge. The man, not surprisingly perhaps, felt that he had been unfairly treated. He nursed a grudge against the flight-lieutenant and he serviced the plane a week later when the officer took off and was killed.

A routine inquiry failed to reveal the cause of the crash and the unofficial view held on the airfield was that the fitter had 'doctored' the plane; but this was never proved although the fitter certainly had both opportunity and motive.

Everybody thought that the affair had ended, until some airmen reported seeing a ghost. Other reports followed and the mysterious figure, dressed in a flying suit and goggles, was glimpsed by many servicemen.

Soon the ghost airman became accepted and almost part of normal life at the station. The flight-lieutenant had come back, it was thought, to haunt the fitter who had caused his death; and new arrivals at the station were warned to watch out for the ghost airman at night-time.

Four years later, in 1946, an experienced serviceman who had seen action in France, Belgium, Holland, Germany, Denmark and Japan arrived at Montrose. He was told about the ghost and laughed at the story for he had heard many weird and wonderful war stories and had learned to take them with a pinch of salt. Then he was put on guard duty.

Guard duty at Montrose in those days meant armed patrol in twos, taking in the airfield, aircraft and the hangars. The way to the hangars lay by a morgue, which everyone gave a wide berth. But on this particular night an aircraft had just landed and had been parked close to the control tower and opposite the morgue; the new arrival was detailed to keep a special eye on it.

At three in the morning he and his companion were standing on guard close to the aircraft. A quiet smoke seemed to be in order and it was arranged that they would each nip round the corner to smoke a cigarette.

The new arrival's mate went first and as the new man stood there alone, the doors of the morgue (which had been checked and found secure only moments before) suddenly flew open and a figure emerged, an airman with a dead-white face wearing goggles, helmet and a flying suit.

The new guard's rifle clattered to the ground and he stared at the figure, frozen to the spot. Then, as suddenly as it had appeared, the figure vanished; with a loud bang the doors slammed shut and everything was quiet again.

Soon the mate returned from his smoke but the experienced and tough war veteran never related what he had seen to any of the airmen at the station. He was wondering, for one thing, whether the whole business hadn't been a hoax.

Only years later, talking to another man who had been stationed at Montrose, did he learn that the ghostly flight lieutenant had years before emerged from a building later converted into the morgue, to walk to the plane for his last flight. Sir Peter Masefield saw the 1913 accident re-enacted in May 1963, fifty years to the day after it happened.

MORAR, INVERNESS-SHIRE

A correspondent told me an experience that befell her at a small local hotel, overlooking the beautiful white sands at the mouth of the river near the extraordinarily deep Loch Morar.

This loch, only thirty feet above sea level, has a depth of a hundred-and-eighty fathoms and it is said to be the deepest hollow on any part of the European plateau except for the submarine valley that skirts the south part of Scandinavia.

My informant told me that during the early part of the Second World War she and a girl friend shared a room here for one night. As they moved around, preparing to retire by the light of two candles for there was no electricity, they became increasingly aware of sounds suggesting the presence of someone else in the room with them.

It seemed to be someone tramping about in heavy boots, moving objects and creaking the floorboards. The girls said nothing to each other and finally they went to bed, both feeling very nervous. Lying still, they listened intently.

Now that they were making no noise at all themselves, the third presence in the room was quite clear and definite. My informant tells me that she was petrified with fright, unable to stir although longing to reach out and relight the candle. Her companion started to scream and clung to her friend. The noise set off a dog barking wildly, that was tied up outside somewhere, but no one attended to it nor came to see what was the matter with the screaming girl.

Throughout the night they saw nothing, either by candlelight or in the darkness, but for hours they heard heavy footsteps circling around the room, and round their bed, pausing occasionally to touch things.

In the morning they rose early and left the hotel without saying anything about their experience; but they gained the impression that the residents who must have heard some of the commotion, probably knew the reason and were not surprised—nor inclined to be disturbed or discuss the matter.

The bedroom was at the back of the hotel, where a grassy slope rose steeply behind the building.

MOTHERWELL, LANARKSHIRE

Here, deep in the coal mining area of Scotland, there is, appropriately enough, a ghost that wears dungarees and boots. It was reported in November, 1968, from the Ravenscraig Steel Works, and workmen stated that the apparition, which sometimes seemed to resemble a complete workman and at other times appeared to be headless, was always seen in the vicinity of Number 2 blast-furnace.

MULL, ISLE OF, ARGYLLSHIRE

Lochbuie, in the south-east of the largest island of the Inner Hebrides, is associated with one of the best-known family ghosts in Scotland. The desolate road through the great glen here, travelled from time immemorial by pilgrims to Iona, is haunted by a headless horseman whose appearance heralds a death in the Ewen family.

Due north of Lochbuie stretches a chain of tarns and on the farthest north of these, Loch Sguabain, stands a ruined castle built so long ago that nobody can say with certainty just when it was erected. But here before the middle of the sixteenth century lived Eoghan a' Chin Bhig, Ewen of the Little Head and his wife, the proud daughter of a laird.

Some say her father was MacDougal of Lorne, others claim he was chief of the MacLaines; at all events she was forever grumbling about her circumstances since marrying Ewen and goading her husband to wrest the estate from her father. One day there was a stormy confrontation between Ewen and his father-in-law and soon afterwards Ewen began to collect followers for a showdown with the laird.

The evening before the conflict in 1538 Ewen is said to have seen a little woman by a stream. She was dressed in green and was busy rubbing away at a bundle of blood-stained shirts. Ewen realized that she was a fairy-figure and asked her whose shirts she was washing.

'The shirts of those who will fall in the fight' came the reply and when Ewen asked whether his shirt was among them, he was told that it was, 'but', added the fairy woman, 'if your wife offers you bread and cheese with her own hand, without your asking for it, on the morning of the conflict, you will win the fight.'

On the morning that the armies were to meet Ewen's wife was in a bad temper; she offered her husband neither bread nor cheese and he dared not ask for it. He and his men fought bravely and desperately but they were no match for their adversaries and at last Ewen met his end. His head was cut clean from his body and his black horse galloped away with its headless rider on its back.

And always now, before a Ewen dies, a ghostly headless horseman is said to ride, sometimes seen and sometimes only heard, down Glen More, on the shores of Loch Sguabain near the ruined castle or at Lochbuie where the phantom is regarded as an ill omen fortelling sickness to one of the Ewen family.

Certainly the headless horseman was seen and heard before the death of three Ewens within living memory. Although the galloping feet of the ghostly black horse seem to thunder over the ground, no hoof-prints are ever found to mark the soft earth.

One old member of the family used to complain before he died that he constantly heard a horse galloping close at hand and after his death unexplained noises and movements of furniture took place in the room where his body lay while servants and others passing the door told of weird screechings and the presence of ghostly hands which were attributed to Ewen of the Little Head.

Lochbuie House used to be haunted by a phantom black dog which Dr Duncan MacDonald encountered on a visit to the house. Another medico, Dr Reginald MacDonald, also met the Black Dog of Lochbuie; while a guest at Lochbuie House once recorded briefly the presence of a ghost dog that was seen and heard, 'so horrible' that the visitor felt unable even to write about the experience.

NANNAU, MERIONETHSHIRE

The old residence of the Vaughan family, said to stand upon the highest ground of any country seat in the land, is haunted to this day by the victim of a murder long, long ago.

In those days the occupant was one Howel Sele, a first cousin of the Welsh prince, Owen Glendower; but the cousins had never been good friends. Their antagonism came to a climax, according to legend, when they were out together hunting, while guests of the Abbot of Kymmer who was striving to reconcile the two kinsmen.

As they rested on their way Owen noticed a doe feeding down below them and remarked that here was a fine mark for Howel who was regarded as one of the best archers of the day. Without a word Howel took aim on the doe and then suddenly turned and shot the arrow straight at Glendower!

The prince, however, wore armour beneath his clothes and the arrow glanced harmlessly off him. Enraged at his kinsman's treachery, he drew his sword and after a short and sharp exchange, killed Howel.

Once the deed was done there was no undoing it, but where to hide the body? Medog, Glendower's companion, who had been following at a distance, now reached the scene of the fight and suggested that a nearby blasted oak tree would conveniently contain Howel's body in its hollow interior.

In the days that followed Howel's servants searched for him high and low while his sorrowing wife shut herself up in solitude in the gloomy castle.

The years passed with no news of the missing Lord of Nannau, although from time to time there were terrifying accounts of the ghostly form of the chief being seen in the vicinity of his ancestral home.

Some witnesses maintained that he stalked the upper stories of the castle on dark nights, others that he haunted the grounds of the ancient house he loved, others again that they saw him on a nearby mountain, and still others on a neighbouring shore.

There were persistent stories of hollow groans and strange, incoherent mutterings heard in the locality of the blasted oak. His old nurse in particular, used to say that she often saw his form flitting about the garden on moonlit nights and that she heard his unmistakable footsteps about the house.

After some ten years Glendower died and on his deathbed besought Madog to reveal his secret to Howel's widow and give the remains a Christian burial. Madog carried out his friend's washes, revealing to the horrified and still hoping wife that she was indeed a widow. Then he led Howel's retainers to the hollow oak which was rent open to reveal the bleaching skeleton.

The remains were borne home and duly buried but still the ghost of the vanquished Lord of Nannau was seen from time to time, while the blasted oak, until its fall and destruction on July 13, 1813, was referred to as 'the hollow oak of the demons'; a tree haunted by a gruesome secret for over ten years.

NEWCASTLETON, ROXBURGHSHIRE

In this wild and beautiful border country known as Liddesdale, a valley traversed by Liddel Water, stands, on bleak moorland the remains of squat, massive and haunted Hermitage Castle.

The oldest part was built early in the thirteenth century by Nicholas de Soulis probably for the purpose of repelling the frequent assaults of the English. In the reign of Robert Bruce (1274-1329) the castle was held by William de Soulis, known as the Bad Lord Soulis and he is said to haunt the place to this day.

Soulis the Bad was reputed to have studied sorcery under the celebrated wizard Michael Scot (c.1175-1234) in the mysterious Eildon Hills.

On his return to Hermitage Castle he practised Black Magic and was credited with many evil and blood-thirsty crimes, including the murder of the Cout of Keilder (Keeldar Mangerton), so-called because of his enormous size and strength.

It would seem that one day the Cout was invited to visit the notorious Lord Soulis. In spite of warning from his wife and a well-known local seer, the 'Brown Man of the Moors', he accepted the invitation to Hermitage relying on his strength and charmed weapons for protection.

After feasting and making merry the treacherous Lord Soulis gave a secret signal to his men who had been seated between each of the visitors. In a moment all of the guests had been stabbed and were either dead or dying, but the Cout of Keilder, ever mindful of the unreliable Soulis, saw the signal, sprang on to the table and escaped in the tumult, reaching the door of the dining chamber by running along the laden tables.

He fought his way from the room and out of the castle, pursued by the retainers of Soulis; but in attempting to leap to safety over the river, he fell into the deep waters and was held under by the spears of his adversaries until he drowned. To this day the place is known as Cout's Pool.

Near to the castle keep, in the ancient burial ground, the gigantic grave of the Cout is still pointed out to visitors, indicated by two stones set far apart, one said to mark his head and the other his feet.

But the death of the Cout brought about the end of the Bad Lord Soulis for so terror-stricken were the local inhabitants after the treacherous murder of Cout's men that they petitioned the king for permission to destroy him.

King Robert I of Scotland, irritated by constant complaints about Soulis is said to have replied: 'Hang him, boil him, do anything you like to him but for Heaven's sake let me hear no more about him.'

More than satisfied with such an answer, the petitioners returned to Liddesdale and lost no time in taking Soulis by surprise. They dragged him, none too gently, to the ancient circle of stones known as Nine Stone Rig (of which remnants still remain) and there they thrust him head foremost into a cauldron of molten lead.

Robert the Bruce quickly repented of having spoken hastily. Fearful, lest the headstrong men of Liddesdale should take his words literally and actually boil Soulis, he despatched messengers to prevent such a frightful act taking place. But they were too late—awful retribution had already overtaken Soulis the Bad.

So runs the legend although it is by no means certain that Soulis met such a horrible end. According to historical records, he was arrested for conspiring against Robert the Bruce in an attempt to get the crown for himself on the grounds that he was descended from an illegitimate daughter of Alexander II, and ended his life imprisoned in Dumbarton Castle.

Yet the more dramatic version has been accepted for hundreds of years. Whatever his end may have been, it is believed to this day that Soulis haunts Hermitage Castle because of the wicked deeds he perpetrated there and that he is destined to do so until Doomsday.

There used to be stories of a room in the castle that was sealed where, on certain nights of the year, his ghost returned and frolicked with other evil spirits. Local inhabitants and visitors who have chanced to be within the castle precincts, or even passing near the building on these unspecified nights, testified that they heard unearthly screams and diabolical laughter.

Another ghost of Hermitage Castle is that of the gallant Alexander Ramsey, Sheriff of Tevitdale, who was decoyed to Hermitage Castle by his one-time companion-in-arms, Sir William Douglas, Lord of Hermitage and natural son of the king from whom he had received the castle in 1358. There the noble sheriff was set upon, thrown into a dungeon and left to die of starvation.

Poor Ramsey is thought to have prolonged his misery by eating grains of corn that fell from the granary situated above his dungeon for during the early days of the last century a mason broke down part of the wall of the old granary for the purpose of using the stone and found, when he explored the dungeon he had unearthed, a quantity of chaff, some human bones and a rusty sword.

Even today it is possible to meet local people who maintain that they have heard heartrending cries, groans and anguished whispering, when they visit the gaunt but proud structure at night-time.

Sir William Douglas forfeited the castle in 1491 when he was caught in treachery and it was subsequently bestowed upon the Earl of Bothwell. When the Bothwells were in turn disgraced, King James VI gave the property to the Buccleuch family who retained it until it passed to the nation.

Other reported ghosts at Hermitage Castle where, over the years, a great number of men and women have met cruel and violent deaths, include a regal figure in white who may be Mary Queen of Scots. She was here when James, Earl of Bothwell, owned the castle and lay seriously wounded and thought to be dying.

There are rumours, too, of unidentified and terrifying ghosts in blood-stained armour glimpsed for a moment or two only, within the castle precincts both on dark and stormy nights and during the hours of daylight whenever there is lightning and the clash of thunder in the area.

Vague and unsubstantiated reports of headless apparitions

have also been associated with this picturesque but grim castle in Liddesdale.

NIGG, NEAR FEARN, ROSS AND CROMARTY

An old cottage with a curious ghost story used to stand on a ridge known locally as the Hill of Nigg. Remnants of the cottage, which almost overhung the sea, could still be traced a few years ago.

There were once two young girls who grew up together and were much attached to each other. One day they visited the home of a relative who had recently died. They were shocked and distressed at the light heartedness and indifference shown by some women employed in dressing the body. The two friends agreed that, should one outlive the other, the survivor, and no one else, would lay out the corpse of her friend.

Some years later one of the girls was the mistress of a solitary farmhouse on the Hill of Nigg. One day she was informed, by chance, that her old companion who had also married a farmer and lived in the neighbourhood of nearby Fearn, had died in childbirth the previous night.

Recalling her promise, she spent an anxious day worrying about the matter for she was unable to fulfil her pledge. She now had an infant who needed attention and no one with whom she could leave the small child; her maid had gone out only shortly before she heard the sad news, having gone to a neighbouring fair; her husband and his ploughman had also gone there.

She resigned herself to the fact that she could not keep the pact that had been made but told herself that her friend had probably forgotten all about the childhood promise long ago.

Evening drew on and her thoughts turned again and again

to her friend and the unfulfilled promise. She went out and stood on a little hillock beside the cottage, giving her a view over the moor her husband and servants would cross on their way home. After a while she saw a female figure approaching through the deepening twilight and. supposing that it was her maid and unwilling to appear anxious for her return, she went back into the house.

As she entered she noticed that some nearby farm animals were restive, as though some stranger were about. But she continued on her way and entered the cottage where she was astonished to find the figure that she had spotted out on the moor! Now, close at hand, she saw that the tall figure was wrapped from head to foot in a winding sheet.

It stood, silent and unmoving as she halted, stunned with surprise, in the doorway. Slowly the figure crossed in front of the fireplace towards a chair where it seated itself, raised its chalk-white arms and uncovered its face, disclosing the features of the deceased girlhood friend.

To add to the horror there was an expression of anger on the features, lit up by the flames of the fire. As the dead and glassy eyes turned to her old friend, the housewife instinctively snatched up her child from the cot in the corner of the room and gazed, fascinated, at the apparition.

She said afterwards that she could distinguish every fold of the winding-sheet; she described the dead, black hair drooped carelessly over the forehead; the livid and unbreathing lips drawn apart, as if no friendly hand had closed them after the last agony; and the reflection of the flames seemed to rise and fall within the eyes, varying by its ceaseless flicker the statue-like rigidity of the features.

As the fire burned slowly down, the woman threw some sticks on to keep the flames burning, without taking her eyes from the frightening spectre in front of her. She had almost exhausted the firewood and was dreading the thought of being left in the darkness with the silent form of her old friend, when she heard voices approaching the cottage.

At the same time the apparition rose from the chair and glided towards the door where the farm animals again set up a commotion as she passed. This time a cow kicked out at it with one of its back legs and, uttering a faint shriek, the phantom disappeared.

The farmer entered the cottage in time to see his wife fall to the floor in a swoon. Having recovered, next day she set out to pay her last respects to her old friend and on examining the body, she discovered on it the unmistakable mark of a cow's foot.

OBAN, ARGYLLSHIRE

A couple of miles to the north, on the banks of Loch Etive, and commanding the entry to the loch, stands the ruined castle of Dunstaffnage. According to tradition it was once the royal seat of the Dalriadan kings, built by Evanus at the time of Julius Caesar.

For long it housed the famous Stone of Scone, thought by some to have been the stone that was the pillow of Jacob when he dreamed of a ladder to Heaven, the coronation stone of Scottish and English kings from time immemorial. The stone was moved to Scone near Perth and then to Westminster Abbey, by King Edward I, in 1296.

Dunstaffnage Castle, captured by Robert the Bruce in 1368, became the stronghold of the Campbells and the MacDougals;

then an English military station during the risings of 1715 and 1745, while Flora Macdonald, the Jacobite rescuer of Bonnie Prince Charlie, was imprisoned here for ten days in 1746. One of the old guns among the ruins was raised from a Spanish galleon in Tobermory Bay.

With such a history and background small wonder that the ruins are haunted. When the Campbells lived at the castle a notorious phantom, 'the Green Lady' haunted the place. She was known as the Scannag or Elle maid.

The reason for her haunting is now forgotten, but the figure invariably exhibited sorrow before the death of a member of the family and joy before an event which brought happiness to the family. In addition, the appearance was sometimes accompanied with poltergeist-like activities.

There are many accounts of 'something' teasing children of the Campbell family when they were in bed, especially the younger folk, of loud stamping and banging on the flooring which seemed to shake the rooms and disturbed many a night's rest.

PENCAITLAND, EAST LOTHIANSHIRE

Haunted and romantic Pencaet Castle has several ghosts including one known to the family as 'gentleman John' who is believed to be a former occupant; a royal ghost in the 'shape' of King Charles I who may have visited and whose bed is certainly here; and more than one unidentified figure.

The late Professor Holbourn acquired the property now known as Pencaet Castle or Fountainhall House in 1923. His widow Mrs Marion Holbourn has been good enough to pass on to me many details of the apparently paranormal manifestations that have taken place at the picturesque rubble-built structure boasting a forestair leading from the courtyard and a circular tower. The early sixteenth-century structure is practically in its original condition.

There are many things of interest at Pencaet apart from the ghosts: a crusader's helmet, a Spanish treasure chest, part of the chair used by Mary Queen of Scots when she abdicated the throne, sixteenth-century tapestries and much furniture in keeping with the period.

Also, a four-poster, presented to Professor Holbourn by his students that is reputed to have once been occupied by King Charles I. Altogether Pencaet Castle is acknowledged to be one of the most interesting mansions of southern Scotland and I am indebted to the Society for the Recording of Abnormal Happenings and to Edinburgh Psychic College for permission to include details from their reports devoted to paranormal activity at Pencaet.

The property was at one time owned by Sir Andrew Dick

Lauder who was terrified as a child at seeing an apparition standing by the fireplace in an upper room. Another former occupant, John Cockburn, either committed murder or was himself murdered centuries ago by one John Seton, to whom he was related by marriage.

Cockburn is credited with being the instigator of some of the disturbances here, including most of the various inexplicable noises of many kinds that have been heard by numerous people on many occasions.

Sounds of footsteps have frequently been heard echoing through the castle together with the sounds of furniture being moved. Such noises were heard in 1923 soon after the Holbourns moved in. Next year various people occupying the house while Professor and Mrs Holbourn were visiting the Island of Foula, complained of loud shrieks and groans.

Doors, securely closed at night, were found open in the morning, even when they had been locked and barred. One girl refused to sleep another night in the place after a full night of strange sounds and unexplained happenings.

As time passed the noises and disturbances became less violent and assuming that the originator was John Cockburn, Professor Holbourn would call out whenever a continuous rattling or tapping was heard: 'Now John, that's childish. Stop it.' And the sounds invariably ceased. Such a well-behaved ghost soon became known as 'the perfect gentleman'.

On Christmas Eve, 1923, the family and guests were gathered around a roaring fire in the music room, singing carols, when in full view of them all and verified by everyone present, a piece of carved oak bearing the family crest emerged from its place on the wall, paused for a moment and then returned to its normal position. The size of the block was seven inches by six inches. This manifestation was regarded as a greeting to the new inhabitants.

After the four-poster bedstead was brought into the house noises, comparable to someone moving about the room, using the bed and shifting the furniture, seemed to emanate from the King Charles Room.

The magnificent bedstead has elaborate carving on the bottom standards which are believed to be taken from the death-mask of King Charles I. Professor Holbourn and his wife occupied the chamber below the King Charles Room for a time and often they heard noises that sounded like someone surreptitiously groping and stumbling above them. The entity haunting the room is thought to be the ghost of Charles I himself, beheaded in 1649.

The royal bedstead appears to have been the scene of paranormal activity. In 1924 a visitor was taken to see the room. The bedclothes were found to have been violently disarranged, giving the impression that the bed had been slept in.

A Mrs Anderson, who was responsible for keeping the room tidy, asserted that she had left the place, only minutes before 'in a decent and proper condition'. Shortly afterwards another visitor, entering the King Charles room to take a photograph also found the bed apparently unmade.

Again, Mrs Anderson was certain that she had in fact made the bed and left it tidy. The photographer discovered that his photograph was under-exposed and when he returned to take another, once again the bedclothes were found disarranged on the haunted bed.

On this occasion, after the bed had been re-made, precautions were taken by locking the two doors giving access to the room and ensuring that all the windows were secured; in addition two bricks were placed against the main door. Next day the bricks were found to have been moved and although the doors were still locked and the windows fastened, the bedclothes were disturbed yet again.

Miss Avis Dolphin (now Mrs Foley), a survivor of the S.S. Lusitania disaster, when nearly two-thousand lives were lost, lived at Pencaet Castle with the Holbourns for some years. One night, while occupying the King Charles Room, she awakened Professor and Mrs Holbourn, who were sleeping in the room directly below, to say that someone was moving about downstairs. Professor Holbourn got up at once; they went down together to find out what was happening.

After an unsuccessful search for the perpetrator of the noises, they were returning upstairs, when they both heard, as they reached the first floor, unmistakable creaking sounds, as of a heavy person turning and tossing in the King Charles bed so recently vacated by Avis Dolphin.

On another occasion Avis Dolphin felt a light touch on her neck as she mounted the stairs in the darkness; she described the feeling as if someone drew the tip of a finger across the throat—light but unmistakable.

About the same period, Marion Holbourn told me, she sometimes saw faint but distinct lights shining in various passages throughout the old house.

One night the sound of birds wings were heard beating violently against the castle windows, terribly loud and insistent. Next day a cousin of the Holbourns who had been staying at Pencaet, died in hospital.

Some time later an elderly lady, recovering from an illness, was occupying the King Charles Room and Mrs Holbourn's brother was at the time using the bedroom immediately beneath this haunted chamber.

One morning at about five o'clock he awakened his sister to let her know that judging by the sounds he had heard from the room above his, he thought the old lady had fallen out of bed and was trying to get help. On reaching the King Charles Room Marion Holbourn found the old lady fast asleep.

Many objects have been moved mysteriously at Pencaet, apparently without human intervention, including large and heavy furniture. A big antique cabinet was shifted from its accustomed place by the wall. A brass ewer and basin, brought to England by Mrs Holbourn's grandfather from Turkey, was found to have been placed on top of a tall cabinet, the ewer on its side.

During the time that Marion Holbourn's son was a student at Edinburgh College of Art, nine students from the college visited Pencaet Castle to rehearse the play, Ladies in Retirement. Mrs Holbourn, spending the night in the Music Room, heard the most appalling noises; her son and daughter-in-law, occupying the dining-room, also heard them and were, in fact, kept awake much of the night. In the morning the two students in the apartment immediately above the Music Room were asked how they had fared during the night.

They replied that their sleep had been much disturbed; they had assumed that some of the other students were playing pranks. They had decided to ignore the noises and assured Mrs Holbourn that they themselves had kept quiet all night.

The two students who spent the night in the King Charles Room, situated above that occupied by Mr Holbourn (junior) and his wife, asserted that they had been continuously disturbed and had hardly closed their eyes all night.

They, too, had suspected a practical joker but had not themselves moved about or made any noise. They complained of the extreme coldness in the room they occupied and described a broad 'and ghastly' stain they had both seen to appear when the commotion was at its height. In the morning when they examined the wall where they had seen the mark during the night, they could find nothing to account for their nocturnal experience. Among the noises they described (and this has been reported on other occasions at Pencaet) was one that sounded like something heavy and soft being pulled slowly across the room at about midnight, accompanied by stealthy footsteps.

One of the occupants of this room at another time had with her a square and most reliable clock that had worked well for many years. At Pencaet it stopped: altogether, it never went for more than five minutes all the time she was at the castle. Marion Holbourn told me that she, too, found difficulty in keeping clocks working when they were placed on a particular wall of the dining-room; once even a watch hung there stopped.

A convincing account of paranormal footsteps was given to me by Marion Holbourn. They were experienced the night of Professor Holbourn's funeral by his widow and their son. Firm and distinct, they appeared to approach the front door along a path and the door was heard to open and shut. Young Holbourn immediately searched thoroughly but could find nothing to account for the noise, although he did find the pet cat hiding beneath a table in a terrified condition.

Mrs Marion Holbourn was away from Pencaet Castle for a period at one time and the house was occupied by her son. Mr Alasdair Holbourn, Mrs Holbourn's bedridden mother, her nurse and the housekeeper, Bella Leadbetter. Miss Lead-better, occupying the room next to the bathroom, called out on one occasion to Alasdair to enquire whether he was having a bath as she could hear the hot water running. Actually he was outside the house at the time. He replied in the negative and said he would see if it was the nurse. He discovered that she had been in bed for an hour.

Entering the bathroom, he found the place full of steam with the windows and mirror blurred but the bath absolutely dry! He also discovered a strange piece of soap which none of the occupants of the house claimed or could explain. Next morning Bella reported that her bath towel had disappeared and it was never recovered.

A Siamese cat was concerned in an incident which took place in the chamber known as the Middle Room. One night Alasdair Holbourn heard the cat scratching at one of the two doors situated at opposite ends of the room.

Rising to open the door, he was about a yard away when the door suddenly threw itself open and at the same time the door at the opposite end of the room also opened and the sound of running footsteps faded away down the passage. Of the cat there was no sign.

An Edinburgh medium visited Pencaet one day and as a result of the various 'impressions' she obtained during a complete tour of the mansion, she had no hesitation in pointing to the late Professor Holbourn as being responsible for the paranormal footsteps and a number of other unexplained happenings.

A curious 'spontaneous manifestation' occurred when a party of members of the East Lothian Antiquarian and Field Naturalists Society were being conducted through the low-beamed Library at the top of the castle.

A domed glass, encasing a model of the castle made years before by Alasdair Holbourn, suddenly cracked for no apparent reason and broke into several pieces. No one was within a dozen feet of the model at the time.

In one letter to me Mrs Holbourn related that the ghost had been active again. She felt that unusual displacement of air might account for some of the reported 'manifestations' and that the forty-one doors in the castle and many more windows had always suggested to her that there could be a normal explanation for some of the curious happenings.

Yet she readily admitted the difficulty of explaining the apparition of a small man dressed in a cloak who was seen by her daughter-in-law to emerge from a cupboard and walk the whole length of a room before disappearing into a solid wall.

Similarly the actual movement of heavy furniture, the stopping of clocks and such activities as the movement of the wooden panel are difficult to associate with draughty doors and ill-fitting windows.

In August, 1972, Mrs Marion Holbourn told me she was really convinced that there were ghosts at Pencaet after the Charles I bedstead was disturbed. A very reliable person was involved. The Holbourns were away on holiday but they left in the house Marion Holbourn's cousin, who lived with them.

He looked into the bedroom one morning and saw that the bed was unmade. He told the daily help, who declared that she had made it. He took her to the room and showed her the bed and she said she must have forgotten.

They made the bed together, but next day it was again unmade. The cousin became frightened and, the bed re-made, he barricaded the window's and locked both doors. When the Holbourns returned home he took them up to the bedroom; together they unlocked the room and looked inside. The bed was again in wild disorder!

There is yet another ghost at Pencaet: an ancient beggar who practised wizardry years ago, named Alexander Hamilton. He is said to have been turned away empty-handed from the castle; in revenge he came back with a blue thread and 'with murderous intent' wound the thread about the gates of the mansion.

A day or two later the chatelaine and her eldest daughter fell victims to a mysterious illness and both died. Hamilton lost his life on Castle Hill at Edinburgh but it may be that his ghost returns on certain nights for from time to time a mysterious and unexplained shadowy form has been seen about the castle gates.

I find that King Charles I visited nearby Winton House in 1633, so it is by no means impossible that he called at Pencaet.

PENICUIK, MIDLOTHIAN

Some five miles south the obsolete Mount Lothian Quarry has long been reputed to be haunted by a galloping horseman.

In the late 1800's, when the quarry was being worked, the lime-burners finished work at dusk. There were recurrent stories of their being startled by the figure of a galloping horseman that disappeared in the direction of Peebles.

Sometimes, late on dark nights, the 'clip-clop' of horses' hooves indicated the return of the mysterious rider.

Those who saw the figure on the occasions when the horse and rider travelled north, quite oblivious to any human watcher, swore that as the galloping horse and intent rider approached the quarry they both leapt high into the air while at the same time a blood-curdling scream rent the air. Then there was silence and the figures were seen no more.

The locally accepted story to account for the singular spectacle concerned a young farm labourer who used to 'borrow' a horse from his master for the purpose of visiting his lady love at a farm near Eddleston on the Peebles Road.

One night, at a corner near the quarry, he came upon a heavily-laden cart that had toppled on to its side, trapping both horse and driver. But despite the driver's anxious cries for help, the love-lorn young ploughman turned a deaf ear and hastened on his way.

A few hours later, when he returned, he again passed the upset cart and rode past it. But this time the cart-driver recognized the young man in the bright moonlight.

When next morning the injured man was found by the quarrymen on their way to work he only lived long enough to tell his story, deeply tinged with the bitterness he felt for the heartless young labourer.

Very soon the young man found himself without a friend in the district. After he lost both his job and his girlfriend, he took to poaching.

One morning his body was found; no one ever knew whether he had died by accident, suicide or murder. Due to strong local feeling his body was not buried in consecrated ground but on a piece of waste land where the estates of Frith, Whitehill and Roseberry meet.

It is hereabouts that clear moonlit nights are still disturbed by the occasional figure of a hurrying horseman, by the clip and clatter of horses' hooves—a phantom horseman hurrying home with the horse before it is missed by its owner.

While in the vicinity, it is worth visiting nearby Roslin Chapel. Here, although they have no ghost, there is a remarkable sculptural decoration, probably by Spanish craftsmen, representing such subjects as the Seven Deadly Sins, the Seven Cardinal Virtues and the Dance of Death.

The Prentice Pillar is said to derive its name from the fact that an apprentice produced it in the absence of his master who, on his return from abroad, slew the 'prentice' with his mallet in a fit of jealousy—so perhaps there should be a ghost here, anyway!

PERTH, PERTHSHIRE

A ghost here appeared night after night because it owed a small sum of money!

In July 1838 the Rev. Charles McKay, a Catholic priest, left Edinburgh to take charge of the Perthshire missions. On arrival he received a call from a Presbyterian woman named Anne Simpson who said she had been waiting more than a week to see a priest.

He learned that she had been much troubled for several nights by the apparition of a dead woman who had materialized in her bedroom. McKay asked the woman whether she was a Catholic and when she replied that she was a Presbyterian, he asked why she had sent for him?

Anne Simpson replied that her 'visitor' had besought her to get a Catholic priest who would pay a certain sum of money that she owed; then she could rest in peace. The priest asked what the sum of money amounted to and was told three shillings and tenpence.

Anne Simpson did not know to whom the money was owed but she was quite emphatic that the visitation was no dream, insisting that she could get no rest because the figure appeared to her night after night. She recognized her as a woman named Maloy whom she had often seen going in and out of the army barracks, near her own lodgings.

The Rev. Charles McKay made enquiries and discovered that a washer-woman from the barracks, named Maloy, had indeed died. He located a grocer with whom she had dealt and who was not aware of her death.

Asking him whether she owed him anything, the grocer

turned up his books and revealed that Mrs Maloy's unpaid account had amounted to exactly three shillings and tenpence. McKay paid the sum.

Shortly afterwards Anne Simpson came to tell him that she was no longer troubled by the ghost of Mrs Maloy; although she did not know that McKay had discovered the debt and paid it. The full story was told in a letter from the Rev. Charles McKay to the Countess of Shrewsbury, dated October 21 St, 1842.

RINGCROFT OF STOCKING, RERRICK, KIRKCUDBRIGHTSHIRE

Ringcroft has now disappeared but it is possible to locate the parish of Rerrick where, nearly three hundred years ago, a poltergeist manifestation was experienced by fifteen responsible people, including six clergymen. The case, written up at the time with great care and attention to detail, came to be regarded as a classic poltergeist infestation.

We have a record of the strange happenings from the pen of the Rev. Alexander Telfair, the parish minister, who published a pamphlet in 1695 recounting the disturbances at the home of Andrew Mackie, a mason.

Initially it was the Mackie's animals that suffered. Livestock was found with the tethers cut or loosened; although these were renewed or strengthened, the same thing happened even when the animals were moved from their accustomed grazing grounds. One morning an animal was discovered suspended from a beam at the back of the house with its feet hardly touching the ground.

Shortly afterwards, in the middle of a quiet spring-time night, the sleeping family awakened to find the house full of smoke. They discovered that a basket full of peats had been tipped out on the living-room floor and set alight.

A few days afterwards, on March 7th, inexplicable stone-throwing began and continued unabated for five days. The stones felt half their normal weight when they were picked up.

A month later the same thing happened; one large stone flew upwards from the floor with such force that it almost penetrated the thatched roof. As it fell back to the floor, breaking in a number of pieces, one struck the Rev. James Monteith, minister of Borgue, in the back.

It was during the early days of the infestation, too, that the Mackie children went running to their parents one evening, frightened by the sight of a shrouded body they found seated by the fireplace when they came into the house.

Their awed faces convinced Andrew Mackie that they had indeed encountered something that scared them. He hastened to the house with the children cowering behind him but whatever had terrified them had by then disappeared. Next day a shepherd's staff and some kitchen utensils were discovered to be missing; later they were found in the shuttered and locked loft.

After church the following Sunday Mr Mackie remarked on the strange happenings to his minister, the Rev. Alexander Telfair, who listened attentively and later visited the house, staying for some time to exorcise the ghost by prayer.

Practically nothing of a ghostly nature happened until the rector was on the point of leaving when two small stones dropped on to the roof of the house and the whole family ran outside to complain that the evil ghost had returned. Mr Telfair immediately went back inside and prayed but even as he did so a number of small stones were thrown at him, seemingly from nowhere.

A few found their mark but without harming him. Soon afterwards, on March 18th, bigger stones were hurled and during the night of March 21st. which the rector spent at the home of the Mackie family, there was considerable alarm throughout most of his stay.

The minister was struck by a stick wielded by unseen hands, not once but several times; articles and furniture in one of the bedrooms were moved and seemed to be alive, to the great consternation of the occupants of the house, the minister and three neighbours who were present.

Later the same night, when engaged in yet another attempt at exorcism, the Rev. Alexander Telfair became aware of a slight pressure on his arm and, looking down, he saw a little white hand and arm that vanished as he watched.

Thereafter the ghost seemed to become more powerful and more vindictive. There were numerous reports, not only from the various members of the family affected but also from friends and neighbours who came to assist, of stones being thrown at them, articles moving suddenly when they were about to be touched and people being hit by sticks and stones.

Once Andrew Mackie was hit on the forehead by a stone and when he tried to dodge some of the repeated missiles with a heavy stick, 'something' gripped him by the hair and scratched him with its finger nails.

At night-time the sleeping children would be awakened by a great noise caused by a stout stick rattling and banging on the wooden chest beside their beds; bedclothes would be repeatedly dragged off the beds and prayer times were disturbed by a noise described as 'whisht—whisht—whisht'.

After Mackie and his neighbour Charles MacLennan went to Buittle and related the story of the disturbances to a gathering of clergymen, two of the ministers, Andrew Ewart of Kells and John Murdo of Crossnrichael, returned with Mackie to Ringcroft.

Here they fasted and prayed in turns throughout the night, but to no avail and they themselves were repeatedly struck by stones that flew at them from nowhere. Ewart was hit so hard on the head that he bled.

That night no member of the household escaped the attention of the ghost. While they were all collected together for evening prayer a peat, alight and burning, was flung among them and as they rose from their knees, stones showered on them from every angle.

During the next few days a barn full of straw was set alight; two attempts to set fire to the house were quashed with the speedy help of neighbours, and William MacMinn, the blacksmith, received a wound on the head from a flying stone.

One evening as Andrew Mackie and his wife were carrying peat into the house, Mrs Mackie stumbled over a slab of the stone floor and discovered to her surprise that the stone was loose for up to that time both she and her husband had always found it perfectly firm.

When they had finished moving the peat, Mrs Mackie turned her attention to the loose stone and, finding that it raised easily, discovered beneath it seven small bloodstained stones and some flesh, enclosed in a piece of old paper.

The Rev. Alexander Telfair recounts that the blood was 'fresh and bright'. Mrs Mackie believed that her interference with these hidden articles resulted in the appearance on the children's bed of a stone so hot that it burned a hole in the bedclothes; it was still too hot to handle when a neighbour was called to the scene.

A letter written in blood was next found by Andrew Mackie; stone-throwing was resumed; a barn door was discovered to have been inexplicably smashed; there was more fire-raising; a spade and a sieve were thrown about the house.

When Mackie succeeded in catching hold of the sieve, the greater part of it was forcibly snatched from him, leaving the rim in his hand. A visitor received a blow on the head that caused bleeding.

During the following days there was continual whistling, groaning noises and stone-throwing at prayer times. Sometimes an invisible force shook the kneeling men backwards and forwards and tried to lift them bodily.

Sheep were found tied together in pairs; ropes were deposited in unusual places and a voice declared that God had directed it to warn the land to repent before dire judgment fell. There were more attempts at setting the house alight and one gable-end of the property was pulled down so that the Mackie family had to shelter for the night in a stable.

Finally the entity or being responsible for all the trouble was apparently seen in the barn at Ringcroft by five of the local inhabitants. They described it as a black thing that seemed to increase in size to such an extent that they thought it would fill the building.

They were terrified but this appearance seemed to signal the end of the disturbances for though next day, May 1st, 1695, an empty sheep-shelter was gutted by fire, thereafter nothing of an extraordinary nature was reported.

The site of Ringcroft of Stocking is marked by three trees that stand a short distance up a side road not far from Auchencairn village. They are known locally as The Ghost Trees.

Some of the foundations of Mackie's haunted farmhouse can still be located in what is now pasture land.

ROSLIN, MIDLOTHIANSHIRE

To the south, on the banks of the North Esk, it is still possible to trace remains of Woodhouselee Castle, the 'haunted Woodhouselee' of Scott's ballad. It stood here on a slope of the Pentland Hills and was persistently haunted by the Lady Bothwell, with a child in her arms. There are reports that she has been seen in the present New Woodhouselee.

The ghost story has its origin in a murder or assassination. There is no doubt that Hamilton of Bothwellhaugh shot and killed the Regent Moray as he passed through Linlithgow on January 23, 1570.

He claimed justification, for while Hamilton was away from home, a favourite of the Regent seized his house, turning out Lady Bothwell and her infant into the cold night where, stark naked, they were found next morning, the child dead and the Lady Bothwell mad.

In the vicinity of the hollow glen beside the river this dastardly act used to be re-enacted: the stark and silent ghost of the mad Lady Bothwell rushing about on cold, moonlit nights.

The apparition was seen so often some years ago that the singular appearances ceased to attract attention and came to be accepted by the inhabitants. This pitiful ghosts seems to have disappeared now although it is still possible to trace people who remember and have seen it.

ST ANDREWS, FIFESHIRE

The town is said to get its name from the shipwreck in the fourth century of a ship carrying the relics of St Andrew himself, but it is not his ghost that haunts the ruined cathedral. Rather, it is an unidentified lady in a long white dress with a veil, holding a book in her clasped hands. In May, 1968, she was reported to have been seen near the Round Tower by an arts student, Miss Alison Grant and by medical student Mark Hodges.

SANDAY ISLAND, ORKNEY

In October, 1970, Mrs Anne Searancke and her family moved into a lovely old cottage that stands by itself with glorious views extending almost the entire fourteen miles' length of the island. They had been there only a couple of days when they heard faltering footsteps accompanied by a strange tapping noise.

They could discover no cause or reason for the sounds which were heard most often at night but sometimes during the day. Then the sound of an organ playing was added—with no such instrument for miles.

No recorded music was being played and no organ music was being broadcast at the time. Soon afterwards a friend, staying for the weekend, went for a walk in the evening and on his return saw a figure entering the back door.

Realizing that it was no member of the family he quietly followed and watched as the female figure entered the house, crossed the kitchen and stood silent and unmoving in front of the stove. As quietly as he could he rushed away to get his camera but as he turned to look again at the mysterious figure, he discovered that it had disappeared.

Afterwards several members of the family saw the same apparition: an old woman in a long dress with her hair curled behind her head and a shawl thrown around her shoulders.

One of the rooms in the cottage is reported to have a most unpleasant atmosphere and dogs have refused to enter the room which has a cupboard, ominously bricked-up.

It seems that one previous occupant of the house used to walk about the place with faltering footsteps and tapping stick, as she was almost blind.

SANDWOOD BAY, CAPE WRATH, SUNDERLAND

This extreme north-east tip of Scotland is a strange and isolated place where one can walk for a whole day among the rocky hills and great lumps of stone slowly disintegrating through the ages, without meeting another living soul. But, if repeated reports are reliable, one might meet the ghost of an irascible old sailor.

Here the utter silence of miles of deserted sand beaches is broken by the continual roar of breaking waves and the high-pitched screaming of gulls, bringing to mind the age-old belief of sailors that these birds were the souls of drowned mariners.

A few years ago a crofter and his son were out with their pony gathering driftwood for fuel. On this particular occasion they wandered further than usual and were busy near the sea-shore in this wild and desolate place—over fifty miles from the nearest railway station.

They had collected a good supply of timber and kindling from unfrequented Sandwood Bay and were thinking that it was time to turn towards Old-shore More and home, for the watery sun was sinking and darkness would be all about them soon, when they became aware that their pony, a quiet and calm creature, had turned suddenly restive. The next moment, father and son both became aware at the same time of a large and bearded man, dressed in the uniform of a sailor, standing close beside them on the sands.

Before they could recover from their surprise at the soundless and sudden appearance, the figure commanded them in a loud voice to take their hands off what did not belong to them and to leave his property.

Horror-struck, for they both immediately felt that there was something uncanny and inexplicable about the sudden appearance of the mysterious figure in that deserted place, the two men dropped the wood they had spent hours gathering. Then they fled from the presence of the sailor—although not before both had noticed the brass buttons on his tunic, the worn sea-boots, the faded sailor's cap and the dark, weather-beaten clothing.

A few months later, early one afternoon, a similar figure was encountered by all the members of a fishing party from Kinlochbervie, as they rounded one of the big sand-dunes that dot the beach of Sandwood.

Each member of the party clearly saw the figure striding along the crest of a sandy knoll; they all noticed the sailor's cap and saw the glint of brass buttons in the sunlight, before he disappeared behind a hillock. The gillie had his stalking-glass on the form and thinking it must be a poacher, he went off to track him down and see what the man was up to.

The experienced and level-headed gillie returned, ashen-faced and puzzled, to report that there was no one in the bay at all except themselves, nor were there any footmarks or other indications that there had been anyone where they had all seen the figure.

High on a ridge facing Cape Wrath Lighthouse amid bracken and heather and about a mile from the sand-dunes of the bay stand the remains of Sandwood Cottage, untenanted now for many years; probably the most remote and solitary habitation on the mainland of Scotland. No road or even path leads to it and on the north side of Loch Sandwood there is only one other habitation, a deserted shepherd's bothy that is also reputed to be haunted.

Once an old shepherd, who had been with the sheep all day, decided to sleep in Sandwood Cottage overnight—and later told this story:

'I entered the cottage as dusk was falling and after making myself a cup of tea, I locked and bolted the front door and went upstairs to the room above the kitchen, took off my clothes, extinguished the candle and went to bed.

'Just as I was going to sleep, I heard steps, distinct footfalls padding about below. I got out of bed and put my ear to the bedroom door and distinctly heard footsteps padding about below me, seeming to go from room to room and back again, time after time. I said to myself that's queer, for I bolted the door; surely I didn't lock someone into the house who entered before I did: but who on earth would be near Sandwood of all places at this time of night?

'As the tramp, tramp, tramp continued, I dressed, lit the candle, quietly opened the door and proceeded to search every room in the place. I found nothing to account for the noises which had ceased as I descended the stairs. I went back to bed and heard nothing more.'

Nothing could convince the old man but that something subhuman was with him in the cottage that night and he even had an explanation for the cause of the footsteps.

Some years before a wealthy Australian had stayed at Sandwood Cottage while fishing Sandwood Loch. He seemed to have fallen completely under the spell of the place and had come back again and again whenever he could, year after year; each time he was more loath to leave.

Soon after the last of his visits to this bleak but beautiful area, he died in Australia and the old shepherd believed that his spirit returned to the place he loved so much.

One night an old fisherman found himself in the bay and as it was so late, he decided to spend the night in Sandwood Cottage. He had been helping to collect some sheep for a friend and he made himself as comfortable as he could in a room on the ground floor.

Around midnight he was awakened by his dog barking and he heard distinct, firm footsteps apparently approaching the outside of the cottage, followed by a knock on the windowpane of the room he was occupying. Looking towards the window he saw clearly in the moonlight the face of a bearded sailor gazing into the cottage.

The fisherman particularly noticed the short black coat that the figure was wearing, the brass buttons and the peaked cap. When he opened the door to see who his visitor might be, he could find no trace of any living soul. He carefully searched the whole cottage, inside and out, but saw no one and found nothing to account for the figure he had seen.

One other night the same man spent at Sandwood Cottage, alone, in the same room. This time he awoke at dead of night with the awful feeling that a thick and heavy black mass, like a blanket, was pressing down on top of him. The sensation of being suffocated was not a pleasant one and the old fisherman made sure that he never spent another night at the haunted cottage.

Not long ago two walkers from Surrey made their way from Durness to the Cape Wrath lighthouse and then, following the coast-line southwards, planned to reach Kinlochbervie in time to catch the morning bus to Lairg. But they were very tired—so when they saw Sandwood Cottage as the sun went down, they decided to spend the night there and continue in the morning.

Next day, hat ing fled the cottage at dawn, they told a local postmaster, the first person they met, about the ghastly time they had had in Sandwood Cottage. In the middle of the night they were roused from their slumbers by a fearful noise so loud that it seemed as though all the windows and doors in the place were being smashed; the whole cottage vibrated as if in a violent storm.

While the rocking and crashing sounds still continued a noise like a horse stamping and pawing seemed to come from the room above them. As near as they could judge, the noise lasted four or five minutes and during this time every part of the cottage seemed to come apart and close up again; the very foundations appeared to rock and sway and the two hikers were so terrified that they could not move.

Afterwards they sat, huddled together, dreading further disturbances, until dawn broke and they, like others before and after them, fled from the haunted cottage at Sandwood Bay, the cottage that does not like to be visited.

Quite recently I heard of an Edinburgh woman who received a small piece of wood from the broken staircase at Sandwood Cottage, as a souvenir of the remotest dwelling in Scotland.

Since the remnant of the cottage has been in her possession she has had several alarming experiences in her London flat, while some very strange things have also happened in her Edinburgh house.

Crockery has tumbled to the floor for no apparent reason, knocks and the sound of heavy footsteps have been heard at night-time; once she noticed a strong smell of alcohol and tobacco and caught a glimpse of a bearded sailor who turned and faced her before disappearing near her sitting-room window.

The odd thing is that the recipient of this piece of wood from Sandwood Bay, a much respected member of society not prone to exaggeration, has never visited the cottage herself yet she asserts that the portion of wood itself now rattles and moves on occasions. She keeps the relic locked up in a drawer and says wild horses could not drag her to haunted Sandwood Bay.

SELKIRK, SELKIRKSHIRE

Some three miles to the east there are a succession of stagnant pools bordered by rushes and a few gnarled alder trees growing out of the peaty slime. It is an unobtrusive piece of marsh-ground that has a beauty and mystery all its own, especially at dusk when a mist often hovers there.

Ghostly whispers and half-interpreted sounds have been reported and some unexplained figures have been seen at the place called Murder Moss, or Murder Swamp.

It is said that over two hundred years ago, in the black year of 1745 when the English were continually crossing the Scottish border, sacking and burning, one of the villages so attacked was Bowden where there dwelt a certain Davie Bonnington who had a lovely young daughter.

Eighteen-year-old Kirsty had many local suitors but only one found favour with her father, a prosperous but forbidding and morose man known as Geordie o' the Mill.

He was a strong and rough man, somewhat feared on account of his habit of disappearing for days at a time on his horse. Where he went no one guessed although his knowledge of the surrounding countryside was unequalled.

Kirsty, perhaps in deference to her father's wishes or perhaps because the mature Geordie fascinated her, did not discourage his wooing, until there returned to Bowden, Will Hob who had left the village as a boy of fifteen and came back a prosperous and handsome man; a man who was enchanted by Kirsty's beauty.

Before long the young pair were often walking together over the Common on summer evenings or sitting by the village stream. Geordie, whom Will disliked from the start, seemed to bear no resentment, always greeted the couple politely and made no show of disappointment when the couple announced their forthcoming wedding-day.

On the eve of the wedding friends and neighbours had gathered, as was the custom, at Bonnington's home to sing and dance and drink and eat as an expression of their good wishes.

It was a wild and stormy night and the revelry was at its height when the distant sounds of galloping horses and shouting told the villagers that the dreaded English raiders were upon them. Hurriedly, lights were extinguished and men and women struggled to return to their homes or run to the moor to hide.

Will took Kirsty's hand and led her through the confusion and darkness to the back of the house where his horse was stalled. He mounted, drew Kirsty up behind him and told her to 'hold tight' for he knew that their only hope of safety lay in instant flight. Suddenly the shape of a mounted man loomed up in the darkness which, with relief, they recognized as Geordie.

'Oh! Geordie, save us' cried Kirsty. 'Right', replied Geordie, 'I'll save you. There's a fine shelter I know where you'll never be found. Come on.' So saying he laid hold of the reins of Will's horse and galloped off with the lovers into the darkness, across the wild countryside that he alone knew so well. A number of villagers saw them depart.

Next day Geordie returned to the village but without either Kirsty or Will. He said that he had set them on the way to Leith and Davie Bonnington started out to look for his daughter. At length he returned to say that he could find no trace of them; all successive searches and extensive enquiries failed to locate the missing pair.

As time passed, suspicion grew that Geordie was responsible for their disappearance; it was even whispered that he had enticed the English to the village and that he had betrayed the young couple to them.

Then, months later, a still more sinister suspicion was aroused by the finding of a woman's handkerchief which a village lad fished out of one of the pools outside the village; a handkerchief that was recognized as having belonged to Kirsty.

Geordie had no friend in the village and he grew more and more sullen and morose. He seemed to be a haunted man and it was noticed that ever more frequently would he ride westward out of the village in the direction of the lonely pools and marshes.

Finally he was seen no more but a few days later the same lad who had returned to the village with Kirsty's handkerchief, came running into the village terror-stricken by what he had seen. He had again visited the silent pools and was half-scared out of his wits.

The villagers could get little sense out of the ashen-faced lad, so a party of the men set out and reached the lonely pools as darkness fell. There, in the moonlight and through the swirling mists, they clearly saw the figure of a man submerged in the water to his waist, motionless and silent, his eyes protruding with terror, glazed and staring... it was Geordie!

Those were superstitious days and it was commonly believed that the man who had caused the death of the young lovers had been forced to revisit the scene of his crime and that he, too, had become inexplicably engulfed in the treacherous swamp.

Thereafter the place was known as Murder Moss and people who venture there on moonlight nights say that they hear ghostly whispers and long drawn-out sighs. Occasionally, as darkness gathers about the black pools, phantom forms seem to stalk among the rushes at this scene of tragedy.

SKYE, ISLE OF

From time immemorial there have been stories of phantom kilted armies on Skye. One of the more recent accounts concerns two young men: Sir Patrick Skipwith and a student from Oxford who were making a geological survey of the island.

They were camped in a deserted glen at Harta Corrie when something awakened Sir Patrick soon after midnight. He got up and went outside where he was astonished to see groups of kilted men, dozens of them, scrambling along the mountainside within fifty yards of the two tents.

He was about to call out when he suddenly realized that he could hear no sound. He woke his friend and together they watched the kilted men for nearly ten minutes before the figures faded away and were gone.

Some nights later Sir Patrick and his friend camped again in the vicinity of Harta Corrie, celebrated in the history of the island for the Bloody Stone that marks the scene of a bitter battle between the MacDonalds and the MacLeods some three hundred years ago.

Again, in the early hours of the morning, they both saw the kilted Highlanders, a phantom army in retreat, in bright moonlight.

The island also has a phantom car that travels at great speed along the hill road from Sligachan. All witnesses agree that the car is a 1934 Austin with lights blazing but no driver. The soundless form vanishes suddenly.

One of the first reports came from Dr Allan MacDonald who saw the 'car' in 1941. 'I was motoring along the road,' he said, 'when I noticed a car travelling very quickly towards me over the hill. Its speed really was terrific and I drew in to let it pass but it never came abreast of me. I waited a while, then proceeded forward and found that the car had completely vanished! There was simply nowhere for it to have gone.'

Donald MacKinnon from Sconsa also saw the same car quite clearly and saw it vanish before his eyes; his son Donald John MacKinnon also saw it, travelling far too quickly for a normal car.

Lieutenant Donald Campbell, of the island's Observer Corps, was driving home to Broadford from Portree when he saw the 'car' tearing towards him with lights blazing—but it never passed him. It vanished before reaching him: one moment it was there, the next it was gone, although there was nowhere for it to have gone to.

Postman Neil MacDiarmid saw it too. He said at the time: 'I had been out with mail to Sligachan. There had been a full moon but it had gone down. As I drove along a cold chill suddenly swept over me. I looked to the shore side and saw an old Austin travelling very fast with one light burning bright at the front and a kind of dim glow inside the car. I could plainly see that there was nobody at the wheel. It tore ahead of me and veered to the right; and then just disappeared.'

STIRLING, STIRLINGSHIRE

The castle, built on the site of a Roman station, occupies a commanding position on the River Forth with remarkable views from the walls, including the field of the Battle of Bannockburn (1314). Many foul and bloody deeds have been perpetrated here over the years and many are the reports of ghosts and ghostly happenings within these ancient walls.

Perhaps the best known ghost is the castle's Green Lady, a phantom reputed for centuries to walk these sombre passages and corridors and to appear in the most unexpected places. Reports in quite recent times include the experience of an army cook, busy in the officers' mess kitchen, until he became aware of the feeling that he was being watched.

When he turned round, he was startled to find a misty-green figure of a lady standing at his elbow, apparently absorbed in his activities. Dinner was late that night for the cook fainted with fright and afterwards swore that he knew nothing of the Green Lady ghost until he saw 'her' himself.

There is a story that the real 'Green Lady' was an attendant to Mary Queen of Scots and that one night she had a premonition that the Queen was in danger. She rose from her bed and rushed to the Royal bedchamber to find the draperies of the four-poster on fire and the Queen asleep inside.

Any appearance of the Green Lady is taken seriously at Stirling Castle for it seems that many of these have heralded a disaster of some kind. Serious fires at Stirling have followed a reported sighting of the silent figure and it is recorded that after the Queen was rescued from the burning bedstead, she recalled a prophecy that her life would be endangered by fire while she was at Stirling Castle.

Alternatively, it has been suggested that the original Green Lady was the daughter of a governor of the castle who was betrothed to an officer garrisoned at the castle who was accidentally killed by her father. In despair and anguish the unfortunate girl is said to have thrown herself from the battlements to her death on the rocks hundreds of feet below.

The massive section in the Upper Square of the castle, known as the Governor's Block, has a room at the top of a flight of stairs where footsteps echo across the ceiling although there is no room, passage or corridor above the apartment.

In 1946 the footsteps were heard at infrequent intervals by an officer of the Argyll and Sutherland Highlanders and in 1956 by a major occupying the room, a particularly hard bitten officer who had fought in Burma and many other parts of the world; not a man who frightens easily.

In the regimental history a curious incident is recorded which may be connected with the mysterious footsteps. In the 1820s there was a 'sentry beat' along the battlement that existed at that time 'above the Governor's Block'.

One night a sentry taking over guard duty found the previous guardsman dead at his post, slouched on the ground, mouth open, a look of utter terror on his face. There is no explanation, no record of a medical report, just a note of several subsequent 'disciplinary cases', before sentry duty above the haunted Governor's Block was discontinued.

STRACHUR, ARGYLLSHIRE

There is a curious story of a remarkable vision associated with the Manse at Strachur.

A certain captain spent a single night here when the property was occupied by some of his relatives. The house had no reputation of being haunted at the time.

Soon after retiring, the visitor was surprised to see the bed curtains open and somebody look in on him. Assuming that one of the residents must be unaware of his visit, he took no notice but when the 'visitor' returned two or three times, the captain at length called out from his bed:

'What do you want?' 'I come,' replied the form in a hollow voice, 'to tell you that this day twelvemonth you will be with your father.'

Although his father was dead, the captain was not particularly disturbed and decided that he had experienced an hallucination or dream of some kind. He lost no sleep over the matter, although he did relate the experience to his host in the morning.

It so happened that a year later to the day he was again at the Manse of Strachur, on his way north to cross the ferry at Craigie. The day was stormy but he decided to proceed. His kinsman accompanied him to the ferry but on arrival they discovered that the boat was moored at the side of the lake; the boatman assured them that it was impossible to cross until the storm lifted. The captain had important business to attend to and insisted on being ferried across.

After much argument it was arranged that the old ferryman's son would attempt the crossing. The captain stepped into the boat— with the ominous warning that they would never reach the other side and that both he and the young man would both be drowned.

The boat set off with the captain, his servant and horse. Although the distance was not great the storm grew in intensity and half-way across it was found impossible to proceed.

After all efforts at tacking had failed, it was decided to return to the point of departure but during the turning the boat capsized throwing the three men and the horse into the water. The captain, who was a strong swimmer and not afraid for himself, shouted to his servant to keep hold of the horse for safety.

Then he set out to swim to the shore, no great distance — but he was encumbered by a heavy topcoat, his boots and his spurs. He seemed to be winning until his coat caught in his spurs and he was gradually dragged below the water. Although he reached the shore, where his relative had anxiously watched the mishap, it was only to make a gesture before he expired which seemed to say, 'You see, it was to be!' The young boatman was also drowned although the servant, aided by the horse, escaped.

STRANRAER, WIGTOWNSHIRE

The oddly shaped peninsula known as The Rhinns of Galloway is a green and enchanted land. It may well be that long ago the arm of land that joins the mainland of Wigtownshire lay under water and The Rhinns was an island.

There are numerous remnants of ancient earthworks, castles and early Christian relics here. The road to the north tip runs by the west coast of Loch Ryan; the main road more or less ends at the village of Kirkcolm. It is said that a former minister of the village had so powerful a voice that his sermons could be heard at Cairn Ryan, on the other side of the loch!

His strong voice was the means of exorcising the ghost that sorely troubled the district for many years. Caldenoch Castle seems to have been the home of the ghost but it is credited with seizing old women whenever it could and dousing them in any burn or water that might be handy.

Attempts by other clergymen had always been frustrated by the ghost who out-sang the psalms and drowned the prayers of those who tried to lay it; but the minister with his formidable voice was too much for the troublesome ghost. After a night trying to out-sing the new clergyman it gave up and was duly exorcised—or at any rate troubled the area no more.

STRATH CONON, ROSS AND CROMARTY

A stretch of the beautiful River Conon with its deep and wide ford, not far from the seventeenth-century (modernized) Brahan Castle (built by the first Earl of Seaforth), has long had the reputation of being haunted by a water-wraith. Legends abound and many of the fatal accidents that used to occur near Conon House were said to have been due to the murderous malice of this local 'elemental'.

One of the most reliable accounts of such a spectre concerns a servant of a Lord Seaforth who, late one night after a party, was accompanied on his way by two friends. In the light of the full moon the servant, described as a young and vigorous man, mounted on a powerful horse, entered the ford and rode in a slanting direction across the full stream.

When he was nearly halfway across a loud cry of terror, followed by a frightful snorting and plunging of the horse, alarmed the servant's companions waiting to follow in his footsteps. Wide-eyed, they watched what appeared to be a tall, dark figure start out of the water, lay hold of their friend and drag him off the horse and into the water!

A moment later they watched the terrified horse struggle towards the opposite bank while its ill-fated rider wrestled with some invisible adversary in the stream for a few seconds and then disappeared forever beneath the water.

TAIN, ROSS AND CROMARTY

Ancient Balnagowan Castle is haunted by at least two ghosts: wicked 'Black Andrew' and a murdered Scottish princess. There are several skeletons somewhere within these grey-pink walls, the remains of the Scottish princess, a man who died of the plague and one of the Rosses who were here for centuries.

My friend James Wentworth Day has told me of the night he heard footsteps, heavy and ponderous, that clumped along the Red Corridor and woke him at midnight. The footsteps were also heard by actress Hermione Baddeley who was staying at the castle at the same time and by another guest, Lady Duff. They have been heard, too, by the housekeeper whose family have served at Balnagowan for three centuries.

The footsteps are said to be those of 'Black Andrew' whose real name was Andrew Munro, a laird in a little fortress in the middle of the sixteenth century. He is reputed to have made the village women work in the harvest field stark naked and he was credited with murders and rapes for miles around.

Eventually the Chief of Clan Ross put an end to 'Black Andrew'; he was thrown out of a high window with a rope around his neck and breathed his last gasp dangling outside one of the bedroom windows of the Red Corridor. Always a 'devil for the women', he comes back and walks the Red Corridor (so it is said) whenever a new lady visitor stays at the castle.

Jimmy Wentworth Day told me that he was shown up to Muniment Room at the top of the tower, accompanied by a black Labrador owned by Bill Hunter who manages the estate.

At the threshold of the room the dog suddenly stopped in

its tracks; its hackles rose, it growled in terror, snapped and backed away. 'He always does that,' his owner said. 'I'm certain this is the room where they put the rope round "Black Andrew's" neck and pushed him out of the window. The dog knows.'

Lady John Conyngham once saw the ghost of the murdered Scottish princess. She was alone in the castle at the time and was eating her dinner when she heard a rustling sound, as of a dress.

She turned and saw a female figure dressed in grey emerge from a corner of the room. The apparition had copper-gold hair and green eyes. She seemed to be a very friendly and gentle ghost. She silently beckoned to Lady John who rose from the table and followed the figure into the drawing-room where it disappeared.

There is no portrait of the mysterious Scottish princess at Balnagowan but a hairy old man with burning and malevolent eyes glowers at all who pass along the Red Corridor; almost as though 'Black Andrew' still watched for women as he did all through his evil life.

TARBAT, NEAR FEARN, ROSS AND CROMARTY

There used to be a muddy lake in the north of the parish of Tarbat which shrank considerably during the summer months, with the remains of a farmhouse still discernible near one edge.

Long ago a young pedlar who was well known in the district disappeared without trace. Some years later, during a dry summer which reduced the lake to half its normal size and depth, a human skeleton was found amid the mud and rushes at the bottom.

Long before this discovery, however, the farmhouse near the lake was reputed to be haunted by a restless and mischievous spectre, which appeared to be wearing some kind of grey woven material. So troublesome did the ghost become inside the house that the property was soon deserted, began to fall into decay and for over half a century no one lived there.

Then a young man bought the site and remains of the cottage, rebuilt it and moved in with his young wife. On the third evening of their married life the young couple were disturbed by strange noises apparently emanating from an adjoining room.

Shortly afterwards the door of their bedroom opened and a figure entered, dressed in some grey plaid or material. The young man leapt from the bed and made for the intruder, calling as he went: 'Who are you? Who are you?' The spectre stepped back and replied in a deep voice:

'I am the unhappy pedlar who was murdered sixty years ago in this very room and my body was thrown into the lake yonder.

But I shall trouble you no more. The murderer is now dead and in two hours the permitted time of my wanderings on earth will be over for had I escaped the cruel knife, I would have died in bed this evening, a grey-haired old man.'

The form slowly disappeared as it spoke and from that night was never seen or heard again.

TIREE, ISLE OF, ARGYLLSHIRE

A wild and lonely beach on the northern shore has long been reputed to be haunted by a phantom black dog. It has the unnerving habit of following people and occasionally barking once or twice; a weird, echoing bark never forgotten by those who hear it. If a third bark is heard, according to tradition, the phantom dog will overtake the hearer.

The same form has been seen on the moor near Kenna-varra, crouching near a sand-dune. One witness, the morning after he had seen the figure, went to the spot in daylight and discovered the prints of huge paws at the place where he had seen the Black Dog.

A similar ghost-dog is said to haunt another part of the island, in the south-west; a strange, wild place known as Hynish Hill where it was seen and heard by two boys some years ago. A curious, naked, semi-human form with a grotesque head and face is seen sometimes in broad daylight on a sea-girt rock close to Balvaig.

There is on Tiree a cavern known as the Lair of the Faery Dog. Loud and unexplained barking, as of a huge dog-like creature, has been repeatedly heard here by the islanders and, occasionally, by visitors.

WATHERSTON, MIDLOTHIANSHIRE

A phantom lorry is said to travel along the busy road between Edinburgh and Stow and its unaccountable presence has been the source of many local reports, published in the Edinburgh papers in recent years.

One such report dates from a warm and sunny day not long ago when a local inhabitant noticed the swift and silent approach of a lorry travelling in the direction of Edinburgh, driven by an evil-looking man.

The witness watched the rather old-fashioned lorry make its quiet but quick way along what was little more than a sheep-track to Watherston Hill where it joined the main road.

Several Scottish newspapers published readers' accounts of a similar vehicle on this particular stretch of road where, it has been noticed, a number of accidents have occurred that could be explained by motorists following this phantom lorry round a bend and off the road.

I approached the spot with some caution when my wife and I travelled over this stretch of road in 1970 and it was just as well that I did—for we suddenly came upon an accident as we rounded a blind corner. Whether or not this particular mishap was caused by the phantom lorry I do not know.

WHITBURN, WEST LOTHIAN

A few years ago the Town Council of this coal and iron district investigated a psychic manifestation at the home of a Mrs Maule and Mrs McClusky in Townhead Gardens.

The two ladies shared the house and became so mystified by apparently inexplicable rappings that Mrs Maule's son went for the police—and returned with two Town Councillors. These practical and hard-headed men searched until three o'clock in the morning in an attempt to discover the source of the noises.

During the course of their investigation they made what was described as 'Miner's Taps': three taps, followed by two short taps. Each time they received answering taps which seemed to originate in the vicinity of a bed occupied by Mrs McClusky's twelve-year-old daughter who disclaimed responsibility for the knockings.

On the following night a further enquiry produced the same result. Afterwards one of the councillors stated that old mine workings ran underneath the house but added that they were about two hundred fathoms down. 'It doesn't seem possible that sound could travel that far through the ground,' he added. 'In any case there are no men working there.'

Mrs McClusky said that the curious tappings began on a Monday and, before they started, vibrations were felt throughout the house. On the Thursday of the same week a further investigation was carried out but this time nothing was heard and thereafter all was quiet.

There has long been a theory that occasional raps and other noises and perhaps displacement of objects may be due to geophysical causes such as underground streams, tides and earth movement. In the case of this particular report it sounds very much as though some such explanation may be applicable.

IRELAND

ANTRIM, CO. ANTRIM

Derelict Antrim Castle dates from 1662; it was rebuilt in 1816 after a fire and was again destroyed accidentally by fire in 1922. A loud hissing or breathing sound, apparently localized in the right wing of these picturesque ruins, has been reported by hundreds of people. Intrepid investigators have ascended the castle walls with ropes and ladders to dislodge owls and other night birds but have failed to discover the origin of the noise. Underground caverns and porous stonework might possibly repay study.

BIRR, CO. OFFALY

Grim, grey and bare, nearby Leap Castle, commanding a fine view of the Slieve Bloom mountains to the east, has been described as the worst haunted mansion in the British Isles.

One of the ancient strongholds of the O'Carrolls, Leap was badly damaged by fire in 1923 but originally the central portion (which comprised the entrance hall) was a square and solid castle of the usual type. Later wings were added on either side, one of which terminates in what is known as the Priest's House. The whole edifice is built on rock and gives the impression of enormous strength.

There is an age-old story that treasure is hidden at Leap Castle. Legend has it that a former inhabitant, due to be taken to Dublin to be tried on a charge of rebellion and fearful that he would not return, made the most of the time left to him by burying somewhere a crock or earthenware pot full of gold and precious jewels.

After years of imprisonment he did, in fact, return home but his long and cruel confinement had deranged his brain and he could never remember where he had hidden his wealth so skilfully.

From time to time various methods have been tried to locate the treasure but so far all have been unsuccessful. One lady who was psychic, though she did not find the money and jewels, as she made her way through the wide hall, suddenly walked towards one wall, laid her hand on the old stones and said: 'There is something uncanny here but I don't know what it is.' It was at this spot in the walls of the castle that two skeletons were discovered, walled up.

The top storey of the central tower is known as the Chapel; it is a big, well-lighted chamber and was probably used for religious purposes at one time. At one end of the apartment there is, or was, an oubliette, a secret dungeon into which prisoners were thrown through a trap-door and then conveniently 'forgotten'.

Often people walking along nearby roads, or in the neighbouring fields, have seen the windows of this chapel lighted up for a few seconds at a time as it would be if many lights were suddenly brought into the chamber. The possibility that the lights originate from servants can be discounted for I have been told that for years they shunned that part of the castle after dark.

One psychic message at a seance stated that the Leap treasure would be found in the chapel room under 'the tessellated pavement near the altar'. But no trace can now' be found of any altar in the apartment, nor any chequered pavement unless this lies beneath the mass of debris where a former roof collapsed. It would be well-nigh impossible to establish this fact now.

Many visitors to Leap Castle have had experiences that they cannot explain. After staying at the castle one man wrote to say that he found himself awake in the night with an extraordinary and violent cold feeling in the region of his heart. As he turned in his bed to ease the pain, he became aware of a tall female figure, clothed from head to foot in some red material, with her right hand raised menacingly in the air.

The figure seemed to be illuminated from within itself. As the visitor lit a match and prepared to get out of bed, he realized that the room was empty. He put out the light and went back to bed and although he did not see the 'Red Lady' again, he experienced several times the same cold feeling that seemed to grip his heart, while his body seemed warm to his touch.

Then there is the inexplicable and unpleasant 'something'

that is usually referred to as 'It'. Several owners, residents and visitors have described identical experiences of this vile ghost.

Not many years ago the lady of the house was in the gallery that runs round one side of the hall and connects with some of the bedrooms. She was leaning over the balustrade, looking down into the ancient hall and thinking of nothing in particular when suddenly she felt two bony hands laid on her shoulders!

Twisting sharply round she saw 'It' standing close beside her. It seemed to be human in shape but only about four feet high; the eyes were like two black holes in the face. She had the impression that the whole figure was made of cotton-wool but the most objectionable part of the experience was the accompanying smell, a most appalling stench such as one would expect from a decaying corpse.

After a moment the figure and the odour vanished as inexplicably as they had arrived, but it was a long time before the lady recovered from the shock of encountering the nauseating presence of the nameless horror.

There are other ghosts at Leap Castle. A shaven monk wearing a cowl walks near one window of the Priest's House and makes his way out through another window.

There is an invisible presence that has the habit of lying on the bed beside a human occupant, leaving a deep impression on the bedclothes afterwards and the feeling of a great weight on the bed at the time; a very frightening experience.

A quiet little elderly man has also been seen here, dressed in old-fashioned cut-away coat, bright green in colour with brown breeches and shining buckle shoes. He suddenly appears and disappears just as suddenly, sometimes accompanied by a quaint old lady, dressed in similar ancient-style clothes.

It is thought that they are the ghosts of some long-past servants or visitors, who met their ends unexpectedly and probably violently in this sombre castle.

BUSHMILLS, CO. ANTRIM

Two miles west of this pleasant town, whose River Bush gave its name to a famous pot-still whiskey, stands the extraordinary and romantic ruin of Dunluce Castle, the 'mermaid's fort'.

It is perched on a precipitous detached basaltic rock high above the sea, separated from the mainland by a deep chasm twenty feet wide; a gulf that in ancient times was spanned by a drawbridge and is now crossed by a narrow wooden bridge that has tried the nerves of many people.

The 'strong fort' was probably built in the fourteenth century by Richard de Burgh, Earl of Ulster or by the MacQuillans (or MacUillins) who certainly held for centuries the castle built on the site of a very ancient Irish fortress, until the almost impregnable bastion was taken by the MacDonnells in 1558.

Sorley Boye ('Yellow Charles') MacDonnell was conspicuous in the struggle against the English and although Sir John Perrot took the castle in 1584 after a nine-months' siege, Sorley Boys recaptured it and made peace with the English. His son Randal was created Viscount Dunluce and Earl of Antrim by King James I. The castle was abandoned and allowed to fall into decay during the seventeenth century.

The castle, long reputed to be haunted by the restless ghost of Richard de Burgh who walks on stormy nights, originally consisted of hve circular towers joined by a strong curtain wall with a platform inside and openings in the battlements for the use of archers. Only two of these circular towers remain with parts of two others.

It is noticeable that in view of its exceptionally isolated position no castle keep was necessary.

The ghost of the original owner is said to be doomed to remain earthbound forever because of the unmentionable crimes he committed during his lifetime.

There are some people who credit him with causing part of the castle to fall over the cliff into the sea one stormy night in 1639, carrying with it eight people. The famous Giant's Causeway (q.v.), an incredible formation resulting from the slow cooling into crystalline form of volcanic lava, may be seen here and should on no account be missed.

CELBRIDGE, CO. KILDARE

The fine house to the north-east of this pretty village (where once Esther Vanhomrigh, Swift's 'Vanessa' lived—her hopeless passion for Swift hastened her death) is called Castletown House. It has a ghost that walked downstairs before they were built and once, it seems, the house was visited by the Devil himself.

William Conolly, speaker of the Irish Parliament, 1715-29, said to have been the richest man in Ireland, built the great house in 1722. Having no heir, he left the property to his favourite nephew, William Conolly of Leixlip Castle. In 1733 he had married Lady Anne Wentworth, daughter of the Earl of Stafford, and it was she who first saw the ghost that walked downstairs that were not there.

Castletown House has always been proverbial for its hospitality. George Moore spent a fortnight here and said afterwards: 'I have wined and dined par excellence.... I venture to say that the hospitality of this splendid house is so unbounded that even in Ireland it will long be remembered.'

But once the hospitality was abused during an encounter between young Squire Thomas Conolly, son of William who had inherited the house and a stranger, one cold and wet November evening in 1767.

One afternoon that month he had walked with his wife, Lady Louisa, in the garden of their home. She reminded him that his mother had written in her journal of the 'tall and shadowy man' she had seen standing on the top gallery, before the staircase had been built.

She had described the figure pausing for a moment against the light of the window and then, with a high-pitched laugh, walk arrogantly, with mincing steps, down the staircase that was not there.

Lady Anne had the impression that the man was marking Castletown House for his own; that the ghost was taking possession. The figure, its derisive laughter still ringing through the hall, seemed to have the power of sight—even foresight—since it confidently descended a staircase that did not exist, taking the right turns and following the shallow treads.

When the staircase was actually built ten years later (at a time when Lady Anne was away from the house), its graceful and gently mounting sweep and two turnings corresponded exactly to the way the mysterious and chuckling figure had manoeuvred the invisible staircase.

A few days later there was a meet of the Kildare Hounds at Garanagh Cross, two miles from Celbridge. It was a wild, windy and wet morning after a storm that had lasted most of the night. Only a handful of the hardiest sportsmen followed the first 'find' through Garanagh Woods.

The fox proved to be as tiresome as the weather, doubling and redoubling on its tracks until the hounds were dizzy. Afternoon began to wane and cold, driving rain added to the discomfort of the hunt. One by one they went off home to dry clothes and a warm fire until by late afternoon there were no more than five or six huntsmen straggling across the ploughed fields by Rantully Hill.

At a point where the 'Dublin Gap' crossed the Portarlington road Squire Conolly noticed for the first time a man riding a spirited black horse that seemed as fresh as his own horse had been when the day began. The squire looked hard at the rider but could not recognize him as being one of the field that morning.

He turned in his saddle and called out a greeting, asking

whether the huntsman was a stranger to Kildare as he did not recognize him. The tall stranger smiled or rather grinned, disclosing abnormally long and yellow teeth, but neither spoke nor acknowledged the greeting, merely pointing away ahead of him.

As he did so, he turned his horse sharply and set off at a canter up the steep hill. At the same time the hounds, over the hill, set up a great noise that could only mean that they were about to make a kill.

Without a second thought, for he did not want the whole day to be a wasted one. the squire set off in pursuit, determined to be in at the kill himself. As he breasted the hill, he reined in his horse in surprise at the sight that met his gaze.

The stranger, dismounted, stood a little distance away, his feet firmly apart and holding above his head with both hands, a bloody fox, oblivious of its gore dribbling down from his grey beaver hat on to his grey hunting jacket and thigh boots. Still grinning, the man snipped off the brush with his sharp teeth and offered it to the squire. Puzzled, the squire looked about him; the stranger's horse stood proudly nearby but otherwise the hill was deserted. Hounds deserting a kill? It was impossible.

As Squire Conolly turned away from the nauseating sight, the man called out to him in a high, false and unpleasant voice: 'Conolly, if you will not accept the brush, will you offer me a cup of something hot at your great house—Castletown?'

Squire Conolly never refused hospitality to anyone and, unattractive as he found the man and his manners, he could not deny so direct a request. He bade the man follow him and take a cup of hot rum toddy with the rest of the huntsmen.

As they entered the high hall of Castletown House, Conolly noticed that the stranger's eyes darted to the window at the top of the staircase, a window that had given light to the gallery before the staircase was built.

Then the squire watched as the stranger's eyes followed down, step by step it seemed, the massive sweep of the great staircase. A hissing laugh burst from the stranger's lips as he minced across the hall floor towards a chair near the roaring fire.

Several of the squire's friends were already seated about the hall, warming themselves with hot drink while servants busied themselves removing the men's wet boots. As a servant approached the stranger, stretched out now in a comfortable chair, he was rudely ordered away; the odd and high-pitched voice told the servant that its owner was feeling drowsy and did not want to be disturbed.

For the first time, as the man's eyes closed, Squire Conolly looked hard at him and he now saw, in the well-lighted hall, that the man was as hairy as a dog. Long, stiff hairs sprouted from his nostrils and great curling tufts of hair hung out of his ears. Even his hands, long-nailed and with tapered fingers, were matted with hair!

An awful suspicion crossed the squire's mind and as the stranger slept, he ordered a servant to remote carefully one of the man's boots. As the steaming boot was drawn from the man's foot—a hairy hoof was disclosed, black and cloven!

Apparently oblivious to the commotion the stranger slept on and Squire Conolly hastily sent a groom to Celbridge to fetch a priest. Just as the holy man arrived, the stranger awakened from his sleep. As soon as he saw that his boot had been removed, he leapt to his 'feet' and, with gait even more unseemly wearing only one boot, he limped towards the fireplace.

There, spreading his arms on the mantelpiece, he dared the priest to do his worst. At the squire's entreaty to exorcise the fiend, the priest mumbled an incantation, but he was too gentle and his words had no effect except to provoke the Devil to laughter.

Angered by this reception, the priest called on the figure to be gone in the name of all that was holy but still the hall shook with Satanic laughter from the figure in front of the fireplace. This was too much for the priest who threw his missal at the leering face.

The book missed its mark and smashed the mirror hanging over the fireplace but this attack had the desired effect for the fiend leaped high into the air and disappeared in a cloud of sulphurous fumes. His vanishing point was a blackened crack in the creamy marble of the hearthstone that remained to remind successive occupants of Castletown House of the strange happenings there one November day in 1767.

CLONCURRY, CO. KILDARE

There is a strange ruined church here and a curious mound or barrow with a tree growing on top of it. Nearby stretches what used to be the dreary wasteland known as the Bog of Allen, now largely reclaimed as pasture. This most-famous of all Irish peat-bogs was once a place of brown turf and stagnant water; it is still a place of ghosts.

One of the many stories of weird experiences concerns a young man on a walking tour who ran into foul weather in the bleak and lonely place. The rain poured down so hard that he could hardly get his breath and within a few minutes it became so dark that he found it difficult to pick his way in the treacherous bog-ridden countryside.

For a brief moment he glimpsed a hut or cabin and, hoping for shelter of some kind, he made his way towards the building. On arrival he found to his disappointment that it was unoccupied and in a ruinous condition. Without a door or glass in the windows, an earth floor and only half a roof, it offered small comfort but it was somewhere to shelter until the frightful downpour eased and he prepared to spend an hour or two there.

Making himself as comfortable as he could, he ate some sodden sandwiches and was standing against the rotten wall, sheltering beneath what was left of the overhanging roof, gazing at the depressing and barren landscape all around him when his attention was drawn to a dark and swiftly flowing river that wound its sinuous way through the wasteland. A kind of black haze seemed to be rising from one particular part of the river. It was like a fog and yet it was not fog.

He pondered about what it might be but found himself baffled.

He had never seen anything like it before and the very strangeness of it gave him an eerie feeling. It seemed to waver this way and that, almost as though undecided which direction to take. Then, after remaining motionless for a moment, it began to move towards the lonely watcher in the ruined hut.

He watched, fascinated, as slowly, noiselessly and somehow furtively, it came towards him, a tall, shapeless black cloud, opaque, impenetrable and indefinable. Alone in that forsaken spot he began to feel uneasy as it grew nearer. He became more and more sure that it was not merely a vapour or mist but rather that it had an intelligence of sorts, that it had seen him and that it was evil.

He became conscious of the fact that he was frightened and yet he could not take his eyes away from the approaching mass, creeping slowly but surely ever nearer to him. His sense of self-preservation told him to run but when he tried to move, to shrink to one side or hide or, better still, to run, he found that he was powerless to move a limb. He had no alternative but to remain, his heart beating faster and faster as the haze drew closer and closer.

The next moment it had reached him. He had no power to ward it off, to resist the indefinable horror that seemed about to envelop him. It was as high as the cabin, devoid of any scent or smell, unsubstantial but not transparent, immaterial but not without a sense of purpose. It seemed to have arms that reached out and thrust him to one side as the shapeless haze passed him and disappeared into the cabin.

For a moment he stood taking deep breaths—he realized that he must have stopped breathing as the fog or haze reached and passed him—and then he turned to see where it had gone. It had passed through the hut or cabin and was moving resolutely into the heart of the Bog of Allen. He stood and watched as it slowly disappeared into the gloom and shadows of that dreadful place.

Thinking about the experience afterwards he said that he thought it might be some elemental river spirit, a sexless, melancholy, soulless being that roamed forever in the desolate and doleful area that was the Bog of Allen.

CONNEMARA, CO. GALWAY

Connemara was one of the last ancient kingdoms of Ireland to accept English customs; in this country of austere beauty, matched only in Greece, small boys were still dressed in skirts in recent years to deceive the fairies.

Renvyle House, now' an hotel, was the scene of stances in the late nineteen-twenties conducted by W. B. Yeats and attended by people like James Joyce, Augustus John and Oliver St John Gogarty who owned Renvyle; many people believe that the place is still haunted, some that it is the most haunted house in all Ireland.

The present house is about fifty years old and was built by Sir Edward Lutyens on the site of an old Gogarty residence that was burned down in the days of the Irish Troubles.

Yeats is credited with personally raising the ghost of a previous occupant of the house, a man who is said to have strangled himself with his bare hands and whose restless ghost still walks here. More than one visitor has insisted on changing rooms but few ever offer any explanation for wanting to move; often they accept inferior accommodation without protest.

A previous employee at the hotel, beautifully situated between lake and sea, recalls that the whole house had a peculiar and indefinite, almost expectant atmosphere. One particular room always seemed to have been the centre of the disturbances. This is I think No. 27 on the first floor in the centre of the hotel. The informant well recalls several visitors who occupied the room reporting that there seemed to be a non-human 'something' in the room.

Once the apartment happened to be occupied by a sensible lady who chanced to be a personal acquaintance of the hotel employee and she repeatedly complained that sometimes a man looked over her shoulder as she was seated at the mirror making up her face.

Another time, when the room was occupied by the wife of a well-known musician, she expostulated about seeing the reflection of a tall well-dressed man in dark clothes. In fact, a dozen or so visitors, all without previous knowledge of the reputation of the room, reported almost identical experiences.

After the employee and his wife had themselves experienced 'unpleasant sensations', they persuaded a local priest to visit the hotel and say Mass in the room. In the middle of the Eucharist a violent thunderstorm suddenly blew up and everyone began to feel that things were getting out of control. The service ended and the priest left but there was no lasting benefit.

Once, when the haunted room was occupied by a very level headed couple, a loud clinking noise disturbed their rest; a noise that sounded so close that it seemed to originate from the pillow on which their heads were lying. No explanation was ever discovered.

More recently, a frightened maid reported that she had encountered a strange man in one of the upstairs corridors; a man who disappeared into thin air as she watched.

Oliver St John Gogarty related in an article published in an American magazine some twenty years ago the story of Yeats and the Ghost of Renvyle. Once Mrs Yeats, who possessed mediumistic powers, saw a ghostly face at the window of her room.

Another time, during the course of a seance held in a room upstairs, the restive spirit of a young man manifested, a man who had died by his own hand in the room where the seance was held.

A Welsh medium encountered what may have been the same ghost and had the overwhelming impression of madness. He saw the figure, almost boy-like, dressed in brown velvet and a white shirt, standing beside a chair. The medium had the feeling that something awful was about to happen.

Slowly the apparition lifted its hands to its neck and squeezed. The body was violently agitated and it seemed certain to the medium that a suicide had taken place in the room.

Yeats believed he reached the suicide through automatic writing and learned that the ghost objected to strangers occupying the room.

In return, Yeats demanded that the ghost should cease to frighten children; he must not moan in the chimneys and fireplace or wander about the house scaring people with his unexpected appearances and disappearances and he must not move furniture or otherwise terrify those who occupied adjoining rooms.

For a while there was comparative peace as the agreed terms were honoured on both sides but soon a curious stranger succeeded in obtaining permission to occupy the room in question and altogether things are said to have been as disturbed as ever before they gradually faded. Instead a tall figure, thought to be Yeats himself, is still occasionally reported at Renvyle.

CORK, CO. CORK

One of the most charming cities in Ireland, although its ancient churches and abbeys, its old walls and its mellowed castles have all vanished, there are a number of ghosts and hauntings associated with the place and with the nearby fifteenth-century Blarney Castle.

Elliott O'Donnell told me of one interesting haunting he heard about from his grandmother who had known the people concerned. About a hundred years ago there lived in Cork an orphan girl named Amelia Jenkyns who was employed as a maid by a wealthy widow, Mrs Bishop. The lady also employed a young man named Andy O'Leary to do odd jobs around the house.

Andy and Amelia became good friends and after a time began to wonder what their mistress did most days when she would have a cup of coffee in the morning and then leave the house, always dressed fashionably and looking very smart. They learned that she was often seen at one of the finest hotels in Cork. They were puzzled, too, by the fact that she possessed wardrobes of fine clothes, purchased from some of the best shops in Ireland.

One dress in particular was admired by Amelia; it was red with large buttons all the way down the front and a very pretty little collar. Amelia had noticed it one morning and she was holding it against herself and admiring it when Mrs Bishop came into the room.

She was very annoyed and threatened to beat Amelia if she ever caught her touching any of her clothes again. The red dress was snatched away and put inside a wardrobe in a locked room. But she never forgot the angry and cruel look in her mistress's eyes.

Time passed and periodically Amelia and Andy would talk about the red dress and the locked room, wondering what other clothes were kept there. They were also puzzled about the kind of man Mr Bishop had been. One day they asked the milkman who told them that he remembered a distinguished-looking man with white hair who looked old enough to be Mrs Bishop's father.

He seemed to be independent and always had plenty of money. In those days Mr and Mrs Bishop used to winter in the South of France and while they were on one of these visits Mr Bishop died and was buried abroad.

Not long after they had received this information and let their imagination run riot, their thoughts turning again to the mysterious locked room, Amelia and Andy had a further subject to talk about together. One night Amelia had a strange dream in which Mrs Bishop took a key from a secret cavity beside the drawing-room fireplace and proceeded to unlock the room containing the red dress.

In her dream Amelia followed her mistress and tried to slip into the room behind her but she was unsuccessful and found the door slammed in her face. All that she had glimpsed through the open door had been a great four-poster bedstead.

Standing listening outside the room Amelia had heard the clink of coins and on the spur of the moment she had put her eye to the keyhole whereupon she had felt something hot burning her eye and this woke her up.

The dream made a great impression on her; she and Andy would talk about it time and time again. They became convinced that Mrs Bishop was a miser and that she kept hoards of money in the locked room. Gradually they became possessed with the idea of getting in, taking some of the money and running away together.

More than once Amelia set out to see if there was a secret cavity near the drawing-room fireplace but she either became frightened by memory of the cruel look she had once seen in Mrs Bishop's eyes or something happened to prevent her reaching the spot she had seen so plainly in her dream.

Once she thought she heard ominous raps that seemed to follow her as she stealthily crossed the hall towards the drawing-room; another time, as she was creeping downstairs, she thought she heard footsteps following her and she rushed back to her room in terror. Then one day she and Andy entered the drawing-room when Mrs Bishop was out.

They had been talking about all the wonderful things in the world that they had never seen. Amelia, who had never been to the theatre, decided to do some play-acting. As she had gone out, Mrs Bishop had said that she would not be back until evening and half-laughing and half-serious Amelia said she would dress-up in some of Mrs Bishop's lovely clothes.

She ran up to Mrs Bishop's room and picked up a silk dress. She put it on and strutted about the room. She took a big hat and put that on too. She rouged her face, pulled on a pair of French boots with high heels and went downstairs to show Andy. He was delighted and in all the excitement they decided to see whether there was a key to the locked room, as in Amelia's dream.

Hardly daring to breathe they stole across the hall and reached the drawing-room. At the door they stopped and after a moment Amelia tapped, gently at first and then more loudly. There was no sound from within the room. They opened the door and went in. Amelia went straight across to the fireplace and to the spot she had so clearly seen in her dream. She picked at a board and it opened. Inside was a key.

Shivering with excitement she snatched it up and ran with Andy to the mysterious locked room upstairs. Laughing and giggling to overcome their fear they inserted the key in the lock. It turned and they slowly opened the door and entered the room.

In the middle of the room, exactly as Amelia had seen in her dream, stood a massive four-poster bedstead with the curtains drawn back. Also in the room there were a couple of heavily carved chairs, an enormous gilt-framed mirror and in the corner a safe.

Amelia posed in front of the mirror, mimicking Mrs Bishop and admiring herself in the dress and hat, with Andy looking over her shoulder into the mirror with her. They saw the bedstead reflected in the mirror behind them and at the same moment they both saw that it was occupied. An old man lay on the bed on his back, apparently asleep.

He had white hair and a long white moustache. As they stared, open-mouthed and suddenly silent, they saw what appeared to be a large cupboard that they had not previously noticed.

The door opened and a lady emerged—it was Mrs Bishop! And yet, like the figure on the bed, there was something odd and unreal about her. She was dressed in a blue evening gown and she sparkled with jewellery: a beautiful necklace and brooch, rings and a magnificent bracelet. The figure tip-toed towards the bedstead, picked up a pillow and with a cruel, almost insane look on her face that Amelia recognized, placed the pillow carefully over the face of the sleeping man, pressing down with all her strength.

Amelia uttered an involuntary scream whereupon both figures vanished and Amelia and Andy found themselves again alone in the room. They looked at each other. Each was thinking the same thing. They had witnessed a ghostly re-enactment of what had once happened—Mrs Bishop had murdered her husband in that bedstead!

Amelia was the first to speak. In a voice that she hardly recognized as her own she said to Andy: 'I'll get the money and then we'll run away from here.' Andy only nodded; he found himself unable to speak. Amelia tried the safe and after some searching she must have touched a hidden spring for the door flew open. Inside there were lots of jewellery and piles of gold coins. Neither had ever seen such riches. Greedily Amelia thrust rings on her fingers, bracelets on her wrists and necklaces over her head.

In an ecstasy of delight she was dancing round the room when the door opened and Mrs Bishop stood there! Quick as a flash Andy slipped behind the open door. This was the real Mrs Bishop dressed as she had been when she went out a few hours before!

She was livid with rage. She made Amelia remove the jewellery, the hat, the dress, the boots; then catching hold of the girl's wrists in a cruel grip, she pulled her out of the room. Hardly daring to breathe, for Mrs Bishop had not seen him, Andy followed, ever ready to hide should his mistress glance back. But she was too intent on revenge; she took the weeping Amelia out of the house, saying never a word but determined and utterly relentless.

Through the bright moonlit streets of Cork they went and Andy saw that they were heading for the river.

Arriving at the banks of the Lee Mrs Bishop did not hesitate. She hustled Amelia towards a small yacht moored close by, and stepping aboard, dragged the terrified girl after her. Frightened but loyal, Andy crept close and through a porthole he saw Mrs Bishop force Amelia on to her knees.

Taking a piece of wire Mrs Bishop coiled it round the neck of poor Amelia and drew it tighter and tighter. Rigid with terror Andy watched as Amelia fell lifeless to the floor, realizing in an awful flash of comprehension that Mrs Bishop knew exactly what she was doing.

Amelia had no relatives, no friends, no one who would make enquiries about her. In a torment of remorse at not going to her aid, he crept away and fled back to the house. He did not know what to do.

Mrs Bishop returned, composed and acting as though nothing had happened. She told him that Amelia had run away but would probably be back with them soon. Andy just nodded and went on with his work.

He spoke to no one until about two weeks later when he told O'Donnell's grandmother, for whom he occasionally ran errands. Unbelieving at first, for Andy's story was incoherent and unconvincing, she at length told the police.

They questioned Andy who was still very frightened and his confused and unlikely story was not treated seriously. Nevertheless they saw Mrs Bishop and believed her when she told them that Amelia had run away, a thing she had done once or twice before. No further steps were taken in the matter.

Some weeks later Amelia's body was found in the River Lee, too decomposed to establish how she had met her death other than by drowning; but for years afterwards when the moon was full there were reports of a ghostly figure haunting the banks of the Lee; a poorly-clad young girl in black with a white, bloated face and a very frightened look in her eyes.

Five miles from Cork the square keep of Blarney Castle nestles on a lonely stretch of countryside overlooking the River Marta; its walls eighteen-feet thick and a hundred and twenty feet high, with delightful views of the surrounding country from the top.

The well-known Blarney Stone is in fact the sill of one of the machicolated battlements about twenty feet from the summit on the south side. The age-old custom of kissing the stone to acquire irresistible powers of persuasive eloquence, used to be accomplished by dangling head down, one's legs held by a guide.

The term 'blarney' was used by Queen Elizabeth I in referring to evasive answers she met from the castle owner at that time, McCarthy Mor, Lord of Muskerry, a descendant of Cormac Laidhir McCarthy who founded in 1446 the earlier castle that once occupied the site. There is an ancient rhyme that tells of the power of the stone:

> *There is a stone there*
>
> *That whoever kisses,*
>
> *Oh, he never misses*
>
> *To grow eloquent.*
>
> *'Tis he may clamber*
>
> *To a lady's chamber*
>
> *Or become a member*
>
> *of Parliament.*

DERRYGONELLY, NEAR ENNISKILLEN, CO. FERMANAGH

A farmer's cottage a couple of miles from Derrygonelly was the scene of a number of inexplicable happenings witnessed by Professor Sir William Barrett, F.R.S., an early Member of the Ghost Club (founded in 1862) and a former president of the Society for Psychical Research.

The three-roomed cottage consisted of a large living-room and two bedrooms, one of which was occupied by the farmer and his only son and the other by the farmer's four daughters. The eldest daughter, Maggie, was nearly twenty at the time of the disturbances; she was the apparent focus of the phenomena which generally began after all the occupants had retired to bed for the night.

The first noises were described as rappings and scratchings that sometimes lasted all through the night. Not unnaturally, these sounds were at first blamed on rats and mice but before long articles in the cottage were found to have been moved; boots, clothing, candles and cooking utensils being found outside the cottage in the morning after a night of bangs, raps and inexplicable noises.

The farmer, a Methodist by religion, sought advice and according to directions laid a Bible in the affected bedroom, its pages held open by means of a heavy stone. Far from having the desired effect the stone was lifted off the book and seventeen pages torn out.

Things became so bad that no lamp or candle would remain in the cottage and even a lamp borrowed from a neighbour and specially blessed and sprinkled with holy water by a priest disappeared during the night and was never seen again.

Sir William Barrett visited the cottage with a Mr Thomas Plunkett of Enniskillen and reported:

'After the children, except the boy, had gone to bed, Maggie lay down on the bed without undressing, so that her hands and feet could be observed. The rest of us sat round the kitchen fire, when faint raps, rapidly increasing in loudness, were heard coming apparently from the walls, the ceiling and various parts of the inner room, the door of which was open. On entering the bedroom with a light the noises at first ceased but re-commenced when I put the light on the window-sill in the kitchen-cum-livingroom.

'I had the boy and his father by my side, and asked Mr Plunkett to look round the house outside. Standing in the doorway leading to the affected bedroom, the noises re-commenced; the light was gradually brought nearer, and after much patience I was able to bring the light into the bedroom whilst the disturbances were still loudly going on.

'At last I was able to go up to the side of the bed, with the lighted candle in my hand, and closely observed each of the occupants lying on the bed. The younger children were apparently asleep, and Maggie was motionless; nevertheless, knocks were going on everywhere around, on the chairs, the bedstead, the walls and the ceiling. The closest scrutiny failed to detect any movement on the part of those present that could account for the noises, which were accompanied by a scratching or tearing sound.

'Suddenly a large pebble fell in my presence on to the bed; no one had moved to dislodge it, even if it had been placed for the purpose. When I replaced the candle on the window-sill of the kitchen, the knocks became still louder, like those made by a heavy carpenter's hammer driving nails into flooring.'

Afterwards Sir William Barrett paid three visits on consecutive nights to the cottage with Mr Plunkett and the Rev. Maxwell Close, M.A., a fellow-member of the Society for Psychical Research. Each time they all heard noises they could not explain although more than once they carried out a complete search of the cottage and garden.

When the farmer told the visitors that sometimes the ghost answered questions by means of raps ('although it tells lies as often as the truth'), Sir William asked mentally for a certain number of raps. Immediately the correct number was heard. He repeated this experiment on four occasions, with different numbers and the resulting raps were always the number he had thought of.

The end of the disturbances came when the Rev. Maxwell Close, at the request of the farmer, read some passages from the Bible, followed by the Lord's Prayer, to the accompaniment of many knockings and scratching noises. At first these were so loud that the parson's words could hardly be heard; but gradually the noises became quieter and ceased—and no further trouble was reported.

DUBLIN, CO. DUBLIN

There is a red-brick Georgian house in the district of Rathmines, occupied by a German professor in 1970 that has long been haunted. The writers James Joyce (1882-1941) and J. M. Synge (1871-1909) were born in the district. But the disturbances seem to be concerned rather with the living than the dead for it has been noticed that unexplained happenings often took place when the professor was absent from the premises.

On one occasion he returned home to find the house flooded from burst pipes. Another time electrical wall sockets seemed curiously 'alive' with sparks jumping from them when plugs were inserted, yet nothing happened when an electrician examined them and he could find no fault in the electric circuit.

When the professor, who was a widower, went away on holiday a friend (who was very sceptical of the paranormal) stayed at the house to look after it. He soon became aware of doors all over the house unaccountably opening and closing by themselves. Repeated study and investigation failed to solve the mystery. He also found the house inexplicably cold and often encountered a draught in the most unlikely places.

One night, while reading in bed, he watched with widening eyes as his bedroom door slowly and noiselessly opened. After a moment he got out of bed and closed the door, after ascertaining that nobody was in the house. Making sure that the door was securely shut, he returned to bed.

Moments later, as he watched, the door opened again. This continued time after time until the visitor decided to ignore the matter and leaving the door open he went to sleep. In the morning when he awakened it was shut tight.

On his return home the professor related a dream which he felt might have some bearing on the curious happenings at the house.

In the dream his wife, who had been dead for some years, appeared with a vividness that haunted him so much that he modelled a statue on the dream appearance; a statue that has a prominent place in the hall of the house to this day—so perhaps the happenings are related to a dead person after all.

St Michan's Church in Church Street is famous for its vaults containing mummified bodies. It is not surprising that there have been occasional reports of strange and inexplicable happenings here.

Most of the accounts are vague but one visitor told me that while she and her husband were being shown the macabre remains, they all heard bursts of incessant loud whispering, as though a number of people were engaged in a violent argument in the dry and still atmosphere. The verger told them that the sounds were heard quite often but no explanation was forthcoming. They gained the impression that it was one of those things that are not discussed. Another visitor maintains that there is one 'mummy' or his ethereal counterpart, that has been seen in several of the family vaults. Certainly, visitors often become confused when they ask about these particular remains and then find that the body is no longer in the position that it had occupied a short time previously.

There are about thirty mummies in open coffins in the vaults of this small and unpretentious church built on the site of an ancient oak forest which, for some obscure reason, has made the air in the vaults incredibly dry.

There is row upon row of perfectly preserved bodies, dark brown with age. The coffins often disintegrate but the bodies remain. Some years ago a visitor placed a bunch of flowers near some of the pathetic human remains—and bodies within a distance of six feet started to decay, affected by the water in the flowers.

An old house in Fitzwilliam Square has long been haunted by a ghost known as 'Lady Reid', an entity that is blamed for lost objects, articles that are moved from their accustomed positions and various noises and disturbances for which no rational explanation can be found.

Mrs Burnett Smith (the Scottish writer known as Annie S. Swan) told me that during several visits to the house when it was occupied by family friends, she experienced happenings which she was totally unable to explain and for which the inhabitants of the house invariably blamed 'Lady Reid'.

During the course of one visit Mrs Burnett Smith occupied a bedroom with her hostess and in the night a terrific noise awakened her. She discovered that a Venetian blind had been pulled up.

It seemed impossible that it had been done by human hands but Mrs Burnett Smith's hostess was by no means surprised at such happenings, which she said occurred all the time. She merely remarked, 'Oh, it's just Lady Reid,' and went back to sleep.

During the course of her stay on one occasion Mrs Burnett Smith was to learn more about 'Lady Reid's' activities, which she related to me in a calm and detached tone, carrying great conviction and utter acceptance. A blue dinner dress disappeared from a settee and was later found underneath a bed, tightly rolled up and badly creased.

One night all the shoes belonging to everyone in the house were moved into one room. Nocturnal noises, for which no explanation was ever discovered, "were a common experience. Scores of articles were found moved from their accustomed places, usually during the night. Toilet requisites and dressing-tables seemed to hold a particular attraction for 'Lady Reid'.

The guest-room was particularly plagued and things became so bad at one time that no one would enter it by themselves. Servants, attending to the making of beds in the morning and again, turning down the beds in the evening, would make a point of 'doing' this room in pairs, mounting the stairs to the guest-room hand in hand and crossing themselves at every step.

A serious investigation of this room would have been interesting but Mrs Burnett Smith's attempts in this direction on my behalf were unsuccessful. The occupants rather enjoyed their ghost and were reluctant to do anything that might annoy her.

When Number 118 Summerhill was being demolished in 1966 the workmen had considerable trouble with ghosts. Six local men claimed they were persistently kept from completing the demolition. Ultimately they refused to work on the property at all unless they were all together on the same floor —and in daylight. They claimed to have seen the apparition of a tall man on three separate occasions.

One of the men, William McGregor, collapsed in a faint when he saw what he described as a tall man wearing a striped shirt. His fellow workman, Mr Joseph Byrne, claimed that he saw a similar figure in the basement, while a Mr Kearney asserted that he had seen the same apparition on three occasions and each time on a different floor of the haunted house.

Elliott O'Donnell once talked to me about a house that used to stand near St Shepherds Grove haunted by the ghost of an unidentified old woman.

The house, it appears, had stood empty for years before a retired colonel rented it furnished for a year, although it had neither gas nor electricity. Colonel Ward's wife and children moved in early one December and it was arranged that the colonel, who had some business to attend to abroad, would join them as soon as he could; certainly in time for the family to spend Christmas together in their new home.

A few days after they had moved into the house Mrs Ward was quietly doing some embroidery in front of the fire one evening when the children were in bed. Suddenly she was surprised to hear a sharp rap on the front door. Wondering who it could possibly be, she listened carefully, recalling that it was the servants' day off. After a moment there was another knock, sharp and somehow authoritative, sounding as though it was made with bare knuckles.

Mrs Ward put her embroidery on one side and answered the

door. Standing on the step was an old woman wearing a lace mob-cap and dressed in strangely old-fashioned clothes. She was ugly, even repulsive. Mrs Ward was about to shut the door in her face, for the old woman had said not a word but simply peered into the house behind her.

Now she quickly raised a skinny hand in a menacing fashion, leered stupidly, pushed past Mrs Ward and ran across the hall and up the stairs with remarkable agility for someone of her apparent age. Startled, Mrs Ward watched her as she seemed to enter one of the maids' rooms; deciding that she must be a friend or relative of the servant, she closed the door and went back to her embroidery.

Next day Colonel Ward arrived and the same night he sat up late, working on some papers. It was past midnight when he picked up a candle and went into the hall on his way upstairs to bed. As he was about to mount the first step he thought he heard a movement from the direction of the front door.

Turning, he found himself face to face with the old hag whom his wife had seen the previous evening. He said afterwards that an odd light seemed to envelop the figure and her pale old eyes seemed to glow maliciously as they met the colonel's surprised gaze.

'Who are you?' demanded the colonel, thrusting the candle towards the woman, but she made no reply and suddenly rushed past him, leering in his face as she did so and ran up the stairs. Near a bend in the stairway she paused, turned, shook a fist at the colonel, turned away from him and vanished. The colonel searched carefully everywhere but could find no trace of the mysterious figure.

The following day Mrs Ward's brother, Jack Deane, arrived from Sandhurst to spend Christmas in Dublin. That evening he saw the old woman, whom he took to be a servant, as he was carrying his boots to the kitchen to be cleaned.

When he addressed the woman, she stared back insolently at him and did not answer so he tossed a boot towards her, saying, 'Here, clean these, I said.' To his astonishment the boot appeared to pass clean through the woman. He threw the other boot and the same thing happened. Hardly able to believe his eyes, Jack took a step towards the woman whereupon she slowly disappeared as he watched.

As soon as he saw his sister next morning Jack said he thought he must have been overdoing it at Sandhurst and must be suffering from hallucinations. Only then did Mrs Ward tell him that both she and her husband had seen the same figure and were equally unable to account for her appearance or disappearance.

Next day all three were in the hall in the evening discussing the party they had arranged for the children the following day when they heard rattling sounds of glass and china. They had previously laid out the china and glasses on a table in the drawing-room and they all hastened there to see what was happening.

As they opened the door they were startled by a tremendous crashing sound. They could do nothing but stand in the doorway and watch as all the china and glass on the table slid to the floor and smashed upon itself.

As they looked round the room they were amazed to see, lying on the floor by the fireplace, the hideous sight of the body of a boy aged about twelve years, almost covered in blood.

Bending over the body, a look of murderous triumph on her face, was a young woman, dressed in clothes of a bygone age, her jewellery and gold ornaments glittering in the weird and inexplicable light that played over the whole scene, while to one side crouched the old hag, leering and swaying backwards and forwards with glee; a devilish and nauseating scene.

As the three people stood horror-stricken in the doorway,

the whole room darkened, the figures disappeared and an uncanny silence reigned. Although it was Christmas, next day the Wards moved out of that haunted house.

ERINGLE TRUAGH, CO. MONAGHAN

The old church has long disappeared and only a couple of ivy-covered gables remained a few years ago to mark the site of the churchyard that was famous for its 'phantom of death'.

William Carleton (1794-1869) the Irish novelist, youngest of fourteen children of a farmer, who acquired an insight into the ideas and feelings of Irish peasantry that has never been equalled, became interested in the haunting, visited Eringle Truagh and wrote afterwards:

I have been shown the grave of a young person about eighteen years of age, who was said about four months before to have fallen a victim to the phantom, and it is not more than ten weeks since a man in the same parish declared that he gave a promise and fatal kiss to the ghost and consequently looked upon himself as lost.

He took a fever and was buried on the day appointed for the meeting, which was exactly a month from the time of his contact with the spirit. Incredulous as it may seem the friends of these two persons declared, at least those of the young man did, to myself that particulars of the meetings with the phantom were detailed repeatedly by the two persons without variation. There are several other cases of the same kind mentioned, but the two alluded to are the only ones that came within my personal knowledge.

The centuries-old tradition that this churchyard was haunted by a handsome young person is one of the most interesting cases of haunting in the annals of Irish ghost-lore. The phantom of death usually appeared in the churchyard and only after the funeral of an inhabitant of Eringle Truagh. To men the phantom appeared as a beautiful young girl and to girls as a handsome young man.

Through all the scores of reports of the appearance of this phantom runs a strikingly similar story. A man or woman, present at the burial of a local person, would linger on in the churchyard after everyone else had left, thinking perhaps to delay for a little while the last parting from someone near or dear to them.

Suddenly they would be confronted by a strikingly beautiful girl (or if it was a woman by a singularly handsome man). In either case the stranger would show the mourner great sympathy and comfort by assuring the bereaved that the dead person was far happier than he or she would have been had they lived. Gradually the sympathetic words and actions would console the sad mourner.

As the two progressed towards the church and then sat side by side in the porch or on the low churchyard wall in the dying sunlight, the magnetic attraction of the mysterious comforter would begin to work its power. From a gentle hand clasp to an arm around the shoulder, from a gentle squeeze of the waist to a light kiss and before long the couple would forget everything but themselves. Alone together in the dusk passionate embraces would follow one after the other until, almost as in a dream, they would make desperate and wonderful love together in the deserted churchyard.

Afterwards, as they promised eternal love for each other, a pact would be made to meet again in the churchyard four weeks hence. After a lingering kiss, the former mourner would depart in a quandary of sadness and happiness.

If he, or she, should chance to look back they would see no sign of the mysterious and beautiful lover. Perhaps then, but only then, would they recall the awful story of the traditional phantom of death in Eringle Truagh churchyard; wide-eyed and panic-stricken, they would rush to relatives, friends, and the parish priest, imploring for something to be done to save them.

But neither prayers, nor the love and friendship of any mortal could save them. The shock that they had suffered and the suspense of waiting for the four weeks to pass would make them ill; they would fade and die and, on the very date that they had pledged to meet the phantom, they would be taken to the churchyard in a coffin.

There are a few records of the phantom appearing outside the churchyard at weddings, christenings and dances. But always the last kiss sealed a promise to meet in the churchyard four weeks hence—and always the promise was kept by the mortal arriving on the agreed day, for burial.

GIANT'S CAUSEWAY, CO. ANTRIM

This impressive promontory of closely packed greyish-brown basalt columns, the result of crystallization of molten lava thrown up during a volcanic eruption in the Tertiary period, is one of the natural wonders of the world.

There are in all some 40,000 hexagonal and pentagonal columns, perfectly articulated by means of convex and concave joints and the causeway extends almost half a mile into the sea. The bright red bands in the cliffs represent quiescent periods between volcanic eruptions.

The legendary origin of the Giant's Causeway suggests that it was built by Finn M'Coul or Fingal as a bridge between Ireland and Scotland for the giants of those days to cross from Antrim to Staffa, where Fingal's Cave on the Hebridean island has a similar fantastically old and primitive atmosphere

In this area of ruined castles, high towering cliffs and bays that are the graveyards of many stout ships (including at least one vessel from the Spanish Armada) it is not surprising that there are stories of strange mutterings and indistinct words being heard suddenly for a moment and then fading away with the wind.

There are weirdly loud and echoing footsteps, heard when they are least expected. Some of the features of the Causeway: the Wishing Well, the Giant's Organ, the Wishing Chair, Lord Antrim's Parlour, the Lady's Fan, the Mitre and the Coffin, are said to change shape inexplicably at night and disappear occasionally altogether for a while.

KILKENNY CITY, CO. KILKENNY

This city on the River Nore, once divided into two districts, Englishtown and Irishtown, has a thirteenth-century cathedral, ruins of a Dominican and of a Franciscan monastery, a college attended by satirist Jonathan Swift (1667-1745)—and a ghostly woman on crutches.

This singular figure, tall and thin, wears a long coat, no stockings and has long, white, flowing hair. She has been seen repeatedly in the vicinity of St John's Parochial Hall.

A young nurse and her boyfriend saw the figure pass their parked car in May 1967, after they were alerted by a barking dog. As the figure passed they were able to see it clearly, although they could not distinguish the face. A moment later the road was deserted. Frightened, the couple drove a short distance along the road and when they stopped again the same figure appeared, passed the car again—and promptly disappeared.

Other witnesses for the strange figure include a priest and a local couple who have seen the apparition on a number of occasions, usually in the springtime.

KILLARNEY, CO. KERRY

The Irish hero O'Donoghue is said to haunt this world-renowned beauty spot, beloved by Scott, Wordsworth, Tennyson and Thackeray, mounted on his favourite white horse.

At dawn each May 1st his ghost is reputed to glide over the waters of Lough Leane, preceded by groups of youths and maidens who scatter wreaths of spring flowers in his path.

Among a number of legends associated with the lake and the O'Donoghues, there is one concerning a beautiful young girl who became so completely possessed by her love for the visionary chieftain and his snow-white steed that, sick with love for the unattainable, she threw herself, one May-day dawn, into the lough so that she might join him.

The legend is immortalized in Thomas Moore's 'O'Donoghue's Mistress':

> *Of all the fair months, that round the sun*
> *In light-linked dance their circles run,*
> *Sweet May, sweet May, shine thou for me!*
> *For still when they earliest beams arise,*
> *That youth who beneath the blue lake lies,*
> *Sweet May, sweet May, returns to me.*
>
> *Of all the smooth lakes, where daylight leaves*
> *His lingering smile on golden eaves,*
> *Fair lake, fair lake, thou'rt dear to me;*
> *For when the last April sun grows dim,*
> *Thy Naiads prepare his steed for him*
> *Who dwells, who dwells, bright lake, in thee.*
>
> *Of all the proud steeds that ever bare*
> *Young plumed chiefs on sea or shore,*
> *White steed, white steed, most joy to thee,*
> *Who still, with the first young glance of spring,*
> *From under that glorious lake dost bring,*
> *Proud steed, proud steed, my love to me.*
>
> *While white as the sail some bark unfurls,*
> *When newly launched, thy long mane curls,*
> *Fair steed, fair steed, as white and free;*

And spirits from all the lake's deep bowers
Glide o'er the blue wave scattering flowers,
Fair steed, around my love and thee.

Of all the sweet deaths that maidens die,
Whose lovers beneath the cold waves lie,
Most sweet, most sweet that death will be,
Which under the next May evenings' light,
When thou and thy steed are lost to sight,
Dear love, dear love, I'll die for thee.

There is a statue of Thomas Moore (1779-1852) in the centre of Dublin City. And the Killarney boatmen still refer to the crested waves that rise from time to time upon the lough as 'O'Donoghue's white horses'.

KINSALE, CO. CORK

This picturesque little port, a maze of narrow streets and steep passages, has a rocky coast with a lighthouse which is the first sight of Britain for ships coming from the United States of America. Here the Lusitania was sunk in 1915 and three of the victims are buried in the churchyard, including an unidentified woman.

Charles, or Kinsale, Fort is one of the first examples of military architecture in the world; it dates from 1677, and it is haunted by a 'White Lady'.

The traditional story of the origin of the haunting concerns a certain Colonel Warrender, a man known for his severe disciplinarian outlook. Warrender was appointed governor soon after the fort was built. He had a daughter, a girl with the unusual Christian name of 'Wilful' who became engaged to be married to a Sir Trevor Ashurst.

On the evening of their wedding day, as they strolled along the battlements of the fort, hand in hand, in the still, warm evening, Wilful pointed to some unusual flowers growing on the rocks below the fort. As they passed a sentry the young bride expressed a wish to have the flowers. The sentry, smiling at the newlyweds, volunteered to climb down and pick the flowers, if Sir Trevor would take his place while he did so.

Eager to please his bride Sir Trevor quickly buttoned on the sentry's coat and took his musket while the soldier went in search of a rope to lower himself over the side of the fort. Having secured his line the soldier disappeared over the parapet and Sir Trevor took up sentry duty.

Time passed and Wilful began to complain of the chilly night air. Sir Trevor knew that he must wait for the return of the soldier but his young bride went inside to their apartment. Still the sentry did not return and Sir Trevor, heavy with exhaustion after a tiring day and the jollification of the occasion, soon dozed off to sleep.

He was still asleep when the governor made one of his accustomed rounds of the sentries and receiving no answer to his challenge, he perceived that the man was asleep, whereupon he drew a pistol and shot his son-in-law through the heart.

As soon as she learned of the fate that had overtaken her husband, the distracted bride rushed from the apartment and threw herself over the battlements. On learning of the double tragedy her father shot himself during that awful night.

Over the years there has been some variation in the details of the story. Other accounts give the governor's name as Browne; the initial victim as the governor's son and date the affair around the middle of the eighteenth century. All agree, however, that the ghostly White Lady has its origin in the suicide of a young bride on her wedding day and there are many reports of the sighting of this ghost.

After service in the Peninsular War of 1808-14 a certain Major Black became Fort Major at Kinsale. He related an experience which befell him to a number of his friends and to his physician, Dr Craig, who published the story in Real Pictures of Clerical Life in Ireland.

One summer evening Major Black went to the hall door of his apartment at Charles Fort and was astounded to see a lady enter through the doorway and walk up the stairs. At first he thought she must be the wife of an officer who had somehow entered the wrong apartment, but as he looked closely at her mounting the stairs without making a sound, he observed that she was dressed entirely in white, in a very old-fashioned style.

Filled with curiosity but with never a thought of anything ghostly, he hurried upstairs and followed her within seconds into one of the bedrooms; yet on entering the room he could not find the slightest trace of anyone. Only then did he recall the story of the mysterious White Lady, reputed to have long haunted Charles Fort.

On another occasion Major Black recounted that two of his sergeants were packing some articles for him. One of the men had his little daughter with him and the child suddenly asked: 'Who is that White Lady bending over the banisters and looking down at us?' The two men looked up and saw nothing but the child insisted that she had seen a young lady, dressed all in white, smiling down at her.

Some years later a married staff officer and his wife, living in the apartments known as the 'Governor's House', were awakened by their children's nurse who had been sleeping in a room adjoining the apartment known as the 'White Lady's Room'.

The nurse said she had been lying awake, listening to the children's deep and regular breathing when she suddenly saw the figure of a lady clothed in white glide noiselessly from the direction of the White Lady's Room towards the cot containing the youngest child. After gazing at the child for a moment, the figure placed its hand upon the child's wrist, whereupon it immediately started and cried out: 'Take your cold hand from my wrist!' The next moment the White Lady disappeared.

About a hundred years ago a certain Captain Marvell Hull and his friend, Lieutenant Hartland, were on their way to the captain's room for a drink together. As they reached a small landing on the staircase they both saw in front of them a woman in a white dress.

A moment before she had not been there and they had heard no sound. Startled by the sudden and inexplicable appearance, the two officers stopped in their tracks, whereupon the figure turned, looked at them, then passed them silently and disappeared through a locked door. Afterwards they said that the face was that of a beautiful young woman, but colourless and with a corpse-like appearance.

Fifty or so years ago a surgeon had a more terrifying experience. He had quarters at the fort and returned from snipe-shooting as the fort mess bugle rang out. He hastened to his rooms to change but when he failed to appear for the meal, one of his brother officers went in search of him and found him lying senseless at the bottom of the steps leading to his rooms.

On recovering consciousness he related that as he hurriedly stooped down to retrieve the key of his door, which he kept under the mat, he felt himself dragged violently across the hall and flung down a flight of steps. As he fell, he caught sight of a white figure which he thought looked like a woman in a wedding-dress.

Not long after the surgeon's experience a Captain Jarves was puzzled one evening to hear a strange rattling noise as he approached his bedroom at the fort and he caught a glimpse of a white figure hurrying away.

When he attempted to open the bedroom door to see what was happening, it seemed to be locked and he could not open it. Thinking that some of his brother officers were playing a joke on him, he called out and tried to force the door inwards. At this a gust of wind suddenly passed him and some unseen power flung him down the stairs where he lay senseless for some time.

In recent years visitors have reported seeing a vague white form in the vicinity of Charles Fort, especially on still summer evenings; a form that disappears almost as soon as one becomes aware that it is there.

LOUGH DERG, ON THE BORDERS OF CO. CLARE, CO. GALWAY AND CO. TIPPERARY

The lowest and the largest of the great lakes formed by the River Shannon. It is said to be haunted by several ghosts; indefinite, wispy figures from the past who have never been identified but those who meet such forms along the shores of this beautiful lake never forget the encounters.

The lake is also said to have a phantom boat which always travels northwards, with the sound of its oars dipping the water and faint voices and music plainly audible to passers-by on dark nights, when the boat itself is not visible.

Those who have seen the boat, on still moonlit nights, have always said that it appeared to be deserted although the rhythmic oars carried it swiftly over the deep and dark waters. Once an Englishman, seeing the strange boat with no visible being aboard, threw a stone at it—whereupon the stone was thrown back at him with great violence. He also heard peals of mocking laughter which frightened him so that he fled and has never since returned to the haunted lake.

LOUGH GUR, CO. LIMERICK

A pretty lake where, according to legend, the last of the Desmonds holds eternal court beneath the waves, emerging every seventh year on a silver-shod steed. On the banks of the lake there are castles and cramogs, dolmens, circles and raths; it is an area much associated with the distant past and perhaps it is not to be wondered at that some faint remnants of bygone ages linger in this beautiful and unspoilt spot.

It is said that the last Earl of Desmond, as famed for his magical practises as for his doughty deeds in battle, one day brought his young and lovely bride to his castle. Being as innocent as she was beautiful and ignorant of the forces of magic she came one morning to the chamber where her husband studied and practised the black arts, imploring him to let her see some of the wonders which he said he could perform.

For a time he refused but he was much in love and could deny his young bride nothing for very long; so eventually he agreed but warned her that whatever happened she was not to speak or utter a sound.

She gave him her solemn promise and with a last warning gesture he moved into the centre of the chamber, muttered an incantation—and feathers sprouted thickly all over him. His face contracted and became hooked, his head shrank, his arms disappeared; the air became filled with a cadaverous smell and in the place of her husband, a huge vulture rose in his place. It swept round the room on heavy, beating wings, threatening every now and then to pounce with its great claws and beak.

But still, with tremendous effort, the Countess remained still and calm and she uttered not a sound. The vulture alighted on the floor near the door, ruffed up its feathers, shook itself, shrank and then swelled in a peculiar way; the next moment a hideous and horribly deformed hag crouched in its place, the flabby and discoloured skin hanging about her face, with thin, yellow hair and great bloodshot eyes.

Dwarfish in stature, she waddled towards the Countess on tiny, thick crutches, her toothless mouth slobbering, her grimaces and contortions becoming more and more frightening as she approached. Suddenly, a few feet from the Countess (still by superhuman effort keeping motionless and silent) the hag gave a screech and collapsed on the floor.

No sooner had she done so than she turned into an enormous snake, rising up and towering over the Countess, seemingly about to strike at any moment. At the instant that the creature struck the snake changed into her husband who stood before his wife, a finger to his lips, motioning her to remain silent.

He then lay full length on the floor and began to stretch himself from the waist: his legs and lower trunk slithered at alarming speed away from the rest of his body while his head and chest drew away in the opposite direction until his feet touched one end of the chamber and his head the other.

As his head rolled and seemed about to become detached from his body the Countess's fortitude gave way and she screamed with every ounce of her strength. Immediately the walls slid downwards, the whole edifice sank into Lough Gur and the dark waters closed over the castle.

One night in every seven years the ghost of the last Earl of Desmond—and some say his lovely wife, too—emerge from their watery grave. Mounted on a coal-black horse they ride back and forth across the waters with the silver shoes of the horse shining in the moonlight. As dawn breaks, they plunge back into the depths of Lough Gur for another seven years and they are doomed to return again and again until the silver shoes of their steed wear out.

OUGHTERARD, CO. GALWAY

Nearby are the ruins of the principal stronghold of the O'Flahertys, Aughnanure Castle. This family was such a scourge in the Middle Ages that the whole area of the rock-bound uplands of Iar Connacht was known as the country of the Flahertys. Over the west gate of Galway City stood the inscription: 'From the fury of the O'Flahertys Good Lord deliver us.'

The great banqueting hall and keep tower of Aughnanure Castle date from the sixteenth century. It is from here that an

O'Flaherty was setting out one night on a foraging expedition when he heard the family banshee singing sadly from one of the castle turrets. He said nothing to his wife but the following night she, too, heard the lament.

Two days later her husband's body was brought back to the castle; he had been killed in a clan feud. Here too, it is said, several banshees were heard singing sorrowfully before the death of the wife of an O'Flaherty clan chief.

PORTLAW, CO. WATERFORD

Curraghmore House, to the west, is the seat of the Marquess of Waterford and memorial to the famous legend of 'The Tyrone Ghost'. A manuscript account of the tale, firmly accepted by successive generations, is preserved at Curraghmore. It was written by the Lady Elizabeth Cobb, grand-daughter of the Lady Beresford to whom Lord Tyrone is said to have appeared after his death.

Lady Beresford's son, Lord Tyrone, and her daughter, Lady Riverston (who both died in 1763) were with their mother at the time of her death. They removed from her wrist the black tape which she had worn on all occasions and at all times, even at Court, a fact repeatedly vouched for by witnesses. There existed for many years an oil painting of this Lady Beresford at Tyrone House, Dublin, with a black ribbon visible on one wrist.

This painting, incidentally, disappeared in a peculiar manner. It hung, with other family portraits, in the main drawing-room at Tyrone House and when Henry, Marquis of Waterford, sold the family's town residence to the Government, he arranged for Mr Watkins, a well-known dealer in pictures, to collect the paintings and objets d'art for removal to Curraghmore.

Mr Watkins was interested in the legend and saw to it that this particular picture was carefully packed for transportation. When the consignment was received at Curraghmore, however, the picture had disappeared and in spite of considerable exertions and inquiries on the part of Mr Watkins and the Tyrone family, it has not been located to this day.

John le Poer, Lord Decies (1665-1693) succeeded as Lord Tyrone in 1690 and is the ghost of the story. This Lord Tyrone made a serious pact with Nicola Hamilton, the daughter of Hugh, Lord Glenawley (who married Sir Tristram Beresford in 1687) that whichever of them should die first, would—if possible—appear to the other with the object of proving life after death.

In October 1693 Sir Tristram and Lady Beresford were visiting the latter's sister, Lady MacGill at Gill Hall. One morning Sir Tristram rose early leaving Lady Beresford asleep and went for a walk before breakfast.

On his return his wife joined him and their hostess but she seemed agitated and embarrassed. Her husband asked after her health and questioned her as to what had happened to her wrist which he and others present had noticed was tied up with black ribbon. Lady Beresford implored her husband and others not to question her, either then or later about the reason she wore the ribbon, adding, 'You will never more see me without it.'

After breakfast she was anxious to know whether the post had arrived. It had not and Sir Tristram asked her whether she was expecting any particular letter that day. She replied that she expected to hear of Lord Tyrone's death, which she felt certain had taken place on the previous Tuesday.

Sir Tristram concluded that his wife must have had a vivid dream and said so, adding that he had never considered her to be a superstitious person but perhaps he should now revise his opinion!

Within minutes a servant brought in the post including one envelope sealed with black wax. 'As I expected,' exclaimed Lady Beresford, 'he is dead.' The letter was from Lord Tyrone's steward to inform them that his master had died in Dublin on Tuesday, October 14th, at 4 p.m.

Sir Tristram consoled his wife, distraught at the news and yet somehow relieved and easier now that her uncertainty had become fact. She then told her husband that she was with child, adding that she would have a son. A boy was born the following July; Sir Tristram survived the birth by only a few years.

Lady Beresford continued to reside, with her young family, at their home in Co. Derry. She seldom went out and had few friends, with the exception of a Mr and Mrs Jackson of Coleraine. Mr Jackson was a leading local citizen and, through his mother, related to Sir Tristram. Mrs Jackson was descended from Sir Adam Lofters, and a relation of theirs, Richard Gorges, married Lady Beresford some three years later, in 1704.

They had a son and two daughters before his wild and dissolute conduct forced Lady Beresford to seek a separation which she obtained. Four years later her husband, then General Gorges, expressed repeated regret for his misdeeds. On the strength of solemn promises for the future, Lady Beresford agreed to his return and she became the mother of another boy.

A month after the birth of this infant, on the occasion of Lady Beresford's birthday, she sent for her eldest son, Sir Marcus Beresford, then twenty years old and her married daughter Lady Riverston. She also invited Dr King, archbishop of Dublin (an old friend) and the elderly clergyman who had christened her and who had always maintained a kindly interest in her life.

During the course of conversation with the clergyman Lady Beresford remarked that she was forty-eight that day, whereupon her old friend said 'no' she was forty-seven. He went on to say that Lady Beresford's mother had a discussion with him once about her daughter's age and he consulted the registry; so he could say with complete certainty that she was forty-seven that day.

This news brought consternation to Lady Beresford who told

her friend that what he had said was in effect a death warrant. She implored him to leave her for she was convinced that she did not have long to live and had a number of things to settle before she died. She asked for her son and daughter to be sent to her immediately.

When her two children were in her presence Lady Beresford told them that she had something of great importance to communicate—before she died. She reminded her son and daughter of the friendship and affection that existed in their early life between Lord Tyrone and herself. She revealed the pact they had made that whichever of the two died first should, if possible, appear to the other as proof of life after death.

One night, Lady Beresford said, many years after this, she was sleeping with the children's father at Gill Hall when she suddenly found herself awake and saw Lord Tyrone sitting on her side of the bed. Lord Tyrone told her that he had died the previous Tuesday at four o'clock and said he had been permitted to appear to assure her of the truth of life after death.

He was further allowed to inform her that she was with child and would produce a son who would marry an heiress, that Sir Tristram would not live long and that she would remarry and die from the effects of childbearing in her forty-seventh year.

Lady Beresford begged Lord Tyrone for some convincing sign or proof of his presence so that in the morning she would know that it had not been a dream; whereupon Lord Tyrone hooked up the bed hangings in an unusual manner through an iron hook and wrote his signature in her pocket book.

But still she was not satisfied and, after she had asked for still more substantial proof, placed his hand, which was as cold as marble, on her wrist for a moment and immediately the sinews shrank and the nerves withered at the touch. Warning her never to let anyone see the mark. Lord Tyrone vanished. In the morning, after Sir Tristram had gone for an early walk,

Lady Beresford arose and with great difficulty succeeded in unhooking the bed curtains.

She bound up her wrist with black ribbon and went down to breakfast, quite certain that Lord Tyrone was indeed dead and had visited her that night. She stated that under the impression she had passed her forty-seventh birthday, she had consented to a reconciliation with her husband but now that she knew she was only forty-seven that day, she was certain she was about to die. She instructed her two children, after her death, to unbind the black ribbon and look at her wrist before it was consumed in her coffin.

An hour later Lady Beresford was dead and after everyone had left the bedroom, her son and daughter untied the black ribbon and found their mother's wrist to be exactly as she had described it; the nerves withered and the sinews shrunk. She was buried by her clergyman friend in the Cathedral of St Patrick, Dublin, in the Earl of Cork's tomb, where she lies to this day.

Lady Beresford's son Sir Marcus later married Lord Tyrone's daughter and both he and his sister always swore to the truth of the story for the rest of their lives. Lady Elizabeth Cobb, grand daughter of Lady Beresford, preserved both the ribbon and the notebook with the signature of a ghost, for many years at her home in Bath.

RANDALSTOWN, NEAR ANTRIM, CO. ANTRIM

During the summer months there are motorboat trips from Antrim, with its beautiful French garden and one of the only two complete Round Towers in Ulster, to Shane's Castle by Lough Neagh. This is the largest inland lake in the British Isles; the waters are reputed to have petrifying qualities and pieces of fossilized wood are often to be found on its shores.

Sixteenth-century Shane's Castle was built on the site of the Castle of Edenduffcarrick, mentioned in the Annals of Ulster under the date of 1470 and destroyed in 1490. Shane's Castle was the ancient stronghold of Shane O'Neill of the O'Neills of Clandeboye and the estate is still owned by Lord O'Neill.

Although most of the later castle was destroyed by fire in 1922, a fine square tower still exists and in the remaining south wall, about thirty feet from the ground there is the sculptured head known as the Black Head of the O'Neills. For centuries there has been a tradition that if this head should be injured, the O'Neill family would come to an end.

The O'Neills have a banshee which has been known to appear at Shane's Castle in the form of a beautiful young woman, seen in one particular room at the castle, pacing to and fro, wringing her hands in sadness and singing a soulful lament. Such an appearance invariably heralded the death of the member of the O'Neill family who heard the banshee wailing.

It is related that a young O'Neill once heard the singing voice just before he set out on a long journey; a few days later he ran into an unexpected skirmish and was killed.

RATHFARNHAM, CO. DUBLIN

The pond in the grounds of the old castle is haunted by the ghost of a dog.

In the severe winter of 1840-41 a skating party was enjoying the seasonal weather. Among the skaters was a man who had with him a 'very fine curly-coated retriever dog', and the animal seemed to be enjoying the fun as much as its master.

At the height of the sport the ice gave way and the man disappeared into the freezing water. Without hesitation the dog went after his master but both man and dog were drowned.

A monument was erected to perpetuate the dog's heroic self-sacrifice and although today no more than the pedestal remains, the ghost of the faithful dog haunts the grounds of the castle; its form has also been seen many times on the public road between the gates of the sixteenth-century castle and Dodder Bridge.

RATHLIN ISLAND, CO. ANTRIM

Five miles north of Ballycastle, across a tide-race that can often be treacherous and is always exciting, this island, shaped like 'an Irish stocking', has seen many historical events. Now its massive cliffs offer sanctuary to numerous sea birds.

The island has often served as a stepping-stone between Scotland and Ireland. One of Marconi's early successful attempts at radio communication took place between Ballycastle and Rathlin and there is a cave near the lighthouse which has long been regarded as the place where Robert the Bruce (1274-1329, King of Scotland) had his famous encounter with a spider. The king's body was buried at Dunfermline, his heart at Melrose.

There are those who maintain that the ghost of Robert Bruce has been glimpsed, motionless, at the shadowy far end of a cave on Rathlin Island where, reputedly, he so often silently meditated during his lifetime.

If his ghost has been seen here, it is such an indistinct, wispy, half-materialization that no witness is entirely sure whether shadows and uncertain light cannot account for what they have seen.

SKERRIES, CO. DUBLIN

A few miles inland there is a field, part of a large estate, that has not been cultivated or used since time immemorial. It comprises a clearing in the centre of a luxurious plantation and it has been suggested that the trees were originally planted to conceal the unused and unusable land.

In the centre of the field there is a very large depression which extends to an area of some forty square yards and has a depth of about two feet. Legend has it that in the very early days of Christianity in Ireland a devout and holy woman and her selected followers had a foundation here.

The woman was called Maeve or Mavoe or Mevee (referred to in those days as Saint Mevee) and her establishment were known for their piety and goodness and for the many miracles for which they are said to have been responsible, miracles that made the very ground here hallowed and secret.

Years passed and the well-loved foundation of Sister Mevee was no more than a memory when the land passed into the possession of a man who laughed at local awe and superstition concerning the holy field.

Time and again he was quietly warned against desecrating the soil but undeterred he put plough to it and began to work, repeating a mocking ditty as he strode across the virgin soil: 'Saint Mevee or Saint Mavoe, I'll plough this up before I go.'

Hardly had he reached the centre of the field before the ground opened and swallowed him, together with the horse and plough, closing over them, leaving the depression in the untilled field that can be seen to this day.

STRABANE, CO. TYRONE

The railway station here has (or had) a ghost that was seen by many local workmen.

One report described the appearance of the ghost to three people two nights running. The three men, named Pinkerton, Madden and Oliphant, were working in the engine house one October night when, soon after midnight, they heard a tremendous knocking noise which seemed to come from all the doors of the workshop, accompanied by unearthly and blood-curdling yells and screams.

They went to one of the doors and wrenched it open and saw there the form of a massive man, staring at them. They shouted for help and a nearby signalman came running to their aid, armed with a crowbar. He made a dash at the figure but even his crowbar had no effect and the mysterious form hovered about the shed until shortly after two-thirty in the morning.

All four men swore that they had seen the figure in good moonlight and inside the workshop; they were so terrified towards the end of the experience that they climbed up on to the engine they were supposed to be cleaning and hid on the roof until the form disappeared.

Next night the same figure appeared at one-thirty in the morning. On this occasion Oliphant, determined to discover whether the figure was material, succeeded in approaching to within a couple of yards of the form, but when the 'ghost' uttered terrible yells he collapsed.

Pinkerton tried to continue with his work but the frightening figure drifted towards him and gazed into his face so that

Pinkerton fell against the engine in his fright. Seven workmen saw the 'ghost' and afterwards found that their clothes, tools and personal belongings had all been thrown about the engine house.

One of the other engine-cleaners stated that once he saw the 'ghost' run up a ladder leading to a water-tank, where it disappeared; another said he thought it seemed to disappear through a window, high up near the ceiling of the workshop.

It was discovered that many years earlier a man had been murdered near the spot where the ghost first appeared. But no description of the murder victim seems to have been obtained so it is difficult to say whether this tragedy had any connection with the figure of a heavily-built man that was repeatedly seen—on one occasion by seven witnesses.

TUAMGRANEY, CO. CLARE

In this wild and romantic mountain country, where you can still walk for a day without meeting a living soul, there is a small lake known as Tier McBran. Great cliffs rise sheer from the water's edge and on the summit of one bluff there are the ruins of an old castle.

The lake itself has long been a mystery for no visible streams flow into it or out of it and it has never been fully explained where its constant water comes from. It is also said to be unfathomable and there is a strange legend associated with these still waters.

Before recorded history when the Fians, a legendary band of warriors, are said to have roamed these parts, a chieftain was out hunting one day when he saw a beautiful white hart suddenly emerge from a shrubbery, its horns and hooves gleaming like gold. Spotting the hunting chieftain it fled like the wind.

He and his fellow huntsmen pursued it, hour after hour, losing sight of the creature and then finding it again. On and on went the hunt and one by one the followers gave up in exhaustion until only the chieftain and his favourite hound Bran remained, following the elusive and apparently tireless hart.

Just as the sun was setting, the hart was trapped on a high cliff overlooking the lake. As the delighted chieftain went forward for the kill, the little white hart paused for a moment, took a last look at its tormentor, and then leaped down and vanished into the green waters far below.

Without hesitation Bran followed it and the chieftain looked down to see what had happened. Astounded, he saw that the hart had changed into a lovely golden-haired girl dressed in white who caught hold of Bran and sank with him to the unknown depths of the lake.

Thereafter the lake was always regarded as being haunted and few people ventured there after nightfall or even dared to fish in daylight.

There are those who maintain to this day that they have seen a giant hunting hound poised on the cliff edge at sunset, a hound that vanished as the sun disappeared beyond the horizon. The cliff from which Bran sprang is known to this day as Craig-a-Bran.

There is a wooded hollow near Tuamgraney (with its interesting twelfth-century church) where many visitors and local people have reported curious happenings often at the end of October, around Hallowe'en.

It is a wild and unspoilt part of the country, fascinating and primitive, yet imparting to the visitor a feeling of awe and foreboding. An air of expectancy seems to linger here and stories of phantom forests and weird experiences abound.

There is, for example, the story of a young man who lived at Tuamgraney and who had once or twice found himself in the vicinity of this strange wooded hollow. But he always became depressed and unusually conscious of himself, so that he invariably turned aside and travelled another way.

One afternoon, however, he determined to walk through the hollow. It was a lush October day, the countryside full of autumn beauty. The place seemed peaceful enough and as he entered the hollow and began to descend through the quiet trees, he thought to himself that he did not feel the acute oppression that he had always noticed when he had been there before.

Suddenly, almost as though he had passed from this world into another, he experienced an overwhelming feeling of sadness and something like terror. He stopped and almost turned back but as he was determined this time to walk through the haunted place, keeping an eye on every tree and bush around him, he cautiously went forward, suddenly realizing that he was walking almost on tip-toe as though not to disturb something.

As he plunged deeper and deeper into the wood he noticed that there were no birds—in fact no sound at all. He felt as though he were the only person alive in the world.

Still he walked warily on, deeper and deeper into the dim hollow, forcing his way through tall grass and bushes. Then he noticed that the overgrown path ahead of him was bathed in a pale light. He stopped for a moment, uncertain what to do. He couldn't understand where the pale but distinct light was coming from.

As he stood still the silence seemed to close in on him and he became conscious of the fact that he had been making the only sounds he had heard for some time. Evening had fallen quickly and there was no moon. Nor was there any hooting of owls, no fluttering of wings, no rustling of grass, leaves or branches; simply utter and complete silence.

He looked more carefully around him. The trees looked somehow strange, tall and slender, waving their long branches like arms, silently and menacingly towards him. He remembered tales of frightful rites being practised in this area long ago, of pagan worship and human sacrifice; of death to those who entered the sacred groves.

Now he seemed to feel hidden eyes watching his every movement as he hesitatingly made his way forward again, telling himself that he would soon be out of the hollow and into the countryside he knew.

Suddenly he saw a movement just ahead of him. A large bush moved and a dog poked its head through the foliage and stared at him. He fought to control his fright and told himself that some stray dog lived in the hollow; but all the time he was looking at the animal and at the expression of evil in its eyes as their gaze met. It showed its fangs and then suddenly vanished.

Before he could overcome his surprise a big black hare leaped on to the path in front of him, gave him one long look that he felt to be an expression of warning and hate rather than fear; then the creature bounded away out of sight. An enormous straw-coloured cat with bushy coat and slowly wagging tail sprang from a tree on to the path ahead of him. It arched its back, glared at him, spat silently, snarled like a tiger and then turned and walked away into the undergrowth.

Other animals appeared from time to time, suddenly and silently, each looking at him with hate before disappearing again into the thick woods. He was sure that lots of other eyes were watching him as he walked on, ever on his guard but determined to make his way through the haunted wood.

The ground began to rise and thankfully he decided that he was coming out of the hollow, when the path turned and he found himself in a glade. No trees grew here but they surrounded the glade so that they seemed to form an audience for a spectacle. Then he saw that the glade or arena was occupied by two animals engaged in a violent yet one-sided struggle. A beautiful and graceful hind, its eyes wide with fright, was being attacked by a ferocious black ram.

There seemed to be something overwhelmingly evil, even Satanic, about the coal-black ram. Appalled, yet fascinated, the young man watched the unequal struggle.

The repeated butting of the ram gave the hind no chance to escape and, beaten to its knees, it gave a pitiful look towards the human being who was watching its torture; its eyes, almost human in expression, imploring for help. Alerted by the mute appeal, the young man snatched up a heavy stick and threw himself between the animals. Just as the ram was making another charge on the helpless hind, he struck at it with all his might but found that his stick struck nothing but the air. The next moment he felt the pain as the ram butted him savagely and then he knew no more.

When he recovered consciousness he found himself lying on the side of a bare and hollow piece of ground. There was hardly a tree in sight. He thought that he must have dreamed the whole experience but when he moved to get to his feet, he discovered that he was very sore, as though he had been butted. He made his way home, thoughtfully and painfully, leaving behind him the haunted hollow.

When he recounted his experience, or dream, to his uncle, who had lived in the locality all his life and remembered stories of the phantom forest that older folk had talked about when he was a child, he learned that such experiences as his used to befall many people who ventured into that strange place around Hallowe'en.

WATERFORD, CO. WATERFORD

There was a Danish settlement here in 853. King John established a mint at Waterford that issued coins for two hundred years; Cromwell was forced to abandon a siege of the town in 1649, while King James II received a famous welcome here.

There is a curious monument to the Rice family in the Christ Church Cathedral with a 'memento mori' representing a decomposing corpse. Ancient Reginald's Tower, probably built in 1003, has a great hall in which the marriage of Strongbow and Eva was celebrated in 1171. With such a history, small wonder that Waterford has a number of ghosts, among them the well-documented return of the dead Jack Hayson.

One Christmas Eve, in a small house close to the River Suir, Eli Hayson was about to go to sleep at nearly midnight when he was surprised to hear the sound of running footsteps along the nearby waterfront.

Something made Eli get up and look out of the window on to the bright moonlit quay where he saw several vessels moored and, racing towards his house from the river, a young man in a grey jersey and dark trousers. As the figure ran frantically towards the house, Eli recognized his twin brother Jack, a seaman whom he thought to be on the Thomas Emery at Cork.

He was about to leave the window to unbolt the door for his brother when he noticed several other dark figures behind Jack, seemingly rising from the water and making after him. Eli tried to shout a warning but found himself rooted to the spot and unable to make a sound.

He saw Jack reach the door and attempt to wrench it open; then the forms closed in on him, clutching and overpowering the terrified and panting man. Eli plainly saw his brother's face convulsed with terror and fear and he heard a single scream: 'For God's sake help me!' but still he could not move an inch.

Within seconds the moon disappeared behind a cloud and all was quiet. When the moon reappeared the waterfront was deserted. Eli came to himself and hurried to the door but there was no sign of his brother nor anything to account for what he had seen and heard. Deciding that he must have had a nightmare, he crept back to bed and was soon asleep.

Within a couple of days news came from the captain of the Thomas Emery to say that Jack, walking in his sleep, had fallen overboard and drowned. Eli and his father attended the inquest at Cork where Mr Hayson testified that he had never known either of his sons to walk in their sleep but several of the ship's crew swore that they had seen Jack get up from his bunk at night and walk about the vessel and a verdict of 'Found Drowned' was returned.

The family were far from satisfied; they made extensive enquiries from the captain and various members of the crew of the Thomas Emery to try to discover what had really happened on the fateful night but all to no avail.

During the years that followed Mr Hayson, senior, died and Eli, left alone in the world, had long given up all hope of solving the mystery of his brother's death when a possible explanation was brought to his notice.

One evening he was having a drink at a bar in Cork, as was his custom and where he was well-known, when the landlord mentioned that an old inhabitant of the town might be able to tell him something of interest. He would say no more but suggested that Eli lose no time in visiting the old man who, it seemed, did not have long to live.

Eli left the bar at once and called at the address given to him by the landlord. There he met a gentle old man named Webster who, however, seemed reluctant to talk once he learned the name of his visitor.

At length, in the middle of idle chatter, he said that he would like to tell Eli something that his son, Tom a watchman on the quay who had died a couple of months before, had been worried about; something that he had seen twenty years earlier and had done nothing about.

It seemed that around midnight one Christmas Eve he had been sitting dozing in front of a brazier, by the side of a shed on the quay, when he was roused by the sound of stealthy footsteps. He got up cautiously, on the look-out for thieves and saw three extraordinary figures walking along the water's edge. Although they had the bodies of men and were clad in sailors' clothing, their heads were those of animals, apes and stags.

For a moment Tom was petrified with fright and surprise but curiosity overcame his fear; making sure that he was not seen, he crept round the side of the shed and followed the strange figures. He saw them descend the quay steps, board a dingy and row off in the direction of a schooner moored nearby.

As soon as he saw them board the ship, he jumped into another boat and rowed himself across. Reaching the schooner, he hauled himself aboard and hid among some of the ship's gear and barrels that lay in the stern of the vessel.

He had hardly settled in his hiding place when his blood nearly froze as he heard loud shrieks of terror accompanied by agonized moans and groans. A moment later a young man of about his own age came leaping up the companion ladder, raced across the deck for his life—with the grotesque trio that Tom had seen ashore at his heels.

It was a moonlit night and as the running man raced towards him Tom could see the awful fear on the man's terrified face.

'Help!' he screamed, 'For God's sake, help me!' Tom rushed from his hiding place but before he could do anything more the frenzied man had jumped overboard.

Tom prepared himself to dive in to do what he could to help but found himself held fast by the three pursuing figures. Now that he was close to them Tom saw that they were indeed men but that they each wore a mummer's mask. It quickly transpired that the whole affair was a plot to get rid of the young man who, in some way that was not revealed, had incurred the bitter animosity of three of his fellow-seamen.

Two of the men were for getting rid of Tom at once but the third, who seemed to be the leader, persuaded them to spare him on condition that he took a solemn oath never to relate what he had seen.

Tom took the oath and amid ghastly threats of what would happen if he ever breathed a word about the affair, he was allowed to go. Only years later, still tormented by the awful look on the terrified man's face, did Tom tell his father about the matter, making him swear never to tell a soul as long as he was alive.

Eli asked whether the old man could establish the exact date of his son's experience and reaching into a chest of drawers Matthew Webster brought forth a pocket book and showed Eli the date. It was the night that he had seen the figure of his brother trying to get into his cottage.

Legend has it that a female vampire is buried at a spot near Strongbow's Tree or Tower, in the little graveyard of a ruined church and that her fatal beauty still lures men to this sinister spot when darkness falls.

WESTPORT, CO. MAYO

About eight miles west, rising in isolation over Clew Bay, stands the graceful cone of Croagh Patrick, the Rech (i.e. rock) of St Patrick, Ireland's holiest mountain of 2,510 feet, an object of pilgrimage since the Middle Ages. On occasions 100,000 people have been known to make the ascent on the last Sunday in July, Garland Sunday, many bare-footed in accordance with tradition.

At the summit which commands a superb view of the Connemara mountains to the south and Achill Island and even Slieve League (1,972 feet) away across Donegal Bay, there is a little oratory and a statue of the saint. Here St Patrick, according to ancient belief, spent the forty days of Lent in the year 441 praying, fasting and banishing from the whole land every snake and other noxious reptile.

Certainly Ireland is today one of the few countries without snakes, toads, polecats, weasels and moles. St Patrick is said to have achieved this result by ringing a bell and then throwing it over a precipice, where it was followed by a swarm of venomous creatures. The bell was returned to his hand each time by angels until the extermination was complete.

There have been a number of reports that elderly pilgrims, while making the strenuous climb, have seen or sensed a gentle and white-robed figure at their side, a manifestation that they have found comforting and helpful on the long ascent to the summit of Croagh Patrick.

On occasions the faint sounds of a ringing bell have been heard in the vicinity of the chapel on the summit when few pilgrims are there but it has only been heard during the month of March or early April, in fact during the forty days of Lent.

WEXFORD, CO. WEXFORD

It was at a large country house called Tullamore, not far from Wexford, the picturesque country town and seaport, that Lord Dufferin, ex-Viceroy of India, saw an apparition that probably saved his life.

A brave and cool soldier, a much-travelled man of the world, self-possessed and unimaginative, he had been relaxing in Ireland after years in India when he was invited to join the house-party of an old friend.

It was close to midnight as Lord Dufferin made his way along the mellowed passage and up the great staircase to his bedroom. He was in a pleasant and cheerful frame of mind as he entered the spacious room with a cheerful log fire blazing in the wide hearth. He felt at peace with the world and having prepared for bed he thought he would read for a while before settling down to sleep.

After half an hour or so he put the book aside but found himself strangely awake and restless. He dozed a little but soon awakened, twisting and turning; a most unusual state of affairs for a calm, clear-headed and practical man who normally fell asleep as soon as his head touched the pillow and slept soundly till morning.

But this night, in 1890, something was wrong and Lord Dufferin eventually felt so restless and disturbed that he got up from his bed.

Crossing the room he reached the window and looked out over the moonlit lawns. It was a cloudless night and the full moon flooded the gardens beneath his window.

He could see every rise and fall of the sweeping lawns, the

well-cropped shrubs and the neat paths. Nothing moved and Lord Dufferin stood for some minutes contemplating the beauty of the night scene; silent, still and mysterious.

Suddenly a movement caught his eye and he watched, fascinated, as the figure of a man stepped from deep shadow into the moonlight. He walked slowly and purposefully straight across the wide lawn, bent almost double by the weight of a long and heavy box that he carried on his back. When the man was in the middle of the lawn, in full view of the watcher at the bedroom window, he stopped, lifted his head and looked straight at Lord Dufferin.

The moon shone down on the man's features and at the sight the hard-headed ex-Viceroy took an involuntary step backwards. So horrible was the face that he shuddered as their eyes met and he was later to describe the face as 'full of horror and malevolence'.

Resuming his task, the man turned away from the window and walked on across the lawn until he was lost in the dark shrubbery; but not before Lord Dufferin, with a quickening of his breath, realized that the object the man was carrying on his back was a coffin!

Lord Dufferin looked at his watch as he turned away from the window. It was nearly two o'clock in the morning and the whole house seemed to be asleep; it was as quiet as death. He turned again and looked out of the window but all was quiet and peaceful and deserted out there now.

There was no doubt in his mind but that he had seen a real person in the garden; for there had been nothing ghostly about the figure he had seen, it had even cast a shadow he had noticed. Nevertheless, he experienced an eeriness such as he had never known before, a feeling that made him realize that he was cold. He returned to his bed and slept soundly for the rest of the night.

Next morning Lord Dufferin recounted his night's experience at the breakfast table. No one took seriously his account of seeing a hideously ugly man carrying a coffin across the lawns at two o'clock in the morning and he was assured that the house had no history of a ghost.

In the years that followed. Lord Dufferin often stayed at Tullamore and occupied the same bedroom but he never again experienced the cold restlessness that had disturbed him on his first visit to the house. And he never again saw the dreadful figure on the lawn—or did he?

Following a number of diplomatic engagements Lord Dufferin was appointed Ambassador to France. One morning, when he was to address an important gathering of diplomats on the fifth floor of a Paris hotel, he arrived with his secretary and was escorted by the manager to the lift.

The lift rattled to a stop, the doors opened. Lord Dufferin, deep in conversation with his secretary, hardly noticed that a number of people entered the lift ahead of him. Then he stepped forward and as he did so he saw the uniformed lift attendant for the first time. The man was facing him and at the sudden shock and amazement, Lord Dufferin stepped back and out of the lift: for the face of the lift attendant was the face of the man he had seen in Ireland carrying a coffin across the lawn.

Now once again Lord Dufferin felt a chill dread seep into him. He was visibly shaken and much to the astonishment of the hotel manager, waved the lift away. As he waited for it to return after depositing the occupants at the various floors, Lord Dufferin heard a sudden harsh clang, then a loud banging noise followed by an awful screech and a tremendous thud that seemed to vibrate through the hotel.

The lift had just reached the fifth floor after leaving Lord Dufferin but the doors were never opened there. The wire suspension cable snapped and the loaded lift plunged to the bottom of the shaft. Five people died, among them the lift operator whose face had stopped Lord Dufferin from entering the fatal lift.

Later Lord Dufferin discovered that the lift operator had only been engaged for that single day, replacing the regular attendant; and no one ever discovered his real name or where he came from.

A later Marquess of Dufferin and Ava said a few years ago: 'The story is perfectly true but my grandfather could never explain it. We have always believed the story and puzzled about it, because he did not believe in ghosts.'

ACKNOWLEDGEMENTS

The author gratefully acknowledges permission to use photographs in this volume from: Peter G. Currie, George J. Edwards, Alasdair Alpin MacGregor, Dame Flora MacLeod of MacLeod, Mrs J. Maxwell-Scott, Donald Ross, Board of Management for Glasgow Western and Gartnavel Hospitals, Irish Tourist Board, Northern Ireland Tourist Board and Scottish Tourist Board.

He also gratefully acknowledges invaluable help in providing information from: Lady Alexandra Airlie, Peter G. Currie, the Marquess of Dufferin and Ava, Miss Theodora FitzGibbon, Tommy Frankland, Affleck Gray, Frank W. Hansell, Norman F. Haynes, Mrs Marion Holbourn, Colin F. McIntosh, Mrs Patricia MacGregor, Dame Flora MacLeod of MacLeod, the Very Rev. Lord MacLeod of Fuinary, Mrs Cathy Mott, Commander G. R. Muir RN, W. T. G. Perrott, Captain Sir Hugh Rhys Rankin, Donald Ross, Julia Lady Seton (Julia Clements), Miss R. M. Simpson and the Earl of Southesk.

ABOUT THE AUTHOR

Peter Underwood

Peter Underwood was President of the Ghost Club (founded 1862) from 1960-1993 and probably heard more first-hand ghost stories than any man alive. He was a long-standing member of The Society of Psychical Research, Vice-President of the Unitarian Society for Psychical Studies, a member of The Folklore Society, The Dracula Society and the Research Committee of the Psychic Research Organisation, he wrote extensively, and was a seasoned lecturer and broadcaster.

He took part in the first official investigation into a haunting; sat with physical and mental mediums and conducted investigations at seances. He was present at exorcisms, experiments at dowsing, precognition, clairvoyance, hypnotism, regression; he conducted world-wide tests in telepathy and extra-sensory perception, and personally investigated scores of haunted houses across the country.

He possessed comprehensive files of alleged hauntings in every county of the British Isles and many foreign countries, and his knowledge and experience resulted in his being consulted on psychic and occult matters by the BBC and ITV. His many books include the first two comprehensive gazetteers of ghosts and hauntings in England, Scotland and Ireland and two books that deal with twenty different occult subjects.

Highlights from his published work include 'Nights in Haunted Houses' (1993), which collects together the results of group investigations, 'The Ghosts of Borley' (1973), his classic account of the history of 'the most haunted house in England', 'Hauntings' (1977), which re-examines ten classic cases of haunting in the light of modern knowledge, 'No Common Task' (1983), which reflects back upon his life as a 'ghost hunter', and 'The Ghost Hunter's Guide' (1986), which gives the reader all the advice necessary to become one. Born at Letchworth Garden City in Hertfordshire, he lived for many years in a small village in Hampshire.

BOOKS BY THIS AUTHOR

Ghosts Of North West England

The ghostly little monk of Foulridge and the giant apparition from Heaton Norris are just two of the denizens of the North-West you might not care to meet on a dark, stormy evening. But for those intrepid souls whose hearts quicken at the thought of eerie footsteps and muffled groans Peter Underwood has assembled an impressive collection of traditional legends.

Ghosts Of Kent

The first expert exploration of the haunted houses and authentic ghosts of Kent, this volume is filled with fascinating true ghost stories from times past. Read about the curious case of Anne West of Old Bayhall Manor, who 'was always worried that she might be buried while yet alive', or the 'ghostly old gentleman' of Cleve Court in Minster, who, when he turns up, is treated 'more as a guest than a ghost' - because 'the dear old thing means no harm'.

And there is Lympne Castle, where Underwood once took a party of Ghost Club members: 'I had just obtained a description of the room, when one of the Club members rushed into the kitchen begging me to accompany her to one of the towers where "something horrible had once taken place"…'.

Hauntings: New Light On The Greatest True Ghost Stories Of The World

In this fascinating account of the best-attested cases of haunting - Hampton Court, the demon drummer of Bedworth, the Wesley ghost, Glamis, Borley Rectory and many others - Britain's foremost ghost-hunter has brought to light a wealth of valuable new evidence. Using the results of many years of research and personal investigation, and providing detailed plans and original photographs, new theories are put forward to change our ideas about these hauntings.

This Haunted Isle

Peter Underwood has personally visited the historic buildings and sites of Britain, and here presents a wealth of intriguing legends and new stories of ghostly encounters from more than a hundred such throughout the United Kingdom.
From Abbey House in Cambridge to Zennor in Cornwall, this is an A to Z of the haunted houses of Britain. At Bramshill in Hampshire — now a police training college — there have been so many sightings that even sceptical police officers have had to admit that the place is haunted. Beautiful Leeds Castle in Kent has a large, phantom black dog; there is an Elizabethan gentleman (seen by a Canon of the Church of England!) at Croft Castle; a Pink Lady at Coughton Court; a prancing ghost jester at Gawsworth; a spectre in green velvet at Hoghton Tower; six ghosts at East Riddlesden Hall; a headless apparition at Westwood Manor; and then there are some little-known ghosts in Windsor Castle, Hampton Court Palace and the Tower of London, and the strange ghosts of Chingle Hall, perhaps the most haunted house in England.

Exorcism!

Throughout history, the practice of exorcism has been used for the purpose of driving out evil spirits and demons though to possess human beings and the places they inhabit. But there are more startling instances where exorcism has been used: to cure a trawler that seemed to be cursed; to expel demons from Bram Stoker's black 'vampire' dog' even to rid Loch Ness and the Bermuda Triangle of their evil ambience. Peter Underwood explores this frightening ritual in relation to witches, vampires and animals, while his far-flung researches have unearthed dramatic cases in Morocco, Egypt, South Africa and the United States, as well as the British Isles.

Death In Hollywood

The Hollywood way of life has long been a potent mix of scandal, secrecy and sensation: exactly like the Hollywood way of death...

In this unique study, Peter Underwood charts the lives, loves and deaths of thirty of Tinseltown's most glittering stars. Many deaths were sad or senseless; some were tragic; others were the revenge of old age, while a few were the revenge of something altogether more sinister...

Many of the film industry's most amazing people have died in Hollywood, some simply as the result of old age, others in sad, bizarre or senseless circumstances. Marilyn Monroe's last hours remain a mystery to this day; Jean Harlow's mother, a devout Christian Scientist, refused her daughter medical help until it was too late; Ramon Novarro was brutally murdered; and Sir Alec Guinness preicted James Dean's death a short time before the fatal car crash.

For anyone interested in the stars who made the movies, 'Death in Hollywood' will add an extra dimension to many a performance.

Peter Underwood's Guide To Ghosts & Haunted Places: Cases From The Files Of The World's Leading Paranormal Investigator

Based on 50 years' expert study and investigation, this collection of cases from the files of Peter Underwood - an acknowledged expert and experienced investigator of haunted houses - represents a unique exploration of the world of ghosts, apparitions and psychic phenomena. If you want to satisfy your curiosity about the subject or simply enjoy a riveting read, this guide is for you.

No Common Task: The Autobiography Of A Ghost-Hunter

This is the autobiography of a man who has spent thirty-five years of his life covering scientific psychical research, with detailed investigations into all kinds of manifestation that might be supernatural or paranormal in origin, including spiritualism, ESP, telepathy, hauntings and other occult phenomena. Many of the true experiences from the author's casebook are published here for the first time.

Dictionary Of The Supernatural

An A to Z of Hauntings, Possession, Witchcraft, Demonology and Other Occult Phenomena...

The entries cover all known (and some very little known) organisations, individuals, periodicals, terms of reference, and significant cases, events and incidents relevant to the subject. Under each entry there are notes on other appropriate books and further reading.

The Ghost Hunter's Guide

What are the qualities which make an ideal ghost hunter? You need to be part detective, part investigative reporter, a scientist, with a measure of the psychologist thrown in...

In this book, which is the first real guide to the hunting of ghosts, Peter Underwood manages to cover just about every aspect of this intriguing and mystifying subject.

Ghosts Of Hampshire And The Isle Of Wight

Peter Underwood, an acknowledged expert and experienced investigator of haunted houses, presents a selection of hauntings throughout Hampshire and the Isle of Wight. A formidable collection of ghoulies and things that go bump in the night.

This edition includes a foreword by author Alan Williams, as well as an interview Williams conducted with Underwood in 1997.

Jack The Ripper: One Hundred Years Of Mystery

Jack the Ripper still causes a shudder, synonymous as it is with violent murder and mutilation. But also of mystery and speculation - for the gruesome series of killings in London's East End in that horrific Autumn of 1888 have never been finally solved.

Into The Occult

Despite all the answers that conventional science can provide to the earth's mysteries, there remain certain phenomena for which no explanation can yet be found outside the occult. For this reason exploration of the occult and paranormal provides endless fascination.

Here is a survey of all the different aspects of this complex and intriguing subject, including an entire chapter on the relationship between sex and psychic phenomena, a subject on which, until recently, there has been an unwillingness to talk.

Deeper Into The Occult

'In an age when voodoo dancers have appeared in London, when Robert Williams, chief psychologist at Kansas State Industrial Reformatory admits to being a practising war-lock; when moon-astronaut Edgar Mitchell conducts extra sensory experiments in space; when the course of a £1,000,000 road is altered to save a 'fairy tree'; when a ghost is officially registered on a census form; when Americans can 'dial-a-horoscope' for a twenty-four hour prophesy; and when the complete skeleton of a cyclops is unearthed by archaeologists — is it surprising that there is a growing interest in the occult, for research in many fields simply proves that things are not what they seem?'

Nights In Haunted Houses

For over thirty years, in his position as President and Chief Investigator of the Ghost Club of Great Britain, Peter Underwood was actively involved in undertaking night vigils and carrying out research into ghosts and paranormal activity in controlled, scientific conditions.

The Vampire's Bedside Companion: The Amazing World Of Vampires In Fact And

Fiction

The Vampire's Bedside Companion is a riveting compendium of new facts and fiction on the 'undying' theme of vampirism.

Here is a new theory on the genesis of Dracula (surely literature's most compelling and macabre figure?); thoughts on allusions to vampirism in Wuthering Heights; first-hand experience of Vampires in Hampstead, London; publication for the first time of the story of a fifteenth-century Vampire Protection medallion that Montague Summers presented to the author; an account by a professor of English at Dalhousie University of a visit to 'Castle Dracula' in Transylvania - The Vampire's Bedside Companion contains these and a wealth of other hitherto unpublished material on a subject that is of enduring interest: The Vampire Legend.

The Ghost Hunters: Who They Are And What They Do

A leading psychical researcher takes an in-depth look at ghost hunters, both past and present. Who are these intrepid explorers of the unknown? How do they probe and examine the realms of the seemingly inexplicable? What are their conclusions? In fascinating detail, Peter Underwood profiles the lives and adventures of some of the most famous names in psychical investigation.

The Ghosts Of Borley: Annals Of The Haunted Rectory

'The Ghosts of Borley' (1973) was the first complete record of the unique Borley Rectory hauntings, detailing all the evidence known about this notorious haunted house from the early days of the Rev. H. D. E. Bull who built Borley Rectory in 1863, through the incumbencies of the Rev. Harry Bull, the Rev. Guy Eric Smith and the Rev. Lionel Foyster, to the investigations by Harry Price and other members of the Society for Psychical Research (SPR).

Queen Victoria's Other World

There have been many books about Queen Victoria but there has never been one that has explored her 'other world' - the world of the strange and unusual, the world of death and her fascination for it, and the world of the unseen and the paranormal that she could never resist.

The Complete Book Of Dowsing And Divining

This comprehensive volume on dowsing and divining - from the twig and the pendulum to motorscopes and bare hands - traces the story of these fascinating and enigmatic phenomena from its origins in the world of fairy tales and mythology to recent theories that the enigma can be explained in terms of present-day psychology.

Printed in Great Britain
by Amazon